Edward P. Evans

Animal Symbolism in Ecclesiastical Architecture

Edward P. Evans

Animal Symbolism in Ecclesiastical Architecture

ISBN/EAN: 9783337234911

Printed in Europe, USA, Canada, Australia, Japan

Cover: Foto ©Andreas Hilbeck / pixelio.de

More available books at **www.hansebooks.com**

ANIMAL SYMBOLISM
IN ECCLESIASTICAL
ARCHITECTURE

ANIMAL SYMBOLISM IN ECCLESIASTICAL ARCHITECTURE

By E. P. EVANS

WITH A BIBLIOGRAPHY AND SEVENTY-EIGHT ILLUSTRATIONS

NEW YORK
HENRY HOLT & COMPANY
MDCCCXCVI

CONTENTS

CHAPTER I

ALLEGORICAL AND ANAGOGICAL INTERPRETATIONS OF NATURE

Impulse given to the study of natural history by Alexander the Great—Scientific spirit fostered by Aristotle—Lack of this spirit among the Romans—Alexandria as a centre of learning under the Ptolemies—The Christian theory of the relation of the Book of Revelation to the Book of Nature—The patristic conception of the visible creation as an image of the invisible world and a mirror of spiritual truth—Animals as religious emblems in Oriental, and especially in Buddhistic, literature—Mineralogical symbolism—Magical and medical properties and religious significance of precious stones—Legends of Solomon's wisdom, and his method of building the Temple—Ceremony of blessing jewels—Speculations of Justinus Kerner and Schubert concerning the occult affinities of the mineral kingdom to man—The typology of precious stones according to the *Physiologus*—Spiritual meaning of the diamond, the pearl, and the Indian stone—Terrobuli in Christian symbolism and architecture ... ... *p.* 21

CHAPTER II

ORIGIN AND HISTORY OF THE 'PHYSIOLOGUS'

Plastic and pictorial representations of animals in Christian art—Literary sources of these representations—*Clavis* of

St. Melito—Epistle of Barnabas—The *Physiologus* compiled by an Alexandrian Greek—The *Hexahemera* of the
Fathers—Adam as the author of a natural history—
Popular character of the *Physiologus*—Origen as an
exegetist—Roger Bacon's views of the place of animals
in Scripture—Expositions and amplifications of the *Physiologus* by Epiphanius, St. Isidore, Petrus Damiani, and
others—Anastasius Sinaita's *Anagogical Contemplations*
—Latin poem on beasts and their mystical meaning by
Theobald of Plaisance, and the English paraphrase—
The *Physiologus* translated into Latin, Ethiopic, Arabic,
Armenian, Syriac, Anglo-Saxon, Icelandic, and all the
principal modern languages of Europe—Brief descriptions of these versions—Prudentius' poems *Hamartigenia*
and *Psychomachia*—The phœnix a symbol of solar
worship used to illustrate the Christian doctrine of the
Resurrection—French bestiaries : Philippe de Thaun's
Le Livre des Créatures, Peter of Picardy's prose version
of the *Physiologus*, and *Le Bestiaire Divin* of William, a
priest of Normandy—Encyclopædias of natural history
based on the *Physiologus*: Thomas de Cantimpré's
Liber de Naturis Rerum, the *Speculum Naturale* of
Vincent de Beauvais, *Liber de Proprietatibus Rerum* of
Bartholomæus Anglicus, *Hortus Deliciarum* of Herrade
de Landsberg, and other compilations—The church
edifice an emblem of the human soul—Symbolism of the
raven and the dove—Albertus Magnus' criticism of the
Physiologus ...   . *p.* 52

CHAPTER III

THE 'PHYSIOLOGUS' IN ART AND LITERATURE

The three characteristics of the lion—Representations of the
lion as a symbol of the Resurrection in architecture—
Beasts often have a twofold signification—The lion and
bear as types of Satan—Diabolification of the dog—

Contents

Strange misconception of the canine character—Lions as
pedestals—Metaphorical use of the lion in poetry—The
lizard in architecture—Artistic delineations of the unicorn
as a type of Christ's Incarnation—Auricular conception of
Christ as the Logos—Supposed anti-toxical virtue of the
unicorn's horn and that of the African viper—The unicorn
in legend and poetry—Characteristics of the elephant—
Symbol of the fall of man—Julius Cæsar's queer account
of the elk—Elephants embroidered on chasubles—Four
characteristics of the serpent—Artistic and poetic uses
of its fabled attributes—The eagle as a symbol of
spiritual aspiration and baptismal regeneration—Allusions to it by Dante and other poets—The fish in sacred
iconology—Significance of the whale in ecclesiastical
architecture—Symbolism of the remora and serra—Importance of the phœnix and the pelican as emblems of
Christian doctrine—Their prominent place in Church
architecture—Import of the fabulous exploits of the otter
and the ichneumon—Panther and dragon typical of
Christ and Belial—Healing power of the "heavenly
panther"—Lesson of self-renunciation taught by the
beaver—Characteristic of the hyena—Symbolism of the
salamander—The partridge a type of the devil—Examples of the charadrius in art—Mystical meaning of the
crow, turtle-dove, ousel, merl, fulica, and hoopoe—Curious
statement of Luther concerning swallows—Why God
feeds the young ravens—Peculiarities of the wolf—The
Physiologus condemned as heretical—Freely used by
Gregory the Great in his scriptural exposition—Virtues
and vices portrayed as women mounted on various
animals—Disputatious scholastics satirized—Tetramorph
—Gospel mills—The ark of the covenant as the triumphal
chariot of the Cross—Cock and clergy—Origin of the
basilisk and its significance—Its prominence in religious
symbology and sacred architecture—Cautious scepticism
of Albertus Magnus—The *Physiologus* from a psychological point of view, as illustrating the credulity of the

CHAPTER IV

SYMBOLISM SUPERSEDED BY SATIRE

CHAPTER V

WHIMSEYS OF ECCLESIOLOGY AND SYMBOLOGY

Universality of the symbolism of the cross—Cruciform phenomena in nature—The sign of the cross in the Old Testament, and its prefigurative significance—Wonderworking power of the cross in Jewish history—Its presence in the Garden of Eden and in the Hebrew alphabet—The cosmos has the form of a cross—Influence of the doctrine of the Trinity upon art—Trinitarian suggestions in the material creation—Mystic meanings in sacred architecture—Symbolism of bells and significance of orientation—Superstitious regard for the points of the compass—Transition from christolatry to hagiolatry

LIST OF ILLUSTRATIONS

ANIMAL SYMBOLISM IN
ECCLESIASTICAL ARCHITECTURE

INTRODUCTION

ONE of the most charming passages in the idyls of Theocritus is that in which Eros complains to Aphrodite of the bees that stung his hand as he was stealing honey from their hive, and expresses his astonishment that such very small creatures could cause so severe pain. Thereupon the Cyprian goddess laughingly replies : " Thou too art like the bee, for although a tiny child, yet how terrible are the wounds thou dost inflict." This witty retort and pat allusion to the pangs produced by the arrows from Cupid's quiver greatly pleased the fancy of the elder Lucas Cranach, who depicted the scene in no less than five different paintings, the most celebrated of which is now in the Royal Museum of Berlin. The same conceit was embodied, at a still earlier period, in one of the poems of Anacreon, who, however, represents Eros as having been stung while plucking a rose in which a bee was sleeping. A Spanish poet of the seventeenth century, Estevan

B

Manuel de Villegas, famous in Old Castile as the
translator and imitator of Anacreon, gives in *Las
Eroticas* a vivid description of a duel between Amor
and a bee, the two ravishers of hearts and flowers.
The combat ended with the painful wounding of
the god and the death of the insect, and thus
ravaged hearts and pillaged flowers were both
avenged.   In a madrigal of the Roman " Arcadian,"
Felice Zappi, Cupids swarm like bees round the
head of the loved one, clinging to her hair, nestling
in her bosom, gathering honey from her lips, and
waving their torches out of her eyes.   In his charming lyric *Die Biene*, Lessing gives a didactic turn
to Anacreon's poem already referred to, and makes
Amor learn a lesson of strategy from his misfor-
tune : henceforth he was wont to lurk in roses and
violets, and, when a maiden came to pluck them,
" flew forth as a bee and stung."   A kiss is also
personified as a bee, which extracts honey from the
lips, and, at the same time, pierces the heart with
its sting.

Curiously enough this simple, sensuous, and
suggestive imagery, which plays such a prominent
part in Greek, and especially in Oriental, erotics, is
wholly foreign to those of the Germanic and
Slavonic races ; it is not native to the poetry of
these nations, and blooms in their literature only
as an exotic.   For the delineation of the tender
passion they preferred a symbolism drawn from
the vegetable kingdom, and the real or fictitious
qualities of fruits and flowers ; the apple, the

peach, the fig, the rose, the lily, the narcissus, the anemone, the violet, and the pink are used to illustrate the attractions of female beauty and the attributes of connubial love. Into Germany, whose pagan tribes seem to have been acquainted with bees, chiefly if not exclusively in their wild state, the art of rearing these insects was introduced with Christianity, and carried on for the most part by the various monastic orders. There was hardly a cloister without its hive, which not only supplied honey and wax for culinary and cultic purposes, but also served as an example to the friars of an ideal life of communistic industry and cenobitic chastity. The superiors of the convents were fond of emphasizing this analogy in their exhortations to the recluses under their charge, and of enforcing it in their religious poetry. Peter of Capua calls the risen and ascended Saviour "apis ætherea"; the saints famous for good works are compared to bees; eloquent Fathers of the Church and expounders of the faith—Chrysostom, Ambrose, Isidore of Spain, and Bernard of Clairvaux—are said to have lips flowing with honey (*mellifluus*); and the virgin queen of the hive is, in the hymns of mediæval mariolaters, a favourite type of the Virgin Queen of Heaven. But notwithstanding the frequency of these allusions in Christian literature, and the consecration of honey and wax to ritual purposes, the bee figures rarely in Christian art. It is found occasionally carved on tombs in the catacombs as a symbol of immortality; in this case, however, it does not express a specifically Christian conception, but is a survival of paganism. In ancient times honey was supposed to be an effective antiseptic, and it was customary to smear with it the bodies of the dead in order to preserve them from putrefaction. Alexander the Great is said to have been thus embalmed, and the same usage formed an integral part of the Mithras-cult, and can be traced still farther back to the solar worship of the Assyrians and Babylonians. Under the Roman empire the mysteries of the Mithras-cult became widely diffused throughout Western Europe; Christian churches were erected over altars dedicated to the old Persian sun-god, as in S. Clemente at Rome, and the gilded bull's head and three hundred golden bees, discovered at Tournay in 1653, in the tomb of the Merovingian king, Childeric III., had their origin in the same system of worship. These bees, which decorated the royal mantle of the living monarch, and embellished his shroud after death, were invested with a traditional sacredness in France as emblems of sovereignty, and therefore adopted by the first Napoleon, in order to give a seeming shimmer of ancient lustre to an upstart dynasty.

Christ, as we have seen, was called the " æthereal bee," and it is an interesting coincidence that Vishnu, incarnate in the form of Krishna, should be represented with a blue bee hovering over his head as a symbol of the æther. It is not probable that this similarity is to be explained on the theory of an historical transmission of ideas, or that there is any genetic connection between these conceptions, except so far as they might grow naturally and independently out of the solar character of both religions. There is no doubt, however, that the Orient is the chief source of our symbolisms, which in migrating westward have undergone such a variety of transformations and adaptations as in many cases greatly to obscure their original significance. In the *Brihat-Kathâ-Sarit-Sâgara* ("Great Ocean of the Rivers of Stories") of Somadeva, there is the tale of a traveller, who fell asleep on a forest tree, and when he awoke saw a tiger lying in wait for him below, and an enormous serpent coiled above his head and ready to spring upon him. At the same time he discovered on a branch by his side some drops of honey from a swarm of bees in the hollow trunk, and in the enjoyment of its sweetness forgot all about the perils by which he was surrounded. Long before the age of Somadeva this allegory of human life was current in India, whence it passed into the legendary literature of Europe, subject to the modifications of an Occidental environment (for example in Jacobus de Voragine's *Legenda Aurea*, and the *Barlaam und Josaphat* of Rudolf von Ems), and is the theme of an elaborate bas-relief on the south door of the baptistery of Parma, where we see a man sitting on the limb of a tree eagerly eating the honey that trickles from the leaves; at the foot of the tree is a dragon, and gnawing at its roots are two mice, white and black, symbols of day and night, the chief divisions of all-devouring time, which ultimately cause every tree of life to fall. M. Henri Gaidoz has shown by strongly presumptive, if not wholly conclusive, evidence, that the Virgin of the Seven Swords is a Christian appropriation and adaptation of the Babylonian-Assyrian war-goddess Istar, who is represented on ancient monuments with seven darts in her shoulders, so arranged as to form with their shafts a halo encircling her head. Pictures of this goddess, brought by mediæval Italian merchants from the East, were supposed to refer to the Virgin Mary, and to the fulfilment of the prophecy of Simeon that a sword should pierce through her soul; and it was not until the fifteenth century that it was slightly modified to suit the Gospel record, and received a permanent place in Christian iconography. The existence of a revered image of the Holy Virgin in remote regions of the East was easily accounted for by the clergy, like many other startling resemblances in religious rites and symbols, as the marvellous and quite miraculous results of the mythical mission of the apostle Thomas.

Indeed, nothing was more common in the middle ages than this Christianization of pagan deities. Thus the eagle as an emblem of Jupiter caused the son of Kronos and sovereign of Olympus to be mistaken for John the Evangelist; Poseidon and Pallas were regarded as Adam and Eve; Hercules with his club passed for Samson with the jawbone of an ass; and representations of Venus were ingeniously construed into those of the Virgin Mary. Under the influence of the Renaissance the newly-awakened æsthetic sense proved strong enough to overrule the scruples of religious sentiment, and the monuments of classical antiquity became models for imitation in the productions of Christian art. We have a striking example of this tendency in a marble relief of the Assumption of the Virgin, which belonged originally to Saint-Jacques-la-Boucherie, and is now in the abbatial church of Saint-Denis. Her graceful figure is almost wholly nude, and resembles Venus rising from the sea rather than the Virgin Mary ascending into heaven; she folds her hands in the attitude of prayer, and stands with one foot on a cloud and the other on the head of a cherub, while four pagan genii as angels accompany her, playing on musical instruments.

It was in the Orient, too, that mythical and symbolical zoölogy, as the natural outgrowth of the doctrine of metempsychosis, attained its most exuberant development. The monstrosities of Indian, Assyrian, Egyptian, and archaic Greek art, sphinxes, centaurs, minotaurs, human-headed bulls, lion-headed kings, horse-headed goddesses, and sparrow-headed gods, are all the plastic embodiments of this metaphysical tenet. The same notion finds expression in heraldry, where real and fabulous animals are blazoned in whimsical devices on coats-of-arms and ensigns as emblems of qualities supposed to be peculiar to individuals or hereditary in families. The man adorned his escutcheon with the bird or the beast which he was proud of resembling or wished to rival, whose rapidity of flight he coveted, or whose ferocity he feared. By this naïve symbolism the primitive chieftain thought to strike terror in his foes, or to strengthen the courage and confidence of his friends and confederates. Out of the same circumstances arose also an uncanny feeling of awe as regards the lower animals, and a superstitious dread of provoking their enmity. Grimm, in his exhaustive discussion of this topic, has called attention to that early stage of society, when the ravenous wolf and the shaggy bear, prowling through the dark glens and sunny glades of the interminable forest, were looked upon, not merely as rapacious brutes, whose physical strength and voracity were to be feared, but rather as incarnations of mysterious and malignant forces capable of inflicting injuries by occult and magical influences, and therefore not to be enraged or irritated in any manner. For this reason they were not called by their real names, but were propitiated by flattering epithets, such as black-foot, blue-foot, gold-foot, sweet-foot, grey-beard, broad-brow, flash-eye, forest-brother, and a variety of similar appellations. The demon-soul revealed itself in the fierce glare of the eye and the long, weird howl, which broke like the voice of an imprisoned fiend on the midnight air, as the beasts were supposed to be holding conference concerning the affairs and destinies of men, into which the immense age many of them were thought to attain would in itself give them more than Rosicrucian insight. This sacred and supernatural character invested all their movements with extraordinary interest and portentous significance. They directed the emigrations of tribes, and determined the places in which colonies were to be planted, watched over the infancy of heroes and suckled the founders of nations, indicated the sites of future cities, showed where temples were to be erected or saints buried, and were selected with the most scrupulous care and circumspection for purposes of sacrifice and vaticination. The presence or sudden approach of certain quadrupeds was an omen of good or evil, and auguries were drawn from the movements or cries of birds. A hare crossing the line of march of an army has sufficed to fill the troops with terror, and cause them to flee in a panic. Among the reliefs in the south porch of the cathedral of Chartres is that of a warrior dropping his sword and running away from this timid quadruped. Finally, animals were transferred to the sky and identified with the constellations, in which form they continued to look down upon the earth with auspicious or malign aspect, and to forecast the fate of mankind.

A natural consequence of this enigmatical and mystical relation of the world of men to the world of beasts was that the latter became at a very

early period objects of worship and mythopoetic
speculation. Zoölatry has existed among all
nations, but this cult reached its highest development among the Egyptians, who adored a vast
Pantheon of deified bulls, rams, cats, mice, ibises,
sparrows, hawks, crocodiles, and a multitude of
mongrel creations of the imagination. Even insects,
flies, bees, beetles, were exalted to divinities.
Monstrosities were held in peculiar veneration.
The union of human bodies with the heads of
beasts or birds is especially characteristic of the
Egyptian religion; similar incongruities are met
with among the most ancient deities of Greece,
and were doubtless of Asiatic origin. Thus the
Arcadian Demeter was represented with a horse's
head, and the Cretan Minotaur with the head of
a bull, not to mention the hosts of gorgons,
harpies, centaurs, tritons, nereids, sirens, and satyrs
formed by uniting a human head with the body
of a beast or bird or fish. The Greek alone, with
his superior æsthetic sense, chaste imagination,
and unsurpassable plastic skill, knew how to give
organic unity to these heterogeneous combinations,
pruning them of excrescences, purging them of
superfluities, and rendering the boldest violations
of the laws of nature beautiful and harmonious as
works of art. These hybrid creatures of the fancy,
like the sphinxes which guarded the portals of the
temples of Thebes, and the colossal winged lions
of Nineveh and Persepolis, originated in the priestly
proclivity to symbolize and to express mystical

ideas in material forms; but their primitive crudeness, refined and transmuted in the crucible of the
Hellenic intellect, emerged as the pure gold of
artistic perfection. As the result of this process
of transformation or evolution, if we may regard
symbols as species and apply to them the catch-
word of modern science, the Greek embodiments
of these conceptions have survived as the fittest
in the struggle for existence, and secured a permanent place in the art and literature of the
civilized world. The fact that they are universally
accepted as "classical" is conclusive proof of their
absolute ascendency.

Alexandria was for several centuries, under the
Ptolemies and the Roman prefects, the principal
channel of commercial intercourse between the
East and the West, and consequently the point
at which Oriental and Occidental ideas came into
constant contact and often into sharp conflict, but
by mutual concession and compromise gradually
developed a certain eclecticism and syncretism of
philosophical speculations and religious systems.
Thus arose the so-called Alexandrian School, in
which the achievements of Egyptian, Hellenic, and
Hebrew culture were commingled and mutually
supplemented. Christianity, however, was too
aggressive in its spirit and too exclusive in its
claims to accept any compromise, or to enter into
any amicable *modus vivendi* with other cults. Its
mission was to put all things under its feet, and to
assert its universal supremacy, and for this reason

it recognized the validity of older forms of worship
and admitted their *raison d'être* only so far as they
could be shown to have a specifically propædeutic
relation to itself as the only true religion. Partly
in application of this principle, and partly as a
matter of policy in order to facilitate its propagation, it appropriated so far as possible the rites
and symbols and ancient traditions of antecedent
religions, interpreting them as anticipations, allegories, prophecies, and prefigurations which had
now been fully accomplished and thereby abro-
gated. Christian proselytes of different races were
eager and adept in making all available currents of
their ancestral mythology tributary to the stream,
whose waters were for the healing of the nations.
Egyptian converts, known as Copts (Copt, Gyptios,
Kyptaios, like Gypsy, is a corruption of Αἰγύπτιος),
found in the sacred records of their progenitors,
as preserved in picture-writing and plastic art, no
lack of ideographic and other symbolical material
which could be easily converted to Christian uses.
Thus the hieroglyphic sign ☥, pronounced *onk*,
and signifying "life," would be readily accepted
as an ansated cross ☥, and naturally give rise to
the simpler form ☥ so often represented on Coptic
monuments ; by a slight change it might be
metamorphosed into the monogrammatic name of
Christ ☧. In like manner an ancient Coptic relief
of the Virgin and Child, described by M. Gayet
(*Les Monuments Coptes du Musée de Boulaq,*
Paris, 1889), and by Georg Ebers (*Sinnbildliches,*

Leipzig, 1892), is a servile imitation of the traditional Egyptian representations of Isis suckling
Horus. The necklace of the Madonna is the
same as that worn by goddesses on the monuments, and by ladies of royal rank in the age of
the Pharaohs. The chair, on which she is seated,
with its back shaped like the hieroglyphic ſ (s),
is an exact copy of that on which Egyptian
deities were wont to be enthroned and Egyptian
sovereigns used to sit in state. The stiff and
angular infant is the very image of Horus; near
by stands Joseph, rather rigidly draped, and holding in his right hand a tree and an instrument
resembling a chisel, which may be intended to
indicate the occupation of a carpenter. Above
their heads extends the ideogram ⊏⊐ (pt), signifying the sky or heavens, and suggesting either
the place of their abode or their divine character.
Over all hovers a female gyrfalcon with outspread
wings, the Nechebt-Ilithyia (Εἰλείθυια), which presides over births and renders parturition easy, as
is stated in the *Physiologus*, by means of the Indian
stone eutokios (εὐτόκιος).

Another striking example of this tendency is the
transformation of Horus slaying Seth-Typhon into
St. George and the Dragon. An Egyptian basrelief of bronze in the Louvre, and a similar one in
clay in the British Museum, represent the sparrowheaded god equipped as a mounted warrior, and
thrusting his spear into the neck of a crocodile, the
emblem and incarnation of his demonic foe. In

Egyptian mythology Horus symbolized the vital energy and reproductive power of nature; he derived his name from the Semitic *Hur*, signifying light, and was therefore properly regarded by Herodotus as identical with Apollo; hence the double name of the Greco-Egyptian priest Horapollo, whose *Hierogly-phica* (edited by C. Leemans, Amsterdam, 1835) is an early and important contribution to symbolical zoölogy. Horus personified not only the vivifying and fertilizing forces of the physical world, and the triumph of life over death, but also the victory of good over evil; his feast was therefore a vernal festival celebrated on the twenty-third of April. Typhon, on the other hand, was the demon of the desert, the producer of drought and sterility and famine. As the counterpart to this delineation we have a rude Coptic relief of St. George and the Dragon, which was discovered at Luxor, and is so thoroughly Egyptian in character that it might be easily mistaken for Horus and Seth-Typhon. Over the haloed head of the Christian hero is an equilateral triangle, a symbol of the Trinity of frequent occurrence on Egyptian monuments; indeed, according to Plutarch, the fact that the ibis was wont to stand with straddled legs so as to form such a figure greatly added to its sacredness. In the background is the bull Apis, with what seems to be a decrescent moon (Ebers calls it a disc of the sun, *Sonnenscheibe*) over its back. The Egyptians worshipped two bulls, both sacred to Osiris, namely Mneuis at Heliopolis, and Apis at Memphis; the sign of the former was the sun, and that of the latter the moon. Above the gateway, through which St. George is riding with the dragon squirming beneath his horse, are two birds having tails resembling the chrysalis of an insect, and it may be, as Ebers suggests, that they are the larva out of which the rejuvenated phœnix was supposed to emerge. It is possible, however, that these queer tails are merely the result of an awkward attempt to draw feathers. The anniversary of St. George, like that of Horus, is on the twenty-third of April, and there is not the slightest doubt that this canonized knight, who figures in hagiology as a Cappadocian prince and blessed martyr, owes his existence to the Christianization of an old Egyptian myth, which, after undergoing this metamorphosis, migrated to Syria, where the saint is reputed to have been born in the city of Lydda, and thence gradually spread over all Asia Minor. Here the crusaders became familiar with the legend, adopted St. George as their patron and pattern in waging the holy war against the Mussulmanic dragon, and brought him to Europe emblazoned on their banners.

It is highly probable, and indeed quite certain, that many ornamentations of Christian architecture, which are now merely traditional and conventional forms and perform a purely decorative function, might be traced to Egyptian and other Oriental sources, where they had distinct significance as signs and symbols. But it is not the purpose of the writer to undertake such a study in comparative symbology, nor are the materials necessary to its successful prosecution as yet available, notwithstanding the rapidly accumulating and extremely valuable results of recent researches in archæology, ethnography, philology, and the critical comparison of religions. The aim of the present volume is a much simpler one, being an attempt to explain the meaning of the real or fabulous animals, which have been put to decorative uses in ecclesiastical architecture, and thus to account for their admittance to sacred edifices. The book is intended to be suggestive rather than exhaustive, showing the origin and signification of the most prominent of these types and symbols, and indicating the direction in which further investigations are to be pursued. The founder or at least the most eminent representative of the Alexandrian School of allegorists was the Jewish philosopher Philo, who, as a mediator between Hebrew and Hellenic culture, endeavoured to discover the teachings of Pythagoras, Plato, and Aristotle esoterically concealed in the Mosaic records, by giving to the latter a far-fetched, figurative interpretation. This hermeneutical principle was adopted by Christian exegetists and apologists, especially by Clemens Alexandrinus in his *Stromateus* (patchwork or miscellany of Greek and Christian literature), and by Origen, who recognized in the Scriptures a threefold sense: literal or historical, moral or psychical, and mystical or pneumatic. Cassian, in the fifth century, wrote a work entitled *Collationes Patrum Sceticorum*, in which he states that there are four kinds of knowledge to be derived from Biblical study : historical, tropological, allegorical, and anagogical. The first of these, being for the most part perfectly plain, was of no importance ; only the last three deserve the name of spiritual knowledge (*intelligentiam spiritualem*) ; or, as Hrabanus Maurus expressed it four centuries later, the historical sense is milk for babes ; the tropological sense is nutriment suited to those more advanced in wisdom ; the allegorical sense is the strong meat adapted to the robust souls whose faith is revealed in good works ; while the saintly persons, who despise all earthly joys and have fixed their affections wholly on heavenly things, are alone fit to receive the "wine of anagogical interpretation" and to be edified thereby. This last and highest degree of spiritual discernment is beyond the reach of " the higher criticism," and, as Cassian observes, is not attainable by severe study and deep erudition, but comes from divine illumination produced by fasting, prayer, and holy meditation. It is an enlightenment of the understanding proceeding from the purification of the heart, and not from poring over commentaries ; a lifting of the veil of the passions that obscure the mental vision.

Not only was the Hebrew cosmogony allegorized and spiritualized, but the same method of exposition was applied to the whole system of nature. Origen, in describing the process of creation, explains the creatures that fill the waters, the fowls of the air, and the creeping things as signifying good or evil

thoughts and feelings, and calls special attention to
the great whales as symbolizing violent passions
and criminal impulses.   In the hermeneutical *Hexahemera* of Basil the Great and his brother Gregory
of Nyssa this zoölogical typology is still more fully
developed, and the various characteristics, popularly
attributed to animals, served to enforce moral teachings or to illustrate theological tenets.   More important in this respect are the so-called *Claves
Scripturæ Sacræ*, which were to be used as keys
not only for unlocking the spiritual treasures of
Holy Writ, but also for disclosing the mystical
meaning of all natural things, the Greek *Physiologus*,
and the numerous mediæval compilations and
poetical productions based upon it, of which an
account is given in the second and third chapters
of this volume.   These works contain an epitome
of the mythical and symbolical zoölogy, botany,
ornithology, and mineralogy gathered from many
nations, and transmitted from the remotest times.
Very early in the Christian era this traditional
material infused itself into patristic literature, and
thus gradually passed from rhetorical decoration in
Christian homilies to artistic decoration in Christian
architecture, where it found expression in fantastic
and often monstrous forms, which can be understood only by tracing them to their sources in the
superstitious notions of ancient and especially
Oriental peoples.   With the growth of religious
scepticism and schism this symbolism gradually
and almost imperceptibly merged into satire, so

that it is often difficult to draw a line of demarcation between them.   Mediæval humour was coarse rather than keen, and better skilled in wielding bludgeons than in brandishing rapiers.   Even the genius of Rabelais hardly suffices to relieve it of a certain boorish grossness and brutality, and render it thoroughly enjoyable to the refined and fastidious modern reader.   The satire of the period of the Reformation was of the same bitter and abusive style.   Luther's wit was notoriously nasty, and even the gentle Melanchthon was capable of indulging in a strain of sarcasm which any cultivated man of to-day would reprobate as extremely vulgar.   It must be remembered, however, that this coarseness was a characteristic of the age, and is not to be regarded as a mark of intrinsic vileness or individual depravity.   It was something wholly external, a mode of expression by no means inconsistent with a robust virtue, as far removed from prudishness as from pruriency.   In our time the fiercest theological polemic would hardly venture to lampoon and caricature his opponents as the reformers of the sixteenth century did the see of Rome, nor would the most rabid apostle of Anti-Semitism seek to propagate his views by adorning Christian churches and other public edifices with filthy sculptures derisive of the Jews.

In the volume now offered to the public the author has endeavoured to show the rise and evolution of this symbolism, and its transition to satire as seen in

Christian art, although, as already stated, he is very far from claiming to have exhausted the subject. The illustrations are derived partly from the bestiaries printed by Cahier in the second volume of his *Mélanges d'Archéologie*, partly from a parchment manuscript psalter of Isabella of France in the Royal Library of Munich, and partly from ecclesiastical edifices. The appended bibliography, taken in connection with the references given in the body of the work, will be found to contain the principal sources of information.

In conclusion, I wish to express my hearty thanks to Hrn. Dr. Laubmann, Director of the K. Hof- und Staatsbibliothek in Munich, Bavaria, as well as to the other custodians of that library, for the uniform kindness and cordiality shown in admitting me to the privileges and in facilitating the use of that magnificent collection of printed books and manuscripts.

CHAPTER I

ALLEGORICAL AND ANAGOGICAL INTERPRETATIONS OF NATURE

Impulse given to the study of natural history by Alexander the Great—Scientific spirit fostered by Aristotle—Lack of this spirit among the Romans—Alexandria as a centre of learning under the Ptolemies—The Christian theory of the relation of the Book of Revelation to the Book of Nature—The patristic conception of the visible creation as an image of the invisible world and a mirror of spiritual truth—Animals as religious emblems in Oriental, and especially in Buddhistic, literature—Mineralogical symbolism—Magical and medical properties and religious significance of precious stones—Legends of Solomon's wisdom, and his method of building the Temple—Ceremony of blessing jewels—Speculations of Justinus Kerner and Schubert concerning the occult affinities of the mineral kingdom to man—The typology of precious stones according to the *Physiologus*—Spiritual meaning of the diamond, the pearl, and the Indian stone—Terrobuli in Christian symbolism and architecture.

ALEXANDER THE GREAT, in addition to his military exploits and political achievements, also gave a new impulse and direction to the development of natural history in Greece by supplying his tutor, Aristotle, with specimens and more or less accurate descriptions of animals native to the lands he had conquered. By means of the material thus obtained

21

the peripatetic philosopher was enabled to extend his researches beyond the confines of his own country, and to correct many false and fantastic notions that had hitherto prevailed concerning exotic, and especially Oriental, fauna, and thus became—at least in a relative and restricted sense—the founder of systematic zoölogy in the modern signification of the term.   His predecessors, as well as his contemporaries, had been wont to speculate about animals chiefly from moral, religious, poetic, artistic, didactic, humoristic, satirical, sentimental, and superstitious points of view, and to prize the lessons of prudence and piety and wisdom which they were supposed to inculcate; but the Stagirite was the first to study them from a strictly scientific point of view.

Still, the scientific field, which Aristotle cultivated with such assiduous care and with so fruitful results, formed only a small evergreen spot, standing oasis-like in the midst of a wide waste of wild conjectures and sterile speculations.   Tyrtamus of Lesbos, surnamed Theophrastus, his favourite pupil and chosen successor as head of the peripatetic school, followed in the footsteps of the great master in this field of investigation, and aimed at the acquisition of positive knowledge by means of exact methods in the study of nature.   Unfortunately, however, the fabulous stories related by Ktesias and Megasthenes in their voluminous descriptions of India and Persia appealed more powerfully to the imagination, and gratified in a higher degree the popular love of the marvellous, than the sober records of accurate observation, and therefore acquired far greater currency.

The Romans brought beasts from the remotest provinces of the empire, not because they felt any rational or scientific interest in them, but solely in order to increase the pomp and splendour of military triumphs, or to minister to the barbarous and bloody sports of the amphitheatre. According to Petronius, the Marmaric deserts and the Moorish forests were scoured for the purpose of procuring ferocious animals to fight in the arena with each other, or with trained gladiators in horrible combat. "The ships from foreign shores," he says, "are crowded with fierce tigers confined in gilded cages, and destined to drink human blood to the frantic plaudits of the populace."

When Cicero was proconsul in Cilicia, he received an urgent letter from the ædile Cœlius, imploring him to send as speedily as possible a cargo of panthers, which were to be used as a "campaign fund" for electioneering purposes. As a means of winning the suffrages of the rabble this sort of expenditure was probably more efficient, and certainly more open and exciting than the modern system of distributing "bunched" ballots, or of purchasing venal voters "in blocks of five." To this entreaty Cicero replied that he would do his best to comply with the request of his friend, and thus contribute to the success of his candidacy, but that owing to the energy and skill of many lovers of the chase, and especially of a certain Patiscus, these beasts of venery were very scarce, having fled for safety from his consular province into Caria. If we may believe their own statements, the Romans accomplished wonders in training beasts and birds for private amusement or for spectacular entertainments. Their passion for pet animals was a matter of fashion, a mere "fad"; and Cato bitterly censured the degeneracy of the times, when ladies frequented the market-place fondling lap-dogs, and dandies strutted about with parrots perched on their wrists. These birds were kept in cages of gold and silver and tortoise-shell, and taught to shout the name of the reigning emperor. The lion learned to play with hares, catching them in frolic and letting them go, and rabbits ran and took refuge in its jaws as in their burrow. Martial, who describes these performances, adds, in obsequious flattery of Domitian, that this gentleness and docility of savage beasts are due less to the art of the tamer (*domator*) than to awe of the emperor (*imperator*), "for the lions know whom they serve." The same poet informs us that eagles were made to act on the stage, taking a boy up into the air without doing him any harm, in realistic representation of the rape of Ganymede on Mount Ida—

> " Ætchereas aquila puerum portante per auras,
>   Illœsum timidis unquibus hæsit onus."
>   *Ep. Lib.* i. 7.

In view of this almost exclusively amphitheatrical

and utterly brutalizing relation of the Romans to
the animal world, it is not surprising to find in the
Natural History of Pliny an encyclopædic compilation of current traditions and popular superstitions, instead of a record of actual observations and
scientific conclusions. In short, the Romans do
not appear to have made any contributions whatever to natural science, although the vast extent of
their dominions afforded them an excellent oppor-
tunity for such investigations. Not even in the
great didactic poem of the keen-witted Lucretius,
De Rerum Natura, do we discover any distinct
traces of the Aristotelian method of inquiry. The
achievements of Roman thought were in politics,
and the cognate department of jurisprudence.

During the reign of the Ptolemies, as well as
under the rule of Roman prefects, Alexandria was
celebrated, not only as the chief commercial centre
of the world, but also as a cosmopolitan seat of
learning, and the principal avenue of intellectual
communication between the East and the West.
Indeed, Egyptian monarchs—at least from the accession of the Nineteenth Dynasty, sixteen centuries before the Christian era—seem to have had a
peculiar passion for establishing museums of curiosities, menageries of exotic beasts and birds, and
other collections of rare and abnormal productions
of nature. The ninth Ptolemy, Euergetes II., surnamed Physkon (Gorbelly), wrote a book full of
curious information about such things. His great
aim, however, was not to discover and record facts,

but to recount wonders, and he is therefore well
characterized by Pitra in his *Spicilegium Solesmense* as a "rerum mirabilium curiosissimus investigator." It was the *mirabilia*, or marvels of nature,
that attracted his attention and stimulated his researches. This sovereign was so zealous in procuring works for the Alexandrian libraries (the
Bruchium Museum and the Serapeum) that he not
only sent special emissaries into foreign countries
to purchase them at high prices, but was also accustomed to take away from travellers any valuable
manuscripts in their possession and add them to
the public collections, giving in return a copy of
the book thus arbitrarily appropriated.

Alexandrian learning embraced unquestionably
a wide range of topics, among which medicine,
anatomy, mathematics, astronomy, and geography
held a prominent place, but the study of botany,
mineralogy, and zoölogy were carried on in an
extremely superficial and desultory manner, and
chiefly for the purpose of discovering in plants,
stones, and animals the occult and magical properties and "strange and vigorous faculties" with
which they were supposed to be endowed. Of the
cautious and critical study and scrutiny of nature,
and the essentially scientific spirit which characterized the Aristotelian method of research, these
scholars appear to have had little or no conception.

It was also in the Greco-Judaic schools of
Alexandria that Christian theology was developed
as the resultant of the contact and conflict of the

Hebrew with the Hellenic intellect. From the
Christian point of view, the Bible was recognized
as the only true source of knowledge. The sacred
volume was assumed to contain unerring information on all subjects whatsoever, provided one could
ascertain its real meaning, which was often wrapped
up and hidden in allegories and obscure similitudes
and symbolisms, like precious treasures kept in
caskets under intricate locks, and concealed in
dark places. Hence the supreme importance of
hermeneutics as the science of sciences, the master-
key, which opens all the secrets of the universe,
and reveals all the mysteries of nature.

It is said of Solomon that "he spake of trees
from the cedar that is in Lebanon, even unto the
hyssop that springeth out of the wall ; he spake also
of beasts and of fowl, and of creeping things and of
fishes." We are not justified, however, in assuming
that he discoursed of natural history in the modern
sense of the term, or that he was familiar with
botany, zoölogy, ornithology, entomology, and
ichthyology, as we understand these sciences. His
knowledge of plants and of animals did not differ
in kind from that of his contemporaries and of the
age in which he lived ; he was superior to others
only in possessing a sturdier common-sense and
shrewder skill, in applying this current lore to
human life and conduct, in apothegmatic illustration
of the folly or wisdom of mankind. What we call
the book of nature was to him a vast and many-
volumed treatise on all phases and features of

human nature, in which the world of lower
creatures was held up to man as a moral mirror,
in order that he might see therein the reflections
of his own vices and virtues.

In the development and enforcement of this idea
patristic theologians surpassed the prophets and
sages of the Old Testament, and even the subtle
scribes and quibbling rabbis, resolving the external
universe into a mere body of divinity or system of
Christian doctrine, written in cipher, which it was
the function of the exegetist to interpret so as to
bring it into harmony with divine revelation, and
make it illustrative and confirmatory of Holy Writ.
According to Origen " the visible world teaches us
concerning the invisible ; the earth contains images
of heavenly things, in order that by means of
these lower objects we may mount up to that
which is above. . . . As God made man in His
own image and after His own likeness, so He created
the lower animals after the likeness of heavenly
prototypes."

This conception of the physical world as a
symbol of spiritual truth is only one form in which
the ascetic contempt of the body, as a clog and
cumbrance to the soul and a hindrance of holy as-
pirations, took expression. The cosmos or material
body of the universe, like the carnal body of the
individual, must be sanctified by its spiritualization
and virtual expression. Paul's statement that " the
invisible things of Him (God) from the creation of
the world are clearly seen, being understood by the

things that are made," was thought to be a distinct assertion and ample justification of this theory, which rendered even the heathen, to whom the gospel had not been revealed, "without excuse."

The Talmud declares that "he who interprets the scripture literally is a liar and a blasphemer." This exegetical principle is, however, not exclusively Talmudic, but underlies and pervades more or less completely all hermeneutical literature. This attitude of mind arises from the fact that sacred books, which are accepted and transmitted from generation to generation as infallible and therefore unchangeable records and repositories of truth, can keep pace with the progress of human thought, and adapt themselves to the growth of knowledge, so as to maintain their hold upon the morally and intellectually advancing races of mankind, only by voluntarily laying aside all claims to strict and literal accuracy, and taking refuge in allegorical and symbolical interpretations.

According to the biblical story the fall of man involved the alteration and corruption of the whole creation, including all forms of animal and vegetable life, and extending even to the soil itself, which thenceforth showed a perverse prolificacy in bringing forth thorns and brambles and every species of noxious weed. These lower organisms were also embraced in the Christian scheme of redemption, and are represented as looking forward with painful longing to its completion, and their consequent release from the degrading penalties of human transgression.

Indeed, one of the most conspicuous signs of the successful issue and perfect consummation of the Atonement is to be the disappearance of all antipathies between savage beasts and their natural prey : the lion will lay aside his fierce animosities and carnivorous appetites, lying down with the lamb, and eating straw like the bullock in token of his regeneration, and universal peace will be restored. Satan will be dethroned as the prince of this world, and the earth resume its pristine state of Edenic innocence and paradisean purity.

Thus the present condition and ultimate destiny of mankind were supposed to be reflected fragmentarily in the lower animals as in a shattered mirror; and it was from this source that the early Christian evangelists and patristic theologians were especially fond of drawing illustrations of spiritual truths and elucidations of scriptural texts. The words of Job : " Ask the beast and it will teach thee, and the birds of heaven and they will tell thee," were assumed to furnish sufficient ground for regarding the entire animal kingdom as a mere collection of types and symbols of religious dogmas and Christian virtues. The apocalyptic monsters of St. John the Divine were also cited as a precedent warranting the wildest vagaries of zoölogical exegesis.

In Oriental literature, and especially in the sacred books of the East, nothing is more common than to put animals to rhetorical, metaphorical, and emblematical uses, and to hold them up to the religious man as models for imitation. Comparisons and correspondencies of this kind were naturally suggested by the doctrine of metempsychosis, in which they have a psychological basis, and from which they derive a peculiar force and cogency, wholly foreign to Occidental habits of thought and feeling.

Thus the Buddhist ascetic is told to pattern in austerity and humility after the ass, which is content to sleep by the roadside in the outskirts of the village, on a dust-heap, a bed of chaff, or a layer of leaves. He is also enjoined to take heed to the squirrel, which, when assailed, uses its tail as a cudgel against its enemies, and to ward off carnal affections and spiritual foes with the staff of steady and earnest meditation. When he goes forth with his begging bowl, he should wrap himself in the vesture of meekness and moral restraint, that he may be free from fear and from worldly contamination, as the white ant covers itself with a leaf when it goes in quest of food. The scorpion has a sting in its tail, which it bears erect; in like manner the religious man should wield the sword of knowledge, and thereby render himself invincible. In the burning heat of summer the pig betakes itself to a pond; so the devotee, when his soul is scorched and inflamed by evil passions, should have recourse to the cool, refreshing, and ambrosial exercise of universal kindliness. Again,

the hog, having gone to a marsh or swamp, digs a
trough in the earth and lies therein; so the yogi
should bury his body in the trough of his mind
by means of profound and passionless meditation.
The owl is the mortal enemy of crows, and is
wont to repair to their nests at night and kill their
young; in like manner the religious mendicant is
the foe of ignorance, and plucks it out of his mind
and destroys it before it has become inveterate.
Like the owl, too, he loves seclusion and the quiet
favourable to calm reflection. The leech sucks
itself fast to whatever it touches, and gorges itself
with blood; so the yogi holds firmly to whatever
he fixes his thoughts upon, and drinks in the
never-cloying fulness of Nirvâna. The spider
spins its web to catch flies; the yogi spreads the
net of unbroken contemplation before the six
avenues of the senses, and takes captive and
destroys every lust that seeks to enter into the
mind. Those who have become the slaves of the
passions live wholly in them, moving about in a
world of illusions, the creation of their own desires,
as the spider runs to and fro on the filaments of
the web, which it has spun out of its own bowels.
The process of regeneration and emancipation from
the allurements of the senses and the trammels of
the flesh is compared to the action of the snake in
casting its skin. He who is content with sensual
pleasures is like a hog wallowing in the mire and
glutted with wash. The elephant is the type of
patient endurance, self-restraint. Buddha himself

is likened to a well-tamed (*sudânta*) elephant, and
is often spoken of as the great elephant (*mahânâga*).
Another symbol of the pious recluse, who has re-
nounced the world, is the rhinoceros, because it
loves to dwell alone and remote from its kind.

Even inanimate things are moralized and made
to represent spiritual states. Thus the jug (*kum-
bho*), which emits no sound when it is full, emblematizes the man who is full of knowledge, and
walks humbly and soberly in the "path" (*dharma-
patha*), avoiding vain boastings and garrulousness
and noisy ostentation. This idea is expressed in
the following lines from the *Suttanipata :*

> "Loudly brawls the shallow run,
> But the stream that's deep is dumb.
> Noise betrays the empty tun ;
> From the full no sound doth come.
> Empty pitchers like are fools ;
> Wise men are the full, clear pools."

The same figure of speech occurs in *The Lover*
of Sir Walter Raleigh :

> "Passions are likened best to floods and streams,
> The shallow murmurs, while the deeps are dumb."

In these comparisons and injunctions the common
qualities and most conspicuous characteristics of
the animals, which the holy man is admonished to
imitate, are lost sight of, and only certain fanciful
attributes considered. In common parlance it
would not be flattering to speak of a saint metaphorically as an ass, a hog, a leech, or a scorpion.

D

This comical disregard of the prominent points of
resemblance, which would be most naturally suggested by the simile, is not confined to Buddhistic
writings, but, as we shall see hereafter, constantly
occurs in Christian hermeneutical and homiletical
literature, and often renders it very funny reading.

It was also in the Orient that a sort of mineralogical symbolism, based upon certain magical and
magnetic qualities supposed to be peculiar to
precious stones, was first and most fully developed.
Jewels were worn originally, and are still worn in
Eastern countries, as prophylactics and talismans
rather than as mere ornaments. Their purpose
was not so much to adorn as to protect the person,
preventing disease and warding off malign influences, and they were therefore prized more for
their occult virtue than for their brilliancy and
beauty. In Europe, too, they constituted an important part of mediæval pharmacopœias, and were
to be found side by side with mummy dust, "eye
of newt and toe of frog," and many nasty and
nauseous compounds in every well-regulated apothecary's shop. Popular superstition has not yet
ceased to endow bufonite or toadstone with
wonderful medical and necromantic properties.

The urim and thummim (light and perfection)
in the breastplate of the Jewish high-priest were
precious stones remarkable for their luminousness
and purity, and, like the sacred scarabæus worn by
the Egyptian hierophant, had a mystical meaning
and were consulted as oracles. In what manner

the divine will was communicated through them is
not known ; it is probable that the priest by steadfastly gazing on them was thrown into an ecstatic
or hypnotic state, in which he saw visions, and
uttered words that were interpreted as divine
inspirations and supernatural illuminations.

It is curious to note to what extent the once
universal belief in the amuletic efficacy of gems
still survives in modern life and literature.   Thus
the amethyst, as its name implies, neutralized the
intoxicating properties of alcohol, and was therefore
wrought into cups, from which one could quaff the
strongest liquors in the largest draughts without
getting drunk.   It was also supposed, perhaps in
consequence of this anti-inebriant quality, to render
a man energetic and diligent in business and to
insure peace of mind.   The agate disenvenomed
the sting of serpents and scorpions, and when worn
on the left hand made its possessor winsome and
wise ; if placed under the pillow it produced
pleasant dreams.

Boccaccio says in the *Decameron*, that " the
heliotrope is a stone of such strange virtue that it
causes the bearer of it to be completely concealed
from the sight of all present." This power was
also ascribed to the plant of the same name.
Dante describes the spirits of the damned in the
seventh circle of hell as running to and fro naked
and affrighted without hope of hole or heliotrope :

" Senza sperar pertugio o elitropia."

In other words, they found no cleft in which to
hide, and had no heliotrope to render them invisible.   The reference here is not to the plant, but
to the mineral. The ruby absorbed morbid humours,
and was an antidote for catarrh and unrequited
love; no wonder then that it also made a man
socially attractive and companionable. . The carbuncle protected the wearer against the fatal look
of the basilisk and the fascinations of the evil eye,
counteracted the virulence of poisons, purified the
air from pestilential vapours, and, when worn as a
necklace, was preventive of epilepsy.   Chalcedony
imparted moral strength and courage to resist all
evil enticements; the variety of it known as carnelian was believed to be effective in cheering the
heart by its soothing action on the bile and the
blood.   The topaz kept the soul pure and chaste,
and is etymologically related to the Sanskrit *tapas*,
a general term for the purifying process by which
the Indian ascetic purges his spirit and frees himself from sensual desires and worldly affections.
It was thought to exert a calming influence upon
lunatics, and, if thrown into a boiling pot, to stop
ebullition.   With a topaz in his armpit, a person
was deemed capable of passing unsinged through
the hottest flames, and undergoing with safety the
severest ordeal of fire; for this reason witches were
carefully examined before being burned, lest they
might have recourse to this means of impunity.
This stone was often given as a mark of friendship,
and especially as a pledge of troth, since it was

supposed to promote fidelity. The lapis lazuli was used as a necklace for children, because it made them fearless and truthful; corals were employed in the same manner, because they warded off sorcerous arts and withstood the powers of witchcraft. Jasper produced clearness and keenness of vision, stanched blood, healed dropsy and dyspepsia, and was an effective febrifuge. Chrysoprase cured heart-affections both physical and mental. Beryl acted as a cholagogue, and as a natural result of its cathartic and tonic qualities developed a cheerful and courageous spirit. Rock-crystal or "icestone," as it was popularly called, quenched thirst, prevented vertigo, and enabled women to suckle their children. The necklace of clear rock-crystal, still commonly worn by wet-nurses, is a survival of the belief in the lactific virtue of this variety of limpid quartz.

The association of precious stones with the months of the year as amulets and promoters of good fortune seems to have originated at an early date in Arabia. In accordance with this notion the hyacinth or red zircon was worn in January, the amethyst in February, the heliotrope or bloodstone in March, the sapphire and diamond in April, the emerald in May, the agate in June, the carnelian in July, the onyx in August, the chrysolite in September, the aqua marine and opal in October, the topaz in November, and the chrysoprase and turquoise in December. Thus the magic power of the stones serve to protect their wearers, and to communicate to them the hidden properties with which these gems were supposed to be endowed. In modern literature this theme has been treated most fully and suggestively, perhaps, by Theodor Körner in his poem *Die Monatssteine*, written in 1810.

Far more important for our present purpose than the magical and medical properties of precious stones is their significance as symbols of theological doctrines and Christian graces. In a mediæval German poem "Concerning the Heavenly Jerusalem" (Diemer: *Deutsche Gedichte*, pp. 361-372), based on the treatise *De Lapidibus* of Marbodius, and on the twenty-first chapter of Revelation, we have a theological mineralogy corresponding to the theological zoölogy of the *Physiologus*. The two verses (Rev. xxi. 19, 20) that make mention of the twelve stones with which the foundations of the wall of the mystical city were garnished, are expanded into more than two hundred lines of the poem, consisting chiefly of extremely far-fetched allegory. Thus jasper is the foundation of the Church, and acts as a preservative against hurtful phantasms and devilish wiles; it is of a green colour, and signifies those who foster the faith, never letting it wither away and grow dry and dead, but always keeping it alive. Sapphire has a heavenly hue, and symbolizes those who, although on the earth, have their thoughts fixed on heavenly things. Chalcedony shows its lustre only in the open air, and typifies those who fast and pray in

secret, but whose righteousness shines forth among
men. Emerald is native to a cold and arid region,
inhabited only by griffins and one-eyed men
(*monoculi*), who are constantly fighting for the
possession of this stone. It surpasses all gems and
herbs in greenness, and symbolizes the freshness
and vigour of Christian piety as opposed to the
coldness and barrenness of infidelity. The griffins
are the demons that, in the form of winged lions,
flew aloft on the pinions of pride and fell from
heaven into the abyss of hell for their misdeeds.
Their monoculous antagonists are those who do
not walk in two ways, are not double-dealing, do
not serve two masters, are not given to duplicity,
but who have an eye single to the glory of God,
are single-minded, seeking with oneness of purpose
to hold fast the jewel of faith, which the demons
would wrest from them. Sardonyx has three
colours, black below, white in the middle, and red
above; it is a type of those who suffer for Christ's
sake, and, although pure and spotless, are vile and
sinful in their own eyes. Sardius is deep red, and
signifies the blood of the martyrs. Chrysolite
glistens like gold and emits scintillations, and is an
emblem of those who let their light shine in word
and deed. Beryl glitters like the sea in the sun-
light, and illustrates the illuminating power of the
divine spirit. After interpreting in this manner
the symbolism of the other stones, topaz, chryso-
prasus, jacinth, and amethyst, on which the New
Jerusalem is built, the poet turns homilist, and

warns his readers that they can enter the heavenly city only by practising the virtues which the stones shadow forth :

"Nu habent ir alle wol uernomen,
Wi ir in di burch sculet chomen."

No doubt this symbolism is utterly fantastic and absurd, and would be hardly worthy of notice were it not for the fact that it holds a prominent place in sacred art, and determines, to a considerable degree, the kinds of stones used in ecclesiastical architecture, as well as in ornamenting sacerdotal vestments, crucifixes, rosaries, chalices, and other sacramental utensils.

Speculations of this sort began to pervade Christian hermeneutic theology at a very early period, and are traceable in the oldest apocryphal literature of the New Testament. In the latter half of the fourth century Epiphanius, Bishop of Cyprus, wrote a book "On the Twelve Stones in Aaron's Robes," and another "On the Twelve Stones set in the Priest's Breastplate." The same allegorical spirit of interpretation is shown by Anselm, Archbishop of Canterbury, and by Ambrosius, in their commentaries on the Apocalypse.

A similar tendency manifests itself in the symbolical and analogical use of numbers, which sought to trace a recondite relation between the seven seals of the Apocalypse, the seven petitions of the Pater Noster, the seven gifts of the Holy Spirit, the seven beatitudes of the Sermon on the Mount, the seven sacraments, the seven prototypes in the Old Testament, the seven heavens, the seven days of creation, the seven ages of man, the seven liberal arts, the seven signs marking the birth of Christ, and many other sevenfold things. This subject is fully treated in an old poem entitled *Deus Septiformis*, or the Septiform God.

A curious specimen of biblical exegesis in a poem of the eleventh century, called *Praise of Solomon* (Diemer, pp. 107-114), explains how it was possible to construct the Temple so that "there was neither hammer nor axe, nor any tool of iron heard in the house while it was building." A dragon, which had caused a severe drought by drinking all the water in the springs and wells of Jerusalem, evaded every effort to capture it until Solomon ordered the empty wells and cisterns to be filled with a mixture of wine and mead. As the result of this stratagem the beast became so intoxicated that it was easily taken and fettered. On recovering from its drunkenness it promised the king that if he would set it free, it would tell him how he could complete the Temple without the unpleasant din and clatter of masons and carpenters. The wise sovereign accepted this proposal, and learned that there was an animal on Mount Lebanon, with the entrails of which one could cut the hardest stones. Hunters were sent out, who succeeded in killing this wonderful creature, and by means of its intestines the workmen were able to construct the edifice as by enchant-

ment. The poet then describes the splendours of
Solomon's court, to which an allegorical interpretation is given : Solomon is God, who created the
world noiselessly, and in a breath, the Queen of
Sheba is the Church, and the courtiers and nobles
are priests and bishops. The author gives as his
authority for this exegesis a gentleman called Hier-
onymus (*ein herro hiz heronimus*), evidently referring
to the famous ascetic and saint of the fourth century.
Indeed, the term " herro" is admirably suited to
the character of this remarkable man, who com-
bined the austerity of the monk with the elegance
of the man of the world, and thereby rendered
himself so attractive to the fine ladies of Roman
society that many of them exchanged their rich
apparel and luxurious homes for a hair-shirt and
an anchoretic life in the desert.

Pineda, in his *Salomon Prævius*, published in
eight books at Mayence in 1813, describes a worm
called samir, whose blood had the property of soften-
ing stones and glass, so that they could be cut and
carved like wax. This discovery, we are told, was
made accidentally by Solomon, who kept a young
ostrich in a glass cage ; but the parent bird brought
the samir from the desert, and by means of its blood
cut the glass and set the captive free. This circumstance was reported to Solomon, who made further
experiments with this substance, and invented a new
process of working in marble and engraving gems.
According to another account, Solomon had a
plant which had been brought to him by a foreign

embassy, the juice of which possessed the same lithotomic qualities. These legends arose evidently as inferences from the passages already quoted concerning the wise king's vast knowledge of natural history and his method of building the Temple. The Hebrew monarch got the credit of all the marvellous stories of this kind which were current in the middle ages, for the same reason that mediæval chronicles made Charlemagne the hero of all feats of valour and deeds of chivalry; and American newspapers ascribe all good jokes afloat to Abraham Lincoln.

The ceremony of blessing jewels used to be performed by the kings of England in Westminster Abbey on Good Friday, and was supposed to impart to these precious stones a still greater healing power peculiarly efficacious in curing cramps and epilepsy. But long before this custom came to be observed, jewels, as we have already seen, played an important part in ancient and mediæval materia medica as antidotes and amulets, and especially as antitoxicons. In a didactic poem entitled *De Gemmis*, and written by Marbodius, Bishop of Rennes, in the latter half of the eleventh century, more than sixty precious stones are mentioned, and their properties described; the work is, however, chiefly a compilation and Christianization of the opinions of Aristotle, Pliny, Galen, Isidore, Dioscorides, Avicenna, and other authorities on this subject, since his sole aim is religious instruction and edification.

A German poet of the thirteenth century, Der
Stricker, ridicules the popular belief in the magical
and medicinal virtues of precious stones as a foolish
superstition, and thus shows himself to have been
far in advance not only of the ignorant masses,
but also of the cultured classes and scholars of
his day.

Among modern writers Justinus Kerner has
devoted himself most earnestly to this province
of investigation and speculation. He maintains
that in primitive times, when man lived under
simpler conditions and nearer to nature than at
present, he was far more susceptible to her subtle
influences, so that " even the spirit of the stone, now
grown dull and sluggish, was capable of affecting
him." Modern culture, he adds, has materialized
man, and "swathed his soul in a threefold girdle
of grossness, so that only mechanical and chemical
forces can act upon it ; for this reason he is now
driven to the use of poisons, the strongest elements
in the three realms of nature, as medicaments and
healing remedies, they alone being able to penetrate the insulating earthy mass which prevents
spirit from operating directly upon spirit." If
stones, he continues, do not manifest the same
virtues now as formerly, the fault is in ourselves.
In our present vitiated state they exert their real
and inherent powers only when we are under the
influence of magnetism, which corresponds, in a
certain degree, to the original and normal condition
of mankind, since it renders the soul more free from

the bondage of the body. Stones nowadays produce upon magnetized persons the same effects that
were ascribed to them in ancient times, for example in the Orphic *Lithiaka*, where it is said
that nature has endued them with greater virtues
than roots or herbs. The same view is expressed
by Schubert in his *Natural History*, where the
mineral kingdom is represented as a realm full of
occult affinities and spiritual suggestions, and mystical relations to the microcosm, man. Schubert
also declares that the secret and subtle properties
of stones affect the human organism most powerfully when it is in a magnetic or somnambulic
state.

In the *Physiologus* (the character and contents
of which will be fully considered in a subsequent
chapter), as well as in mediæval bestiaries, we find
the queerest exegetical applications of these superstitious notions intermingled with utterly irrelevant
citations of Holy Writ, such as one would now
hear only from the lips of a Hard-Shell Baptist
preacher or an old plantation negro exhorter.
Thus the diamond, or adamant as it is called, is
taken as the type of Christ, because it shines in
the dark, as it is written in Isaiah: "The people
that walked in darkness have seen a great light;
they that dwell in the land of the shadow of death,
upon them hath the light shined." Again, we are
told that the diamond is so hard that neither iron
nor stone can penetrate it, but it penetrates all sub-
stances, "for all things were made by Him, and

without Him was not anything made that was made." Likewise the apostles have said of it: "I saw a man upon a wall of adamant, and in his hand a stone of adamant." (Here the apostles are confounded with the prophets, as the quotation is from the Septuagint version of Amos vii. 7.) We are furthermore informed that "the diamond can be cut and polished only after it has been soaked in the warm blood of a he-goat." In this case the he-goat is typical of the crucified Christ, and the diamond represents the hardness of a world stubborn in sin, which nothing but the warm blood of the Saviour can render tractable and reformable. As early as the third century St. Cyprian, Bishop of Carthage, in his *Liber de Duplici Martyrio*, accepts this notion on the authority of the naturalists of his day, and uses it to illustrate the efficacy of the Atonement. "Those who are versed in the knowledge of natural things tell us that adamant does not yield to the hardness of steel, and can be malleated only after being macerated in the blood of a he-goat. But no adamant is harder than the stony heart of the sinner; nevertheless the blood of Christ softens this stony heart, this iron heart, this heart harder than adamant." In this way the marvels of the material creation were made to elucidate the mysteries of the spiritual world, and to confirm the truths of divine revelation. The *Physiologus* also asserts that no demon can enter a house or habitation of man in which there is a diamond, and adds: "So it is with the heart

wherein Christ dwells, whose presence protects
it against all approaches and assaults of the
devil."

It is said of the pearl-fishers, that they attach an
agate to a cord and let it down into the sea, where
it is drawn towards the pearls by a mysterious
attraction, so that by following the cord the fishers
discover them and remove them from their shells.
Here the agate typifies John the Baptist, who
pointed the way to the pearl of great price, saying :
" Behold the Lamb of God, which taketh away the
sin of the world." The author then tells how the
pearl is produced. The sea-creature, which contains this precious substance, is described as having
two appendages like wings, and has therefore been
mistaken for a bird ; it is evident, however, that
a bivalve is meant. Just before the dawn this
oyster comes out of the deep water to the shore,
and, opening its shell, receives a drop of dew
from heaven, which the rays of the rising sun
change into a pearl. The reader would naturally
expect this story to be a symbolism of the Incarnation or the Immaculate Conception; but the writer
indulges in an elaborate theological, or rather ecclesiastical, interpretation, in which the sea is the
world, the fishers are the saints and doctors of the
Church, and the bivalve stands for the Old and
New Testaments joined together into one Bible or
Book of Revelation, and containing the pure pearls
of divine truth. As we shall have occasion to
observe, the similitudes of the *Physiologus* are not

only hopelessly and often ludicrously mixed, but readily shift at every turn of thought like the figures of a kaleidoscope.

Dante in one of his sonnets (xxxv.) uses a metaphor based on this theory of the genesis of the pearl in a modified form, and implying that it is an emanation of the stars: *come de stella margherita*. A mediæval Spanish poet also speaks of the pearl as having its origin in a dew-drop, and refers to St. Isidore of Seville as his authority, who, he says, was well informed in such matters:

"Ca assi lo diz Sant Esidro que sopo la materia."

Another type of Christ is the Indian stone (λίθος ἰνδικὸς), which was supposed to cure dropsy by absorbing morbid humours and serous fluids in the body; "so, too, Christ heals us who are spiritually dropsical, having the waters of the devil collected in our hearts." There is also an Indian stone called eutokios or birth-easing, which is round like a nut and rings like a bell. When the female vulture is with young, she sits on this stone, as soon as she begins to feel the pangs of parturition, and its virtue is such as to enable her to bring forth without the pains of travail. In like manner Christ was born of the Virgin unbegotten and without suffering. And as the eutokios is hollow and has within it another stone, which gives out a pleasant sound, so the Godhead of our Lord was hidden in His body and yet made itself manifest. In this connection the expositor quotes several passages of the Scriptures, such as Matthew xxi. 42, and Isaiah xxvi. 18, which do not bear the slightest relevancy to the doctrine he wishes to enforce.

What the *Physiologus* relates of the vulture is reported by Pliny of the eagle, and the stone is called aëtites or eagle-stone, and is said to have been found frequently in the aerie of the king of birds. We may add that in the mediæval Waldensian bestiary a more edifying interpretation of the fable is given, which is explained as symbolizing the help of the Holy Spirit in bringing forth good works.

It is a noteworthy mark of ignorance that both Pliny and the *Physiologus* speak of these accipitrine birds as though they were viviparous instead of oviparous animals, and were to be classed with mammals rather than with fowls.

Among fabulous stones the so-called terrobuli, more properly pyroboli (πυροβόλοι λίδοι) or firestones, play a very prominent part in Christian symbolism and art. They are said to be found on a certain mountain of the Orient, and to be male and female. So long as they are far apart there is no perceptible heat in them, but if they are brought near to each other, fierce flames burst forth and the whole mountain is set on fire. Then comes the moralization designed to inculcate the virtue of monasticism. "Therefore, ye men of God, who would lead a pure life, separate yourselves

E

far from women, in order that the fires of lust may
not be kindled in your hearts ; for these carnal
passions are emissaries of Satan, sent to assail not
only holy men, but also chaste women." Adam,
Joseph, Samson, Solomon, Eve, and Susanna are
then adduced as examples of the wiles and witchery
of women.

The terrobuli are usually represented in art as the

Terrobuli. (*Bestiary.*)

naked or scantily-draped
figures of a man and a
woman, often in the rude
form of a hermes, stand-
ing near each other and
enveloped in flames. They occur in miniature
illustrations of mediæval bestiaries, as for example
in a manuscript of the tenth century in the
Arsenal Library, and one of the thirteenth century
in the National Library of Paris, and a third of
the fourteenth century in the Royal Library of

Sculpture on arch of doorway of old Norman church at Alne.

Brussels. Representations of them in ecclesiastical
architecture are comparatively rare ; there is, however, a fine specimen of the terrobuli sculptured on

one of the voussoirs or arch-stones over the south

Sculpture on arch of doorway of old Norman church at Alne.

entrance to an old Norman church at Alne in
Yorkshire.

Sculpture on arch of doorway of old Norman church at Alne.

CHAPTER II

ORIGIN AND HISTORY OF THE 'PHYSIOLOGUS'

Plastic and pictorial representations of animals in Christian art—Literary sources of these representations—*Clavis* of St. Melito—Epistle of Barnabas—The *Physiologus* compiled by an Alexandrian Greek—The *Hexahemera* of the Fathers—Adam as the author of a natural history—Popular character of the *Physiologus*—Origen as an exegetist—Roger Bacon's views of the place of animals in Scripture—Expositions and amplifications of the *Physiologus* by Epiphanius, St. Isidore, Petrus Damiani, and others—Anastasius Sinaita's *Anagogical Contemplations*—Latin poem on beasts and their mystical meaning by Theobald of Plaisance, and the English paraphrase—The *Physiologus* translated into Latin, Ethiopic, Arabic, Armenian, Syriac, Anglo-Saxon, Icelandic, and all the principal modern languages of Europe—Brief descriptions of these versions—Prudentius' poems *Hamartigenia* and *Psychomachia*—The phœnix, a symbol of solar worship used to illustrate the Christian doctrine of the Resurrection—French bestiaries : Philippe de Thaun's *Le Livre des Créatures*, Peter of Picardy's prose version of the *Physiologus*, and *Le Bestiaire Divin* of William, a priest of Normandy—Encyclopædias of natural history based on the *Physiologus*: Thomas de Cantimpré's *Liber de Naturis Rerum*, the *Speculum Naturale* of Vincent de Beauvais, *Liber de Proprietatibus Rerum* of Bartholomæus Anglicus, *Hortus Deliciarum* of Herrade de Landsberg, and other compilations—The church edifice an emblem of the human soul—Symbolism of the raven and the dove—Albertus Magnus' criticism of the *Physiologus*.

STILL more important than the emblematic significance of precious stones is the place assigned to animals in physico-theology. Christian art, from the fourth century, furnishes numerous examples of this sort of symbolism, as may be seen in the oldest churches of Rome and Ravenna, and in the remains of early sacred monuments now preserved in the Museum of the Lateran and in similar archæological collections.

The literary sources, however, from which the conceptions embodied in these plastic and pictorial representations were derived, are of much earlier date. A celebrated work of this kind was the *Clavis* of St. Melito, Bishop of Sardis in Asia Minor, who lived in the latter half of the second century, under the reign of Marcus Aurelius. It was written in Greek, but now exists only in a Latin translation, or rather a Latin revision and re-digest of the original, since the text published by Pitra in his *Spicilegium Solesmense* is unquestionably a mere re-hash of the bishop's book, dating probably from the eleventh century.

Still earlier is the epistle ascribed to Barnabas, which, although not composed by him, belongs probably to the latter half of the first century. The ninth chapter of this curious allegorization of the Jewish ceremonial contains a list of the unclean beasts enumerated in the Levitical law (Deut. xiv.), with an explanation of their spiritual significance. The chief purpose of the apocryphal epistle was to counteract the Judaizing tendency in primitive Christianity, and to this end the author endeavoured to resolve the legal and ritual prescriptions of the Old Testament into mere pre-figurations and prophecies of Christian doctrines and institutions, and thus virtually abolished them by spiritualizing them. Judaism is thereby reduced to a foreshadowing symbolism of the new religion, by which it is destined to be superseded and ultimately set aside.

The most complete and systematic, as well as the most popular and probably the oldest, of this class of exegetical expositions is the *Physiologus* or "Naturalist," as we would call it, which was compiled by an Alexandrian Greek from a great variety of sources, and doubtless embodied much of the priestly wisdom and esoteric science of ancient Egypt. The early Christian apologists and herme-neutists seem to have been extraordinarily fond of this kind of literature, which served their purpose as an application of the supposed facts of natural history to the illustration and enforcement of moral precepts and theological dogmas. In their frequent references to this work they evidently assume a general knowledge of it on the part of their readers, and it is probable that the *Physiologus* in its present form is made up of fragments of several books of a similar character, which were not only used as text-books in schools, but were intended for the edifica-tion of old and young, and were therefore more simple and attractive in style than the heavy *Hexahemera* or expositions of the six days' work of creation, in which Papias, Justin the Martyr, St. Theophilus, St. Basil of Cesarea, Eustathius, and other patristic theologians delighted to display their ponderous and perverse erudition. In these elaborate commentaries the fable often serves as the text for a sermon, or suggests the theme of a dissertation. Thus in the *Hexahemeron* of Ambrosius the story of the copulation of the viper with the lamprey furnishes the subject of a treatise on conjugal love. In like manner the crow is chosen as the type and pattern of hospitality, the stork is an example of filial piety, the swallow of maternal care and domestic content even in poverty, while the fish, which devour each other, are emblems of greediness.[1]

The Jews claim to have had a natural history by

---

[1] According to Luther the wisdom of the Magi was of this kind. In his sermon on Matthew ii. 1-12, he says : "Denn die hohen Schulen rühmen sich auch wie sie die natürliche Kunst lehren, die sie nennen Philosophia, und lehren doch nicht Affenspiel, sondern vergiftig Irrthum und eitel Traum. Denn natürliche Kunst, die vorzeiten Magia hiess, und jetzt Physiologia, ist die, so man lernet der Natur Kräfte und Werk erkennen ; als dass ein Hirsch die Schlangen mit seinem Athem durch die Nasen aus der Steinritzen reisst und tödet und frisset, und darnach vor grosser Hitze der Gift nach einem frischen Born dürstet, wie solches der 42 Ps. V. 2 anzeigt. Item, wie ein Wiesel die Schlange heraus-locket, wenn es vor der Schlangen Loch wiebelt mit seinem Schwänzlein, und dann die Schlange erzürnet heraus kreucht so lauret das Wieslein oben über dem Loche, und die Schlange über sich siehet nach ihrem Feind, so schlägt das Wieslein seine Zähne der Schlangen in den Hals neben die Vergift und erwürget also seinen Feind in seinem eigenen Loche. In solchen Künsten haben die Magier studiret."

Adam, who as the man first created and especially
commissioned by God to give to the animals names
corresponding to their qualities, was supposed to
have been intimately acquainted with them, and
might therefore be regarded as an original and
infallible authority on the subject.

The fact that the *Physiologus* is usually cited in
the singular number (ὁ Φυσιολόγος) has been thought
to imply that the work was the production of a
single author; but this inference is wholly un-
warranted, since the word may be used generically
to denote naturalists as a class.   Indeed, some of
the Fathers use the plural form, as, for example,
Epiphanius in his commentary on the injunction:
"Be ye, therefore, wise as serpents," cited in his
Panarion or "Bread Basket," a description and
refutation of the heresies of his time, in which he
quotes what the Physiologists say (ὡς φασιν οἱ
φυσιολόγοι) concerning the habits of this sagacious
reptile.

The *Physiologus* may therefore be regarded as a
convenient compendium of current opinions and
ancient traditions touching the characteristics of
animals and plants, which served as a manual of
instruction in zoölogy and botany with moral
reflections, so as to include also the province of
ethics.   In the hands of Christian teachers it was
made wholly subordinate to hermeneutical and
homiletical purposes, and became a mere treatise
on theology, interspersed with pious exhortation.
Whether the statements it contained were authentic

or not was something which the expositor did not
bother himself about.   It was not for him to question the assertion of the naturalist, but to accept it
as one accepts an apologue for the sake of the lesson
it teaches, without any thought of the actuality or
probability of the occurrence.   Indeed, St. Basil
expressly declares it to be a matter of less moment
to ascertain whether such creatures as griffins and
unicorns really exist, than to discover what religious
tenets they inculcate and confirm ; and St. Augustine affirms that it is not for us to find out whether
these marvellous stories are true or false, but rather
to give heed to their spiritual significance.   Thus
he says, as regards the statement that the eagle
breaks off its beak against a stone when it gets too
long : " Sive illa vera sunt quæ dicuntur de aquila,
sive sit fama potius hominum quam verit, veritas
est tamen in scripturis, et non sine causa hoc
dixerunt scripturæ.   Nos quidquid illud significat
faciamus et quam sit verum non laboremus."—*In
Psal. CII.*

Origen was inclined to treat in a similar manner
all the events recorded in the Old Testament,
regarding them, not as historical facts, but as
religious types and symbols.   Thus he characterizes
the idyl of Rebecca as "not a relation of actual
occurrences, but a concoction of mysteries."   This
"adamantine" expositor and "Father of biblical
exegesis," as he has been called, appears in his
youthful ardour and enthusiasm to have interpreted
the words of Holy Writ with strict and uncom-

promising literalness, and to have practised its
teachings in this spirit with a blind fanaticism that
is said to have led to self-mutilation for the sake
of the kingdom of heaven (Matt. xix. 12). The
cooling of his ascetic zeal and the consequent
repentance of his rash act naturally produced in his
mind a powerful reaction against the bondage of
the letter of the Scriptures in favour of a spiritual
and symbolical system of exegesis, of which he
became the most ingenious and daring exponent.

The same views were expressed by the most
eminent and sober-minded physicist of the middle
ages, the Franciscan friar Roger Bacon, who, in his
Opus Majus (ed. Jebb, p. 39), remarks : " All
ancient saints and sages gather in their expositions
the literal sense from the nature and properties of
things, in order that they may educe therefrom the
spiritual sense by suitable adaptations and similitudes. Thus Augustine in quoting the admonition :
' Be wise as serpents,' says that our Lord meant
by these words that as the serpent exposes its
whole body for the protection of its head, so the
apostles were to suffer persecution for the sake of
Christ, who is their head. Every creature, indi-
vidually and generically, from the heights of heaven
to the end of the same, has its place in Scripture
(' ponitur in scriptura '). The former are facts in
nature designed to illustrate the truths contained in
the latter ; and the words of revelation bring out
these truths more clearly and correctly than any
philosophic toil can do."

According to this theory, which still represents the official attitude of the Catholic Church and of many orthodox divines among Protestants, there is a sort of pre-established harmony between science and theology, which can be disturbed only by the aberrations of "science falsely so called." True science, on the contrary, does not aspire to any higher position than that of a handmaid to theology, and should never forget her essentially servile and ancillary functions, or think of questioning the supreme and infallible authority of her mistress, however arrogantly it may be exercised.

Towards the end of the fourth century, the bigoted polemic and bitter persecutor of Origen's disciples, Epiphanius, Bishop of Constantia in Cyprus, is said to have written an exposition of the *Physiologus* in twenty-six chapters, and a work of this kind attributed to him was printed about the middle of the sixteenth century by the learned Augustine friar and famous poet Ponce de Leon. The same subject was treated early in the seventh century by St. Isidore, Bishop of Seville, in his great work on etymology (*Originum seu etymologiarum,* lib. xx.), which became the popular encyclopædia of the middle ages, and the chief source from which the authors of the numerous mediæval bestiaries derived their information. The twelfth book treats of beasts, quadrupeds, birds, reptiles, and insects; the sixteenth of precious stones, and the seventh of plants. In this survey of the animal, vegetable, and mineral kingdoms the author generally confines himself to statements of what was regarded in his day as the facts of natural history; the mystical and moral application of these things was made by his younger contemporary, St. Hildefonse, Bishop of Toledo, who discusses at considerable length their spiritual significance.

Petrus Damiani, Abbot of Fonte Avellana and Cardinal-Bishop of Ostia, wrote in the eleventh century a treatise on the excellence of the monastic state as exemplified by divers living creatures (*De bono religiosi status et variarum animantium*), mentioning about forty marine and terrestrial animals, from the oyster to the elephant, and adducing their real or fabulous qualities in illustration of the desirableness of a cenobitic life. About the year 1215 an Englishman, Alexander Neckam, composed a volume "On the Nature of Things" (*De Naturis Rerum*), in which he discoursed of animals from ethical and doctrinal points of view. In 1498 there was published at Cologne a duodecimo entitled "Dialogue of Creatures excellently moralized and applicable to every Moral Matter in a pleasing and edifying manner, to the Praise of God and the Edification of Men" (*Dyalogus creaturarum optime moralisatus omni materie moralo iocundo et edificativo modo applicabilis, ad laudem Dei et hominum edificationem*). It contains a hundred and twenty-two dialogues, some in the style of Æsop's fables, and others modelled after the *Physiologus*, with coarse woodcuts in elucidation of the text, and is altogether a pretentious but rather inferior production. Anastasius Sinaita, a monk of the famous cloister on Mount Sinai, wrote during the latter half of the seventh century his elaborate "Anagogical Contemplations on the Six Days' Divine Work" in eleven books (*Anagogicarum contemplationum in divini opificii Hexaëmeron*), in which this sort of hermeneutic theology is pushed to the absurdest conclusions. The author's endeavour, as he states it, is "to thresh the ears of Scripture in order to get out the pure kernel, which is Christ." In other words, his work is a contribution to that "science of mystic Christology" which the early Church so assiduously cultivated, and of which Bishop Alexander in his Bampton Lectures deplores the decline. As regards the story of Eden, Anastasius remarks : " Woe be to us if we take it literally, for then we rush constantly from Scylla to Charybdis." This is quite true, and with the advancement of science and the comparative study of religions it is becoming increasingly difficult to sail with safety on this line between the whirlpool and the rock.

In Beaugendre's edition of the works of Hildebert of Lavardin, Archbishop of Tours, who lived during the latter half of the eleventh century, is included a Latin poem on beasts and their mystical meaning, composed, as the title states, by Theobald of Plaisance, whoever he may have been. It has been suggested with some degree of probability that he was the Theobald who held the office of abbot of Monte Cassino from 1022 to 1035 ; there is, however, no confirmation of this conjecture in

the manuscripts, where the author is called Theobaldus Senensis Theobaldus Placentinus episcopus,
or simply Theobaldus Italicus.

This version of the *Physiologus* was exceedingly
popular in the middle ages, as is evident from the
many manuscripts in which it has been transmitted
to us, and from the number of annotated editions of
it which were printed during the fifteenth century.
It was published in 1872 by Dr. Richard Morris
from a Harleian manuscript (Early English Text
Society, vol. xlix., Appendix I., pp. 201-209). The
English bestiary printed in the same volume (pp.
1-25) from a manuscript of the thirteenth century,
belonging to the library of the British Museum,
is a free translation of Theobald's work. It was
first edited by Wright (Haupt and Hoffmann's
Altdeutsche Blätter, ii., and Wright and Halliwell's
Reliquæ Antiquæ, i.), and is also found in Mätz-
ner's *Altenglische Sprachproben*, i. Thierfelder mentions in Naumann's *Serapeum* (1862, Nos. 15 and
16) two metrical versions of the *Physiologus* in
Latin as extant in manuscript; one dated 1493
and written in elegiac verse by a certain Florinus,
and preserved in the University Library of Leipsic,
and the other in Leonine verse by an unknown
author, and now in the University Library of
Breslau.

Perhaps no book, except the Bible, has ever been
so widely diffused among so many peoples and for
so many centuries as the *Physiologus*. It has been
translated into Latin, Ethiopic, Arabic, Armenian,

Syriac, Anglo-Saxon, Icelandic, Spanish, Italian, Provençal, and all the principal dialects of the Germanic and Romanic languages.

One of the oldest and most interesting of these versions is the Ethiopic, which belongs to the first half of the fifth century, and forms, with the translation of the Septuagint, the basis of Ethiopic or Ge'ez literature. It adheres very closely to the original, but contains numerous errors, owing to the translator's imperfect knowledge of Greek. It has been carefully edited from London, Paris, and Vienna manuscripts, with ample annotations, a German translation, and an admirable introduction by Dr. Fritz Hommel, Professor of Arabic in the University of Munich (Leipsic, 1877). As the work is written in classical Ge'ez, it can be recommended as an excellent text-book for beginners in Ethiopic.

Of a somewhat later date is the Armenian translation, which follows the Greek original in the descriptions of the animals and their habits, but deviates from it considerably in the moralizations and religious applications of their characteristics. It has been published by Pitra in his *Spicilegium Solesmense*, iii., and translated into French by Cahier (*Nouveaux Mélanges d'Archéologie*, 1874).

The oldest Syriac version, published by Tychsen (*Physiologus Syrus*, Rostock, 1795), is, in the opinion of Dr. Lauchert, "at least as old as the Ethiopic and more important than the Armenian." [1] It gives

[1] *Geschichte des Physiologus*, von Dr. Friedrich Lauchert. Strasburg, Trübner, 1889. This is the most complete and

the natural history of thirty-two animals, each
section being introduced by passages of Scripture
in which the animal under discussion is mentioned,
but without any moral or religious reflections, or
any attempt at exegetical exposition. It thus
constitutes a sort of biblical beast-book free from
hermeneutical tendencies. There are also several
later Syriac translations, some of which have been
printed, with Latin metaphrases, by Land in his
Anecdota Syriaca, iv. The Arabic version, edited
by Land in his *Otia Syriaca*, iv., observes pretty
much the same order as the Greek original, the
authorship of which is ascribed by the Arabic
translator to Gregory surnamed the Theologian,
better known as Gregory of Nazianz. This statement, however, seems to be a personal conjecture
or vague tradition of no real value.

The Latin version of the *Physiologus* is first mentioned in the so-called *Decretum Gelasianum* or
Index Prohibitorum attributed to Pope Gelasius I.,
and supposed to have been issued by him A.D. 496.
In this catalogue of forbidden books it is characterized as *Liber Physiologus, qui ab hæreticis
conscriptus est, et beati Ambrosii nomine signatus,
apocryphus*. As Ambrosius died A.D. 397, and it is
hardly probable that a work which he did not
write would be ascribed to him until at least a
few years after his death, we are justified in assum-

---

critical history of the *Physiologus* hitherto published, and is
especially rich in bibliographical information.

ing that the Latin *Physiologus* was not composed before the beginning of the fifth century. Professor Friedrich of Munich has shown, in a paper read before the Royal Bavarian Academy of Sciences, Jan. 7, 1888, that the above-mentioned Gelasian Decree was not issued by Pope Gelasius I., but was a private document with no official character whatever, and that it did not exist before A.D. 533. An additional circumstance, which enables us to fix the probable date of the work within still narrower limits, is the fact that in connection with the exposition of the third quality of the ant a list of heretics is given whose teachings are to be avoided, but among them Nestorius, whose doctrine was condemned by the third Œcumenical Council at Ephesus, A.D. 431, is not mentioned. As so prominent a heretic would not have been passed over, we may fitly infer that this Latin version was made before his condemnation, namely during the first three decades of the fifth century. The existing manuscripts of the Latin *Physiologus* belong to the eighth, ninth, and tenth centuries; they do not present a uniform text with variants, and are therefore not copies of the same translation, but rather independent versions, to which each translator has added interpretations of his own; at least they contain expositions not found in any Greek manuscripts now extant. The Latin *Physiologus* has been published by Cahier in his *Mélanges d'Archéologie*, ii.-iv. Another shorter Latin version, known as *Dicta Johannis Chrysostomi de Naturis*

F

Bestiarum, has been printed by Heider in *Archiv für die Kunde oesterreichischer Geschichtsquellen*, ii. (1850), from a manuscript of the eleventh century belonging to the cloister of Gottweih. It is simply an abbreviation and re-arrangement of the text edited by Cahier.

Cassiodorus in his commentary on Psalm cii. 6 says, that the holy man loves solitude like the pelican, and withdraws from human society like the nycticorax or night-raven, and tells the old story of the renewal of the eagle's youth in illustration of Psalm ciii. 5. Gregory I., surnamed the Great, was especially fond of symbolisms of this sort, and made very free use of them in his expositions of Job. So, too, in the beginning of the eighth century, Aldhelm, Abbot of Malmesbury, draws illustrations of his parables from the same source, as does also the Venerable Beda, a generation later, in his interpretation of Job xxix. 18, which he renders : " I shall die in my nest, and I shall multiply my days like the phœnix ; " the Hebrew word *chul* meaning phœnix as well as sand. It also signifies palm-tree ; St. Jerome took it in this sense : "sicut palma multiplicabo dies," and the same interpretation is given in the Septuagint : ὥσπερ στέλεγος φοίγικο πολυν χρονον βίωσω : " like the stem of the palm-tree I shall live a long time."

One of the early Christian poets, Aurelius Clemens Prudentius (A.D. 348—410), in his *Hamartigenia* or Genesis of Sin (v. 518 *sqq.*), gives a detailed description of the birth of the viper in illustration of his theme. Prudentius is also the author of *Psychomachia*, or the " Battle of the Soul," which is one of the first examples of a purely allegorical poem in Occidental literature, and the model of all similar productions in the middle ages. In the proem we have a characteristic specimen of typological hermeneutics, in which Abraham represents Faith, his three hundred and eighteen servants signify Christ (the Greek numerical letters T (300) I (10) H (8) were for this reason a monogrammatic expression for Christ), the heathen kings of Sodom and Gomorrah are types of carnal vices, and Lot, a sojourner in Sodom, is the soul of the pious man beset by the seductions of the flesh. This interpretation was not original with the Spanish Latin poet, but borrowed from the supposititious Epistle of Barnabas, where in the ninth chapter the following passage occurs : " The scripture saith, ' Abraham circumcised three hundred and eighteen men of his household.'[1] Hear the meaning first of the eighteen, then of the three hundred. The ten and eight are represented, the ten by I, and the eight by H. There thou hast the beginning of the name IHΣOΥΣ. But because the Cross, in the form of the letter T, was to carry the grace of salvation, therefore he adds three hundred, which is represented by T in Greek. So he shows forth Jesus in the first two letters, and the Cross in the third." Evidently the Jewish patriarch did not

---

[1] This statement is not strictly correct, but is derived from a combination of Gen. xiv. 14 and xvii. 26, 27.

dream of the profound significance which Christian
expositors would attach to the simple act of cir-
cumcising the members of his tribal family.

A still more elaborate allegorical production of
this class is the hexameter poem *De Phœnice*,
ascribed to Lactantius, but probably of a somewhat
later date. It bears the stamp of paganism rather
than of Christianity, the phœnix being glorified as
a satellite of the sun and a symbol of solar worship.
It begins with a florid description of the home of
the phœnix in the remotest region of the East, in a
grove consecrated to the sun and situated far above
the reach of Phæton's fire or Deucalion's deluge,
where there is neither disease nor death, and where
old age, crime, passion, care, and poverty never
come, and storm, rain, and frost are all unknown.
In this retreat, which is rendered perpetually fresh
and green by a living spring, the phœnix dwells
and greets the dawn with a sacred song.[1] The
peroration is a rapturous apostrophe to the phœnix:
" Oh, bird of happy fortune and fate, to whom the
god himself has granted the gift of self-regenera-
tion. Whether male or female, or neither, or both,
happy is she who enters into no compact with
Venus. Death is Venus to her; her only pleasure
is in death; she desires to die that she may be
born again. She is her own offspring, her own
father and heir, her own mother and nurse, a foster-
child of herself. She is herself indeed, but not the

[1] For a full analysis of the poem see Adolf Ebert's
Geschichte der Christlich-Lateinischen Literatur, i. 95.

same, since she is herself and not herself, having gained eternal life by the boon and blessing of death." [1]

It is easy to see what a prolific source of doctrinal interpretation and illustration the supposed characteristics of this mystic bird would supply to Christian exegetists and homilists. It is well known, too, that the chief features of sun-worship colour the ideas and crop out in the ecclesiastical institutions of Christendom. Christmas, Epiphany, Easter, Whitsuntide, the midsummer feast of St. John, and all the principal holy-days and festivals of the Church are survivals of a solar or stellar cult, and were determined, not by historical facts or traditions, but by astronomical considerations corresponding to the waxing or waning power of the sun, or coinciding with the position of the constellations in the heavens and the influence they were supposed to exert upon the course of the seasons and other sublunary affairs. Constantine remained a sun-worshipper till the day of his death, and the coins of early Christian emperors were often stamped with the image of the phœnix as an emblem of this ancient and once universal cult.

An Anglo-Saxon paraphrase of this poem, supposed to have been made by Cynewulf, has been published by Thorpe (*Codex Exoniensis*, pp. 197-242), together with the Latin text, and also by Grein (*Bibliothek der angelsächsischen Poesie*, i. 215-233). The first part is a description of the phœnix, and

---

[1] Cf. Lactantius, *Opera*, ii. 214-219.

the second part an application of its fabulous qualities to the Christian doctrine of the Resurrection.

It was from the Latin *Physiologus* that all the
translations of the work existing in the vulgar
tongues of Europe were made.   Thus it became
the common property of the people; its similitudes
were no longer confined to hermeneutic theology,
but passed into general literature, and into ecclesiastical architecture.   The oldest of these versions
is the Anglo-Saxon, which dates from the end of
the eighth century.   It has been edited by Thorpe
with an English translation (*Codex Exoniensis*, pp.
355-367), and by Grein (*Bibl. der angels. Poesie*, i.
233-238); and although only a fragment of it has
been preserved, enough remains to show that it
must have been superior to all other versions in
poetic beauty and compact vigour of expression.

There are two German versions of the *Physiologus*, belonging respectively to the eleventh and
twelfth centuries.   The older one is a fragment,
and has been printed several times from a Vienna
manuscript, best perhaps by Müllenhoff and Scherer
(*Denkmäler*, No. 81); the other is complete, and has
been printed last by Lauchert in the Appendix to
his *Geschichte des Physiologus*, pp. 280-299.   Both
versions correspond to the *Dicta* of Chrysostom
with only slight variations.

The Icelandic version, which has been transmitted to us in a very fragmentary condition, dates
from the beginning of the thirteenth century, and
follows the Latin text with occasional additions

and deviations. It was edited in 1877 by Mœbius
(*Analecta Norræna*, pp. 246-251), who also gave a
German translation of it in Hommel's *Ethiopic
Physiologus*, pp. 99-104 ; but the most complete text
of these fragments has been printed, together with
the crude and quaint drawings illustrating the
original manuscripts, by Verner Dahlerup, in his
exhaustive critical bibliography of the *Physiologus*,
which appeared in *Aarboger for Nordisk Oldkyndighed og Historic udgivene af Det kogelige Nordiske Oldskrift-Selskab* in 1889 (ii. 4, 3, 199-290).

The French bestiaries are also based upon the
Physiologus, but have been greatly amplified, not
so much by the introduction of other animals, as
by fuller descriptions and more extended expositions. The oldest of these productions is the
Anglo-Norman *Le Livre des Créatures*, by Philippe
de Thaun, written about the year 1121 and dedicated to Queen Adelheid of Louvraine, and doubtless intended to celebrate her nuptials with Henry
I. of England, which took place at this time.
It has been published from a manuscript in the
British Museum, with an English translation by
Wright in his *Popular Treatises on Science during
the Middle Ages*. Another French translation in
prose was made by a priest, Peter of Picardy, who
states that he undertook the task at the request of
Philippe de Dreux, Bishop of Beauvais (1175—
1217), an item of information which enables us to
assign the work approximately to the end of the
twelfth century. The translator adds that the

Bishop, having little confidence in the fidelity of
poetic versions, wished him to avoid metre in order
to adhere as closely as possible to "the Latin
which Physiologus, one of the good clerks of Athens,
has used."   It has been published by Cahier in his
Mélanges d'Archéologie, ii.-iv.   About the same
time, or perhaps a little later, William, a priest of
Normandy, wrote *Le Bestiaire Divin* in rhyme.
Inasmuch as the author refers twice to the interdict
which Pope Innocent III. laid upon England, "at
the time when Philippe reigned in France," as still
in force, the poem must have been written between
1208 and 1212.   It has been published by Cahier
(*ibid.*), by Hippeau (*Le Bestiaire Divin de Guillaume,
clerc de Normandie*, Caen, 1852), and lastly and most
satisfactorily by Reisch (Leipsic, 1890).

There is also a Greek metrical version of the
Physiologus in two manuscripts of the fourteenth
and fifteenth centuries, both of which are in Paris.
It is probably a production of the twelfth century,
and has been printed by Legrange (*Le Physiologus
en grec vulgaire et en vers politiques*, Paris, 1873).
The fragment of a Spanish *Physiologus* of the fourteenth century has been published under the title
Libro de los Gatos, from a manuscript of the
National Library of Madrid by Pascual de Gayan-
gos, in his collection of prose writers anterior to the
fifteenth century (*Biblioteca de Autores Espanoles*,
lii., Madrid, 1859).   We have also the somewhat
scanty remains of a Rumanian version, supposed
to belong to the sixteenth century, although the

only manuscript of it extant bears the date 1717. It has been printed with an Italian translation by Gaster (*Archivio Glottologico Italiano*, x.). Lauchert mentions a Waldensian *Physiologus* existing in a single Dublin manuscript, and entitled *De las Propriotas de las Animanças*. The author calls himself Jaco, and states in the introduction that the book is designed for use as a manual of instruction, and in accordance with this purpose, the exposition is ethical rather than theological, and aims to inculcate, not so much soundness of doctrine as correct moral conduct in the common relations of life.

Barth has edited from a Paris manuscript in his *Chrestomathie Provençale* some excerpts of a Provençal *Physiologus* under the title *Aiso son las Naturas d'alcus Auzels e d'alcunas Bestias*, treating of the nature of birds and beasts, but with no attempt at exposition of any kind. There is also a bestiary in the Tusco-Venetian dialect, recently published and annotated by Max Goldstaub and Richard Wendriner (Halle, 1892) from a manuscript in the Biblioteca Communale of Padua. It discusses some forty beasts, several of which (as the horse) are not mentioned in the *Physiologus*, and explains their qualities in a moral rather than in a dogmatic sense. Thus the unicorn is a symbol of violent and cruel persons, who can be subdued and rendered gentle only by the grace of God. Saul is adduced as an example of this sort of person. The Biblioteca Ricciardiana and the

Biblioteca Laurenziana of Florence, as well as other Italian libraries, contain numerous codices of bestiaries which have never been printed.

Besides being so frequently translated, the *Physiologus* is constantly cited by mediæval writers, and forms the basis of many bulky tomes, such as Thomas de Cantimpré's *Liber de Naturis Rerum*, written between 1233 and 1248. This work was one of the earliest and most celebrated encyclopædias of natural history, and was freely translated into Dutch about 1280 by Jacob van Maerlant, under the title *Der Naturen Bloeme*, and in 1350 into German by Konrad von Megenberg as *Das Buch der Natur*. Like in character, and hardly less important, are the *Speculum Naturale* of Vincent de Beauvais, completed about 1250, the *Liber de Proprietatibus Rerum* of Bartholomæus Anglicus, dating from the latter half of the thirteenth century, Brunetto Latino's *Li Tresors*, the French translation of a Latin original belonging to the same period, the *Acerba*, a didactic poem by Cecco d'Ascoli, who was burned at the stake in 1327, and other volumes, which treated in a popular style of the occult properties and symbolical significance of birds, beasts, plants, and stones.

An elaborate compilation of this kind was the *Hortus Deliciarum* of Herrade de Landsberg, Abbess of St. Odile, who turned the facts and fables of natural science into the channel of moral instruction and religious edification. It was written during the latter half of the twelfth century, and preserved in a unique vellum manuscript of 648 folio pages, with numerous illuminations and miniatures, in the Strasburg Library, where it perished, with so many other literary and artistic treasures, during the bombardment of that city by the Germans in 1870.

There was also a treatise on beasts and other things (*Institutiones Monasticæ de Bestiis et aliis Rebus*), commonly, though in all probability falsely, ascribed to Hugo de Saint-Victor, in which these symbolisms were wonderfully wrought out, and every feature, member, hue, and habit of the creatures thus allegorized was made to yield a secret and subtle significance. "What Holy Writ inculcates on the learned," says the author of this work in reference to the pictorial representations of such ideas, "pictures impress upon the ignorant; for as the scholar delights in the subtlety of Scripture, so the soul of the simple is pleased with the simplicity of pictures." But this simplicity was often lost in a puzzling maze and winding labyrinth of allegorical and mystical interpretation, which it would be impossible for the wayfaring man, even though he were not a fool, to thread without the *Physiologus* or some later elaboration of it as a clue. Indeed, without such guidance it would be equally difficult for us at the present day to understand what the builder of a mediæval church or an embroiderer of sacerdotal vestments meant by adorning them with seemingly incongruous representations of lions, eagles, phœnixes, pelicans, ravens, doves, partridges, panthers, harts, foxes, hedgehogs, ferrets, ichneumons, lizards, serpents, tortoises, whales, elephants, ibises, crocodiles, unicorns, salamanders, and other real and mythical animals, or to conjecture what conceivable relation they could bear to Christian theology or Christian worship.

The sacred edifice as a whole was regarded as an emblem of the human soul, of which the creatures carved on the pillars and portals were the desirable or undesirable attributes and affections. Thus an ox typified patience and gentleness, a lion sternness and majesty, a turtle-dove constancy and chastity, a ram spiritual leadership, a lily purity, and a rose martyrdom. We have a modern survival of this symbolism in Gabriel Max's celebrated painting, *The Last Greeting*, in which a rose falls to the feet of a young woman as she stands exposed to wild beasts in the amphitheatre.

So, too, the raven and the dove are not mere reminiscences of the Deluge, but emblems—the former of the carnal-minded Jews, who live on the carrion of the Law, the latter of the new principle of Christianity, that finds no abiding-place outside of the ark of safety, but returns to it bringing the olive branch of peace and reconciliation. There is also a distinction between the dove of Noah, the dove of David, and the dove of Christ; the first signifies rest, the second peace, and the third salvation. As the dove separates with its beak the choicest kernels of wheat from the chaff, so it is the office of the preacher to separate the pure grain of Christian doctrine from the husks of

Judaism. Its two wings are love of man and love
of God, compassion and contemplation, the active
and the meditative life; the ring round its neck
is the encircling sweetness of the Divine Word;
the gold and silver of its plumage are the precious
treasures of purity and innocence; its whiteness
intermingled with changeable tints is the spirit of
chastity in conflict with fickle and rebellious passions; its red feet are the feet of the Church stained
with the blood of the martyrs; its two eyes survey
the past and discern the future, looking in upon
the soul and up to God; their yellowish lustre
indicates maturity of thought and reflection, for
yellow is the colour of ripe fruit.

In the middle ages these symbolisms, which
seem to us so far-fetched and obscure, were constantly referred to in sermons and in sacred and
profane literature, as well as in common discourse,
and appear, therefore, to have been generally understood, so that a passing allusion to them in a book
or address was assumed to be intelligible without
further comment. Thus we find in a Latin poem
published by Du Meril in his *Poésies populaires
latines antérieures au XIIe siècle*, p. 191, a line in
which Christ is said to have been put to death by
owls—

"Christus a noctuis datur supplicio."

This is, however, a figurative expression for the
Jews, who, in the *Physiologus*, are compared to the
nycticorax, night-raven or owl, which cannot endure the presence of the sun, as the Jews could

not endure the coming of "the dayspring from on
high," and the brightness of the sun of righteousness, loving darkness rather than light because their
deeds were evil.   Thus we read in the *Bestiaire
Divin* of Guillaume—

> " En cest oisel sunt figuré
> Li fols Gieu maléuré,
> Qui ne voldrent Deu entendre
> Quant il vint ça per nus raendre,
> De Deu, qui est verrai soleil,
> Ne voleient creire le conseil."

About the middle of the thirteenth century
Albertus Magnus wrote a book on animals (*De
Animalibus*), in which he attempted some criticism
of the *Physiologus*, but the narrations he accepts as
true are for the most part quite as incredible and
absurd as those he rejects, so that it is difficult to
determine by what criterion he tests their authenticity.   Thus, for example, he is sceptical as regards
the self-mutilation of the beaver when pursued by
hunters, but puts implicit faith in the fable of the
unicorn and the virgin.

With the translation of the *Physiologus* into the
vulgar tongues of Europe it ceased to be the exclusive possession of theologians and exegetists, and
was no longer confined to the purposes of homiletical and hermeneutical illustration, but became
the common property of the people, and passed
into the general literature of Christendom as an in-
exhaustible source of quaint and often forced metaphor, and sometimes apt, though more frequently
lame and lopsided, simile.

Allusions to it occur henceforth not only in sermons and sacred songs, in devotional works and doctrinal treatises, and in the encyclopædic compilations of natural science, which professed to give information "concerning all things and some things besides" (*de omnibus rebus et quibusdam aliis*), but also in the secular, and especially the erotic poetry of the period.   Indeed, without a knowledge of the *Physiologus*, these allusions would be wholly unintelligible.   The citations contained in Lauchert's exhaustive chapter on this subject (pp. 185-207) suffice to show how widely extended and well-nigh universal was the popularity which the work enjoyed.

CHAPTER III

THE 'PHYSIOLOGUS' IN ART AND LITERATURE

The three characteristics of the lion—Representations of the lion as a symbol of the Resurrection in architecture—Beasts often have a twofold signification—The lion and bear as types of Satan—Diabolification of the dog—Strange misconception of the canine character—Lions as pedestals—Metaphorical use of the lion in poetry—The lizard in architecture—Artistic delineations of the unicorn as a type of Christ's Incarnation—Auricular conception of Christ as the Logos—Supposed anti-toxical virtue of the unicorn's horn and that of the African viper—The unicorn in legend and poetry—Characteristics of the elephant—Symbol of the fall of man—Julius Cæsar's queer account of the elk—Elephants embroidered on chasubles—Four characteristics of the serpent—Artistic and poetic uses of its fabled attributes—The eagle as a symbol of spiritual aspiration and baptismal regeneration—Allusions to it by Dante and other poets—The fish in sacred iconology—Significance of the whale in ecclesiastical architecture—Symbolism of the remora and serra—Importance of the phœnix and the pelican as emblems of Christian doctrine—Their prominent place in Church architecture—Import of the fabulous exploits of the otter and the ichneumon—Panther and dragon typical of Christ and Belial—Healing power of the "heavenly panther"—Lesson of self-renunciation taught by the beaver—Characteristic of the hyena—Symbolism of the salamander—The partridge a type of the devil—Examples of the charadrius in art—Mystical meaning of the crow, turtle-dove, ousel, merl, fulica, and hoopoe—Curious statement of Luther concerning swallows—Why God

80

feeds the young ravens—Peculiarities of the wolf—The *Physiologus* condemned as heretical—Freely used by Gregory the Great in his scriptural exposition—Virtues and vices portrayed as women mounted on various animals—Disputatious scholastics satirized—Tetramorph—Gospel mills—The ark of the covenant as the triumphal chariot of the Cross—Cock and clergy—Origin of the basilisk and its significance—Its prominence in religious symbology and sacred architecture—Cautious scepticism of Albertus Magnus—The *Physiologus* from a psychological point of view, as illustrating the credulity of the Fathers of the Church—Why "the hart panteth after the water-brooks"—Story of the antelope—Barnacle geese—"Credo quia absurdum"—Modern counterparts of early Christian apologists and exegetists.

THE *Physiologus* begins with the lion, and adduces three characteristics of the king of beasts. "First, when he perceives that the hunters are pursuing him, he erases his foot-prints with his tail, so that he cannot be traced to his lair. In like manner our Saviour, the lion of the tribe of Judah, concealed all traces of His Godhead, when He descended to the earth and entered into the womb of the Virgin Mary. Secondly, the lion always sleeps with his eyes open; so our Lord slept with His body on the Cross, but awoke at the right hand of the Father. Thirdly, the lioness brings forth her whelps dead and watches over them until, after three days, the lion comes and howls over them and vivifies them by his breath; so the Almighty Father recalled to life His only-begotten Son, our Lord Jesus Christ, who on the third day was thus raised from the dead, and will likewise raise us all up to eternal life."

This comparison of the risen Christ to a lion's whelp is also used by Abélard in the following lines—

" Ut leonis catulus
Resurrexit Dominus,
Quem rugitus patrius
Die tertia
Suscitat vivificus
Teste physica."

The appeal of the illustrious schoolman to physics in proof of his statement is clearly a reference to the *Physiologus*.

This last supposed characteristic of the lion appears to have been a favourite symbol of the resurrection of Christ, as well as of the general resurrection, and holds a prominent place in

Relief of a Lion. (*Munich.*)

mediæval architecture.   Representations of it are frequently found in various parts of ecclesiastical edifices, as, for example, on the principal portal of St. Laurence in Nuremberg, in the choir of Augsburg Cathedral, at the foot of a colossal crucifix in St. Nicholas of Stralsund, in the Würtemberg cloisters Maulbronn and Bebenhausen, and in a large relief, which dates from the latter half of the thirteenth century, and doubtless belonged originally to some church or cloister, probably to the old chapel and hospital of the Holy Ghost (built 1251-66 and burned 1327), but which now adorns the façade of a house Im Thal near the Marienplatz in Munich, and the origin and signification of which have excited no little discussion among Bavarian antiquarians and ecclesiologists. So, too, a stained window of the minster of Freiburg in the Breisgau contains a painting of the Crucifixion, at the top of which is a pelican feeding its young with its own blood; above the pelican stands a lion breathing upon three whelps, which are just beginning to show signs of life. Underneath the lion is the inscription: *Hi[c] Leo Forma S[alvatoris]*, showing it to be a type of the quickening power of the voice of Christ. A stained window of the thirteenth century in the cathedral of St. Etienne at Bourges represents the pelican below on the left and the lion and whelps on the right of the Crucified; above, on the corresponding sides, are Jonah delivered from the whale and Elijah restoring to life the son of the widow of Zerephath (see Frontispiece). In the central lancet window of the chapels dedicated to the Virgin in the cathedrals of Le Mans and Tours are similar symbols of the death and resurrection of Christ, in which the phœnix rising from its ashes takes the place of the pelican. Also the central lancet window in the apsis of the cathedral of Lyons has a border of medallion paintings referring to the same subject, among which are a lion and his whelp running at full speed, the latter having evidently been just resuscitated. It was often carved on sacramental vessels, as, for example, on a ciborium belonging to the monastery Kloster-neuburg, near Vienna, a fine specimen of gold-smith's work dating from the beginning of the fourteenth century.

A lion howling over three whelps is one of the

Lion howling over his whelps.
(*Strasburg Minster.*)

series of reliefs representing biblical and mythical sub-jects that ornament a frieze on the exterior of Stras-burg Minster. Besides scenes from the Jewish Scriptures, such as Abra-ham preparing to sacrifice Isaac, but arrested by an angel, who points to a ram entangled in a bush, Jonah cast up by the whale near one of the towers of Nineveh, the brazen serpent, etc., we may mention in this connection several reliefs which are based upon the legends of the *Physiologus*, and the meaning of which will be explained hereafter : a phœnix in the flames, a pelican piercing her breast and feeding her young with her blood, an eagle taking eaglets from the nest to make them look at the sun, and a unicorn with its head in the lap of a virgin, while a man is thrusting a spear into its side. This last sculpture resembles very closely the illustration from the bestiary which we have given in discussing the symbolism of the unicorn.

In connection with scenes from the life of Christ on the bronze doors of the cathedral of Pisa are reliefs of a lion howling over two whelps, an eagle mounting up towards the sun, a unicorn, a hart by a stream of water, a serpent, and an old rhinoceros with two young ones playing in the background, evidently intended to represent the leviathan of the Bible.

At a somewhat later period the lion, as a symbol of the Resurrection, was sculptured on public buildings of a secular character and on private dwellings; it was also engraved on pieces of armour and especially on helmets, often with the legend, *Domine vivifica me secundum verbum tuum*, or some other appropriate device, expressive of the hope of the warrior that, if slain in battle, he might be raised up on the last day,

Durand, in his *Rationale Divinorum Officiorum*, lib. vii., has a chapter on the rubric of the Evangelists (*Rubrica de Evangelistis*), in which he says that Mark's type is a roaring lion, "because his aim is chiefly to give a description of the resurrection of Christ, and that for this reason his gospel is read at Easter. For it is stated that the lion by its tremendous roar calls to life its whelps on the third day, and thus God the Father by His immense power called to life His Son on the third day." Origen has a similar explanation

of this symbolism in his discourse on Genesis.[1]
Indeed, the allusions to this zoölogical myth in
homiletical and hermeneutical literature are so
numerous and unequivocal, and the symbolical
interpretation of it so obvious and uniform, that
one marvels that Bavarian archæologists should
have expended so much rare and recondite erudition and ingenuity of conjecture, and have gone
so far afield historically in search of the origin and
meaning of the Munich bas-relief already mentioned.

A sleeping lion is often brought into typological
relation to the infant Jesus, as, for example, on the
western portal of Notre-Dame de Paris, and in a
fresco in the church of the convent Philotheos on
Mount Athos, where the connection is made clear
by the words of Jacob concerning Judah : " He
stooped down, he couched as a lion, and as an old
lion; who shall rouse him up ? "—Gen. xlix. 9
(Didron, *Histoire de Dieu*, p. 348).

The belief that the lion never closes its eyes in
sleep caused this animal to be placed at the doors
of churches as a guardian of the sanctuary.   This
custom, which was observed for the same reason
by the ancient Egyptians, is thus referred to by a
mediæval poet—

> " Est leo, sed custos, oculis quia dormit apertis
> Templorum idcirco, ponitus ante foras."

[1] " Nam Physiologus de catulo Leonis scribit, quod quum
fuerit natus, tribus diebus et tribus noctibus dormiat, quod
valde convenientur aptatur in Christo, qui tribus diebus et
tribus noctibus in corde terræ sepultus, somnium mortis
implevit."— *In Genesim*, Hom. xvii.

This type of spiritual vigilance is found most frequently in Romanic and early Gothic architecture, from the beginning of the ninth to the end of the thirteenth century. Usually the lions repose on either side of the principal entrance, or stand on pillars in the portico of the edifice, or serve, especially in Italian churches, as pedestals to support the columns of the doorway. Examples of this kind may be seen in the cathedral of Mayence, the oldest churches of Cologne, the so-called Schottenkirche (former church of Scotch Benedictines) in Ratisbon, St. Stephen's in Vienna, and in various structures of an ecclesiastical character at Ancona, Monza, Padua, Parma, Ravenna, Rome, Siponto, and other Italian cities.

In some instances the same beast may symbolize utterly opposing principles, since it embodies antagonistic qualities.[1] The lion, for example, is not only typical of Christ triumphing over death and hell and loosing the seven seals from the book of life (Rev. v. 5), but also signifies the great adversary, the devil, which, "as a roaring lion, walketh about, seeking whom he may devour" (1 Peter v. 8). This is the lion from whose mouth the Psalmist prays to be saved (Ps. xxii. 21), and to which St. Augustine refers when he exclaims in his *Sermo de Tempore* (clxxiv.), "who would not

---

[1] "Secundum regnum ergo Christo adsimilata sunt. Et alia multa sunt in creaturis habentia duplicem intellectum ; alia quædam laudabilia, alia vero vituperabilia ; et differentiam habent inter se atque discretionem, sive moribus sive naturis."

rush into the jaws of this lion, if the lion of the
tribe of Judah should not prevail! It is lion
against lion, and lamb against wolf." The lion of
the tribe of Judah is opposed to the devouring lion,
and the lamb as the type of the meek and lowly
Saviour is opposed to the fierce and insatiable
wolf as the type of Satan. Christ, he adds, "is
a lion in fortitude, a lamb in innocence; a lion because He is invincible, a lamb because He is meek
and gentle." In another discourse (Hom. xxxiv.)
St. Augustine says the devil is impetuous as the
lion and insidious as the dragon, raging openly
like the former and lying in wait secretly like the
latter. In former times the Church fought against
the lion as it now fights against the dragon. In
Sermo clxxix. the lion and the bear typify the
devil, "who is figured in these two beasts, because
the bear's strength is in its paw and the lion's in
its mouth." In Sermo cxcvii. he says that as
David throttled the lion and the bear, which took
a lamb out of the flock, so Jesus Christ, whom
David prefigured, throttled the lion and the bear,
when He descended into hell and delivered the
captive spirits out of their jaws. Thus both these
animals are different embodiments of the Protean
prince of darkness. On the bronze doors of the
cathedral in Hildesheim are reliefs which date
from 1015, and represent the history of sin and
redemption; in one of them a bear stands behind
Pilate, whispering into his ear and filling his mind
with diabolical suggestions. The bear as the type

of Satan is found less frequently in architecture than in illuminated manuscripts and missals, and in carvings on caskets, crosiers, shrines, and other minor objects of art.

Christ trampling on a lion, an adder, or a dragon (Ps. xci. 13) is often used to indicate His triumph over the powers of hell. The same idea was intended to be expressed by sculpturing figures of deceased persons reclining on tombs with their feet resting on a lion, a dragon, or a dog, which was likewise regarded as an incarnation of the evil principle, in conformity with the apostle's assertion, "For without are dogs." At a later period the lion at the feet of a man symbolized manly strength and courage, and the dog at the feet of a woman signified undying love and fidelity. It was the substitution of the Aryan for the Semitic point of view that reversed the meaning of the symbolism.

The diabolification of the dog was due to the Hebrew misconception of its character; and it is a curious fact that the Jews, who endowed a rapacious and offensive creature like the vulture with fictitious virtues, should have had no proper appreciation of one of the noblest and most useful of their domestic animals. The affection and fidelity of the dog seem to have made hardly any impression upon them. This oldest and most trusty companion of man is rarely referred to by them except in terms of contempt, and it is from this source that many derogatory expressions concerning dogs have passed into the common speech of to-day.   When Elisha foretells the cruel conduct of Hazael, the latter exclaims: "Is thy servant a dog that he should do this great thing?"   Job expresses the same scornful feeling when he says: "Now they that are younger than I have me in derision, whose fathers I would have disdained to have set with the dogs of my flock."   Only in the apocryphal Tobit (v. 16; x. 14) is the dog treated in some degree as the friend and associate of man. Thus when Tobias and his companion set out on their journey to Media to collect a debt, it is said: "So they went forth both, and the young man's dog with them"—a simple touch that adds im-mensely to the beauty and realism of the picture. In the New Testament dogs are pariah beasts completely out of the pale of human interest and sympathy.   There is an old legend that Jesus once saw a crowd of persons gathered round the carcass of a dog, and giving utterance to their disgust at the sight of such a loathsome beast.   But as Jesus looked upon it He said: "How white its teeth are!"   The story is intended to illustrate, not His higher and truer estimation of the worth of the animal, but His own nobility of character, and the generous optimism which avoided evil-speaking, and could discover admirable qualities even in so hideous a creature as a dead dog.   Indeed there is nothing in Hebrew or early Christian literature to be compared with Homer's sympathetic description of Ulysses' dog Argus, or Arrian's characterization

of the greyhound Hormê (ὁρμή, "impetuous "), "the
swiftest, sagest, and divinest" of beasts. With
what fine appreciation he dwells upon her cunning
and cleverness, and other excellent traits! Ælian
relates (*De Nat. Animal.*, vii. 38) that a Magnesian
war-hound, which distinguished itself at Marathon,
was honoured with an effigy on the same tablet
that recorded the valour of its master. The Avesta
and other sacred books of the Parsis enjoin the
greatest kindness and reverence towards the dog,
whose sagacity, vigilance, and fidelity are regarded
as the pillars of pastoral society ; and in the Indian
epic, the *Mahábhárata*, the hero Yudhishthira refuses to enter Indra's heaven unless "his faithful
dog shall bear him company."

In the porch of Freiburg Minster are delineations of the deeds of Samson in carrying off the
gates of Gaza, tearing open the lion's jaws, and
performing other exploits supposed to foreshadow
the redeeming power of Christ. In this work the
artist embodies the ideas of patristic exegetists,
who show a vast amount of misapplied ingenuity
in tracing analogies between the career of the
Hebrew solar hero and that of the Sun of
righteousness. (Cf. St. Augustine's *De Samsone*,
Sermo I.)

The column-sustaining lions, so often placed at
the entrance of the churches, or used to support
pulpits, as in Pisa, Sienna, Lucca, Chiusi, and
elsewhere in Italy, and especially in Tuscany,
represent Satan subdued and subjected to the

service of Christianity. The same is true of the lion's head on the doors of the baptistery at Florence, and the cathedrals of Mayence and Hildesheim. In the vestibule of the cathedral of Piacenza, dating from the first half of the twelfth century, as well as in many ecclesiastical edifices in Ferrara, Modena, and Rome, the columns rest upon the shoulders of men with lions underneath them, which have seized other men as their prey. They symbolize heretics, whom the devil has got possession of, but who are overcome by the power of truth, and made to uphold the orthodox faith. Among other sculptures on the doors of a church in Novgorod, is the head of a lion with open jaws, in which are seen the faces of the damned writhing with agony, and above it the inscription : " Hell consuming sinners." St. Augustine, in his *Sermo de Tempore* (lxv.), compares Daniel in the lions' den with the temptation of Jesus in the wilderness ; but it is more commonly interpreted as typical of Christ's descent into hell, as, for example, at the entrance of the church of St. Porchaire in France.

The characteristics attributed to the lion in the *Physiologus* were familiar to mediæval poets, and furnished them with an ample fund of metaphorical material. Thus Wolfram von Eschenbach, in his most celebrated poem, compares the hero Parzival and his half-brother Feirefiz to two lion's whelps roused to life and energy by the roar of battle. Again, in his epic *Willehalm*, he declares that in the fierce combat between Christians and paynims at Alischanz the noise produced by the blare of trumpets, the roll of drums, and the shouts of contending hosts was loud enough to call to life a lion's whelps.

Thomasin von Zircläre, in the *Welscher Gast*, which describes court-life in Italy, and lays down general rules of conduct for princes, says that when sovereigns have done wrong, they should blot out all traces of it by humble repentance and increased beneficence, as the lion escapes pursuit by obliterating its foot-prints with its tail. Elsewhere he advises monarchs never to act on the impulse of the moment, but to give heed to three things before putting any project into practice: listen to counsellors, compare their views, and adopt the best advice, as the lion's whelps lie three days dormant after they are born. The simile, in this case, is ridiculously inapt, but the *Physiologus* gives the key to it, and renders it at least intelligible. The same zoölogical myth was evidently in the mind of the old Spanish poet, Juan de Mena, when he described the mother of Lorenço d'Avalos as lamenting like a lioness ("como al que pare haze la leona") over her dead son. Amorozzo da Firenze expresses the intensity of his susceptibility to the tender passion by asserting that the voice of his lady-love would suffice to revive him from death, as the voice of the lion reanimates its young. A Provençal erotic poet, Richard de Berbezilh, uses the same imagery to illustrate the same sentiment. Another old French poet, Guirant de Calanson, says: "As the lion sleeps with open eyes (*huelks uberts*), so my spirit, even in slumber, beholds thee, O lady."

Meister Stolle, in the *Wartburgkrieg*, would endow princes with the voice of the lion and the eyes of the ostrich, which hatches its eggs by gazing at them, so that they might rouse and animate their followers by word and look, inciting them to noble and knightly achievements. Reinmar von Zweter praises the "ostrich eyes" of the Emperor Friedrich II., as inspiriting and life-giving; and Pierre Espagnol informs us that the eyes of his lady-love are incubatory like those of the ostrich, causing sighs to germinate and spring up in his heart whenever she turns upon him an ardent glance.

The next animal mentioned in the *Physiologus* is the lizard, which, when it gets blind in its old age, creeps into the crevice of a wall looking towards the east, and stretches out its head to the rising sun, whose rays restore its sight. "In like manner, O man, thou who hast on the old garment, and the eyes of whose heart are obscured, seek the wall of help, and watch there until the sun of righteousness, which the prophet calls the day-spring, rises with healing power and removes thy spiritual blindness."

Representations of a lizard running along a wall or peeping out of some chink in it, either sculptured in stone or carved in wood, are not uncommon in mediæval churches, especially among the decora-

tions of the chancel.   It was not the mere caprice
of the architect that put the reptile there, but its
presence is due to its significance as a symbol of
the regenerating and illuminating influence of the
gospel.

The unicorn is another favourite type, and is
thus described by the *Physiologus:* "It is a small
animal, but exceeding strong and fleet, with a
single horn in the centre of its forehead.   The only
means of capturing it is by stratagem, namely,
by decking a chaste virgin with beautiful ornaments
and seating her in a solitary place in the forest
frequented by the unicorn, which no sooner perceives
her than it runs to her and,
laying its head gently in her
lap, falls asleep.   Then the
hunters come and take it captive to the king's palace and
receive for it much treasure."

Herein the unicorn resem-
bles our Saviour, who "hath

Capture of the Unicorn.
(*Bestiary.*)

raised up a horn of salvation for us in the house
of His servant David"; and the work of redemption, which neither thrones, nor dominations, nor
heavenly powers could accomplish, He brought
to pass.   The mighty ones of this world were
unable to approach Him or to lay hold of Him,
until He abode in the womb of the Virgin Mary.
As it is written: "And the Word was made flesh,
and dwelt among us, and we beheld His glory, the
glory of the only-begotten of the Father, full of

grace and truth;" or as this passage is paraphrased in *Le Bestiaire Divin*—

"Sul por la volonté de Dieu,
Passa Deu por la Virgne mère ;
Et la Parole fut char faite,
Que virgineté n'i ot fraite."

In the border of the central lancet window in the apsis of the cathedral at Lyons is a representation of this fable of the unicorn and the Virgin as a symbol of Christ's incarnation. It is rather awkwardly drawn, and the Virgin seems to sit astride of the unicorn's neck, but it was evidently the intention of the artist to have the animal's head lying in her lap. There is a carving of the same kind in St. Botolph's Church at Boston, Lincolnshire, and a series of reliefs of a similar character may be seen in the cathedral at Toledo, in Spain. A curious German engraving of the fifteenth century, entitled "Von der menschwerdong gottes nach geistlicher auszlegong der hystori von dem einhoren," pictures the Annunciation and Incarnation as the chase of the unicorn. The archangel Gabriel, the leader of the hunt, winds his horn, from which is supposed to proceed the melodious greeting : " Hail, highly-favoured one, the Lord is with thee, thou blessed among women !" The unicorn, pursued by hounds, is running rapidly towards the Virgin, who sits with upturned eyes and hands folded across her breast in a state of ecstasy, while the horn of the animal is in perilous proximity to her lap. On her right are an altar with burning candles and a flowing fountain, a symbol of the waters of eternal life.   In the background God the Father holds a globe surmounted with a cross in one hand, and gives His benediction with the other.   The three dogs are Mercy, Truth, and Justice, and denote the attributes of the

Hunting the Unicorn.   (*Old German Engraving.*)

Saviour and the feelings which impelled Him to become incarnate, and to redeem the world from the dominion of Satan.[1]   This symbolism is more fully and clearly expressed in a German painting of the fifteenth or perhaps the beginning of the

[1] Cf. Dr. Ulrich Pinder: *Der beschlossen gart des rosen-krants Marie*, Nürnberg, 1505, Band II., Blatt ix.   Also Cahier: *Caractéristiques des Saints dans l'Art populaire*, Paris, 1844.

sixteenth century, now belonging to the Grand
Ducal Library of Weimar.   In this extremely
elaborate and highly-finished work of art there are
four dogs held in leash and barking at the unicorn,
which is already in the lap of the Virgin; their
collars are labelled respectively Veritas, Justitia,
Misericordia, and Pax; the first two are dark-
brown, the third light-brown, and the fourth white.
The Virgin wears a greenish-brown dress studded
with golden flowers, and a green mantle.   Gabriel
is arrayed in scarlet, and has wings of many
brilliant hues.   Gideon kneels behind her on his
fleece of wool (Judges vi. 36-40).   In the background is a city representing Zion.   To the right
of the Virgin in the sky appears God the Father,
with a large wreath of oak-leaves encircling His
neck and resting on His shoulders, His hands
upraised in the act of blessing, and the Christ-child
descending on a beam of light and bearing a cross.
At the lower end of the beam of light is a dove
hovering over the Virgin's head and its beak
directed towards her ear.   This attitude of the
dove, which is quite common, and indeed almost
universal, in mediæval and early modern pictures
of the Annunciation, is intended to indicate the
naïve notion entertained by patristic writers and
later theologians, that the conception of Christ was
effected supernaturally through the Virgin's ear, so
that she remained perfectly pure and immaculate,
and her maidenhood intact.   This queer theory
had its origin probably in Gnostic speculations and

the Greco-Judaic religious philosophy current in Alexandria, and was the result of a too literal interpretation of the doctrine of the Logos. As God spoke the world into existence, so the voice of the Most High uttering salutation through the mouth of the angel caused the Virgin to conceive, "and the Word was made flesh." But as spoken words are addressed to the ear, and through this organ find lodgment in the mind and thus bear fruit, it was assumed that the incarnation of the Logos was accomplished in the same manner: "Deus per angelum loquebatur et Virgo per aurem impregnabatur," says St. Augustine (*Sermo de Tempore*, xxii.); and this view, which was generally accepted by the Apostolic Fathers, is expressed eight centuries later in a verse attributed to Thomas à Becket—

"Gaude Virgo, mater Christi,
Quæ per aurem concepisti."

The same description of the miraculous event is given by the German mediæval poet, Walther von der Vogelweide: "dur ir ore enphinc si den vil suezen." In the parish church (formerly belonging to the abbey) of Eltenberg on the Rhine, is an Annunciation moulded in clay, baked and painted, in which the infant Jesus, attended by the Holy Spirit, descends from heaven on the breath of God the Father, and enters the ear of the Virgin. Similar representations are to be seen (so far as they have not been destroyed) at Oppenheim, on the portal of the cathedral at Würzburg, and elsewhere. The blast of Gabriel's bugle in the Weimar painting is no uncertain sound, but becomes articulate as: " Ave gratia plena, Dominus tecum," to which the

The Annunciation. (*Parish Church of Ettenberg.*)

Virgin responds: "Ecce ancilla Domini, fiat mihi secundum Verbum tuum."   Indeed the air is full of floating legends taken chiefly from the Song

of Solomon, such as "Sicut lilium inter spinas, sic
amica mea inter filias " (As the lily among thorns,
so my love among the daughters); "Fons hortorum,
puteus aquarum viventium quæ fluunt impetu de
Libano" (A fountain of gardens, a well of living
waters, and streams from Lebanon); " Veni Auster,
perfla hortum et fluant aromata" (Come, thou
south, blow upon my garden that the spices may
flow out); "Turris eburnea" (Tower of ivory), etc.
The Virgin sits behind a wicker fence or palisade
in illustration of the passage : "A garden enclosed
is my sister." Engravings of this painting have
been frequently published ; as, for example, in the
sixth volume of *Curiositäten der physch- literarisch-
artistisch- historischen Vor- und Mitwelt* (Weimar,
1817, p. 133); *Revue Archéologique* (Paris, 1844-45,
p. 462); *Das Evangelische Jahrbuch,* issued at
Berlin ; and in a recent Christmas number of
Harper's Magazine. There is another picture of a
similar character at Weimar; a third was formerly
in the Hospital Church at Grimmenthal on the
Werra ; and a fourth is in the cathedral at Bruns-
wick, painted on one of the folding compartments
of a triptych or altar-piece. The Virgin with the
unicorn in her lap is on the outside, and the angel
as huntsman with horn, spear, and dogs on the
inside. Out of the mouth of the animal proceed
the words : "Quia quem Cœli capere non possunt,
in tuo gremio contulisti,"—a punning form of expression, which may refer either to the incarnation
of Christ, or to the hunting of the unicorn : "Whom

the heavens (highest powers) could not contain
(capture), thou didst hold (take) in thy womb (lap)."
The Virgin has a blue robe, the lower part of which
is reddish ; a basket of manna is at her feet, and
near her the legend : " Fons signatus " (a fountain
sealed).   The angel is dressed in white with a red
mantle floating in the wind, and has four dogs
in the leash.[1]   In the Grimmenthal picture the
symbolism is still more striking.   On the left of
the tall and majestic angel is a lion howling over
two motionless whelps, with the legend " Maria Leo,"
and just before him the eternal city or perennity of
God (*Perennitas Dei*) ; above the gate of heaven
(*Porta Cœli*) God the Father appears in the clouds
between the sun and the moon ; across the disc of
the former are the words "clara ut sol " (clear as
the sun), and issuing from the mouth of the human
face defined in the crescent of the latter the words,
" Pulchra ut luna " (fair as the moon).   On the left
of the painting is a star (*stella maris*), and on the
right a pelican feeding its young with its blood,
and Moses talking with Jehovah in the burning
bush.   In the centre is Gideon kneeling on his
fleece ; behind him is the flowing fountain of the
waters of eternal life ; above it a mirror with the
inscription, "speculum sine macula " (a mirror
without spot).   An engraving of this picture, but
without any interpretation of its symbolism, was

---

[1] Cf. Ribbentrop : *Beschreibung der Stadt Braunschweig*,
where this work of art is ascribed, but without sufficient
reason, to Lucas Cranach.

published in Friedrich Rudolphi's *Gotha Diplomatica oder Ausführliche Historische Beschreibung des Fürstenthums Sachsen-Gotha* (Frankfurt am Main und Leipzig, 1717, p. 310). It was an altarpiece, and was probably the work of Paul Lautensack, better known as Meister Paul of Bamberg, who was born in that city in 1478, and died in 1558 at Nuremberg, as an ardent and rather fanatical Protestant. In the latter half of the fifteenth and the early part of the sixteenth century, Grimmenthal was a noted place of pilgrimage, where many miraculous cures were said to have been effected through the agency of the Holy Virgin. The ruling prince, Wilhelm, of the House of Henneberg, a zealous Catholic, employed Meister Paul to decorate the interior of the church, and the artist devoted himself for ten years to the task, and received twelve thousand florins for his services, a sum regarded at that time as an exceedingly munificent remuneration. People flocked to this wonder-working shrine from all the countries of Europe, and no less than forty-four thousand persons are reported to have visited it in a single year. The maimed, the halt, and the blind were healed of their infirmities, but the medical virtue of the Madonna manifested itself most strikingly as a specific for syphilis, or the Venusseuche, as it was commonly termed. According to an old Latin chronicler, there was in 1503 "a grand peregrination to the Blessed Virgin at Grimmenthal, where an immense concourse gathered, chiefly on account of the French malady, otherwise called acute and burning leprosy ('principaliter propter malum Franzosiæ, alias acutam lepram ac ardentem dictam'), that raged for a period of more than ten years, during which time some three hundred Moorish knights or Ethiops ('quasi 300 Mauri equites sive Aethyopes') passed through Silesia journeying thither."[1] The Reformation naturally tended to check these pilgrimages, and finally put a stop to them altogether. Luther himself felt a strong antipathy to this holy shrine, which he denounced as " ein rechtes Grimmenthal, Vallem furoris." In 1525 the revenues derived from pious offerings were so small that they hardly sufficed to defray current expenses, and in 1547 the buildings, which formerly served to lodge pilgrims, were converted into a hospital, and the church was henceforth used merely for the cure of souls. But, although the method of healing had been officially secularized, the sacred place preserved to a certain degree its traditional reputation in the minds of the people, until in 1767 the church, with all of Meister Paul's paintings, was destroyed by fire. The Virgin with a unicorn resting its head in her lap is quite common in ecclesiastical architecture, especially in stained windows, as for example in St. Redegonde, at Caen. Again, in an Italian engraving of the six triumphs of Petrarch, dating from the fifteenth

---

[1] *Licurii Append. ad Fascicul. Tempor. ap. Pistorii Script. Rerum Germanicarum Vet.*, Francof., 1707, tom. ii., p. 600.

century, and belonging to the Albertine collection in Vienna, the triumph of chastity is symbolized by a virgin seated and a unicorn with its head in her lap. In the background is a hunter blowing a horn, and rapidly approaching with a pack of dogs. In another engraving illustrating the same triumph the car of chastity is drawn by unicorns.

Superstitious notions about the peculiar virtue inherent in the unicorn's horn were quite current in the middle ages. Thus John of Herse, who made a pilgrimage to Jerusalem in 1389, records his observations on this point. "Near the field Helyon in the Holy Land," he says, "is the river Mara, whose bitter waters Moses struck with his staff and made sweet, so that the children of Israel could drink thereof. Even now, evil and unclean beasts poison it after the going down of the sun ; but in the morning, after the powers of darkness have disappeared, the unicorn comes from the sea and dips its horn into the stream, and thereby expels and neutralizes the poison, so that the other animals can drink of it during the day. The fact, which I describe, I have seen with my own eyes." This story furnishes an excellent illustration of the value of human testimony, and the conclusiveness of ocular evidence, showing the little confidence to which the report of an extraordinary event is entitled, even when it rests, not upon hearsay, but upon the positive statement of an honest eye-witness. That John of Herse meant to tell the truth, and thought he observed what he records, there is not the slightest reason to doubt.

On account of this supposed anti-toxical property, the unicorn's horn was used for making spoons (so-called test-spoons), salt-cellars, and especially drinking-cups. Articles manufactured of this material held a prominent or rather an important place in the table-service of mediæval nobles and princes, and were prized as a sure protection against all sorts of poison, as well as a specific for epilepsy and other forms of convulsion. A closer examination of these objects, which are now preserved as curiosities in museums, proves them to have been fabricated from the tusks of the narwal.

Equally spurious are the so-called griffin's claws now preserved as relics in churches or as curiosities in museums, as for example in the churches of Hildesheim, Weimar, Cologne, and Gran on the Danube, and in the museums of Dresden, Vienna, and other European cities. They are simply horns of the Caffrarian buffalo. An interesting specimen of this kind is in the old abbey on the Inde, founded by Lewis the Debonair in the ninth century, and now known as Cornelimünster, because it contains the relics of the canonized Pope Cornelius, among which the saint's horn or drinking-cup, styled the griffin's claw, holds the most conspicuous place. Hagiologists even tell us that a griffin gave it to the holy man out of gratitude for having been miraculously healed of epilepsy. This legend

is related as an historical fact as late as 1755 in
the *Heiligthumsbüchlein*, issued for the guidance
and edification of pilgrims to the sacred shrine.
On such occasions wonderful cures are believed to
be wrought by pouring holy water from this horn
on the sick and infirm. It has been customary
for the last five centuries to exhibit these relics
once in seven years for healing purposes.

Samuel Bochart, in his *Hierozoicon*, written
about the middle of the seventeenth century,
cites a number of Arabian authors, who enlarge
upon the marvellous peculiarities of the unicorn's
horn. Among other curious statements, it is said
that if the horn be cut lengthwise, it will be
found to contain the figure of a man, a beast, a
bird, or a flower, beautifully designed in white,
and filling the whole shape from the tip to the
base.

In the *Parzival* of Wolfram von Eschenbach,
among various remedies employed to heal the
wound of Anfortas, king of the Gral, the heart of
a unicorn and the carbuncle growing under its
horn are mentioned. In the same poem Queen
Orgeluse's lover, Cidegast, whom Gramoflanz has
slain in combat, is extolled as "a unicorn in
fidelity." In Heinrich Frauenlob's *Kreuzleich* (Lay
of the Cross), Konrad von Würzburg's *Goldene
Schmiede* (Golden Smithy), and other poems of the
thirteenth and fourteenth centuries in praise of the
Virgin, God the Father is represented as a huntsman, pursuing the unicorn until it takes refuge in

the womb of the immaculate Mary. Reinmár von Zweter lauds the power of chastity, which was stronger than the Almighty; and Hugo von Langenstein celebrates in florid and somewhat motley allegory the majesty of the maid whose loveliness and purity captivated and conciliated heaven's unicorn, and thus averted the Divine wrath from our sinful world. In a German hymn of the fifteenth century addressed to the Virgin, she is said to have "tamed the unicorn and the hind"; and in a hunting-song, quoted by Lauchert from Uhland's collection (No. 339), the whole scheme of redemption is set forth as the outcome of the fascinations of "ein seuberlichs junkfrewelin."

Metaphors drawn from the fabled habits of the unicorn, or allusions to them, are frequently met with in the effusions of mediæval erotic poets, who, like the unicorn, would fain lay their heads in the laps of their ladies and be enslaved by their charms. The Suabian knight and minnesinger, Burkhart von Hohenfels, likens himself to the unicorn, because a fair woman has allured him to his destruction; and Guido Cavalcanti, the contemporary and friend of Dante, makes use of the same imagery in a sonnet addressed to Guido Orlandi, who was languishing in fatal thraldom to the all-subduing passion. Thibault, Count of Champagne and King of Navarre, describes in one of his lyrics the treachery of the hunters, who catch and kill the unicorn while lying faint and languishing in the virgin's lap, and adds—

"Thus Love and my Lady have done to me,
And my heart can never again be free." [1]

The unicorn, like the lion, has a twofold signification, and in the Waldensian *Physiologus* stands
for Satan, who can be overcome only by purity
and innocence. The enmity of the unicorn to the
elephant, described by Isidore, and enlarged upon
by the author of *Le Bestiaire Divin*, tends also to
confuse the spiritual meaning, since both of these
animals are types of Christ. The elephant is, however, in this case, as we shall see hereafter, a symbol of fallen humanity. The Latin texts and the
later popular versions of the *Physiologus* carry
out the religious symbolism of the unicorn into
the minutest doctrinal detail. Thus the single
horn signifies the oneness of the Father and the
Son, while the smallness of the animal and its
similarity to the he-goat express the exceeding
humility and condescension of Christ in consenting
to become incarnate in the likeness of sinful man.

According to Albertus Magnus, the horn of the
African viper was said to rival that of the unicorn
in its sensitiveness to poisons, and to show their
presence by emitting perspiration; for this reason,
he adds, it was used for the handles of table-knives.
This statement, however, he gives with reserve, as
not sufficiently proven: "sed hoc non satis proba-
tum est" (*De Animal.*, lib. XXV. vi. 667). Of the

---

[1] "Et moi ont fait de tel semblant
    Amors et ma Dame, por voir ;
    Mon cuer n'en puis point ravoir."

antidotal and prophylactic virtue of the unicorn's horn in such cases the erudite Dominican and "doctor universalis" does not seem to have entertained the slightest doubt.

In the *Alexanderlied* of Pfaffen Lamprecht we are told that Queen Candace—whose kingdom was "on the edge of the earth's abyss, where the sky revolves round it like a wheel on its axis"—presented the Macedonian conqueror with a live unicorn, which had been captured by means of a decoy virgin. The animal is described by the poet as a highly heterogeneous and utterly impossible creature, having the body of a horse, the tail of a pig, the head of a stag, the feet of an elephant, and a long horn projecting from its forehead. The carbuncle concealed at the root of this horn is also mentioned, and its medicinal properties, so often described in mediæval pharmacopœias, are extolled.

The elephant, says the *Physiologus*, is a very intelligent animal, but has an exceedingly cold and passionless temperament. Therefore, when the time for copulation comes, the male and female betake themselves to a region in the neighbourhood of Paradise, where the mandrake grows, and eat of this aphrodisiac plant, and thereupon beget young.[1] Now when the period of parturition arrives,

---

[1] The mandrakes which Reuben found in the field were used by his mother Leah for venereal purposes (Gen. xxx. 14-16), and this precious peculiarity is enlarged upon in rabbinical literature. The Greeks spoke of them as anthropomorphic ; and according to popular superstition they spring from human sperm spilled on the ground, and are so

the female elephant goes into a pond until the water touches her breast, and there brings forth her young, as the Psalmist says : " Save me, O God, for the waters are come into my soul." But the male keeps watch in order to ward off the dragon, which dwells in the pond, and seeks to devour the new-born elephant.

The two elephants signify Adam and Eve, who ate of the forbidden fruit of the tree of life, and yielding to the power of sensual passion excited by it, begat children, and brought death and woe into the world.

Another characteristic of the elephant is that when it falls down it cannot get up again, since it is unable to bend its knees. For this reason it always sleeps standing, and leans for support against a tree. The hunters take advantage of this bodily defect and, having discovered its sleeping-place, saw the tree almost asunder, so that when the huge beast leans against it the tree gives way, and the elephant falls to the ground, and there lies roaring helplessly. Then the other elephants hasten to its assistance, but all their efforts to raise it up are in vain; at length a small young elephant comes, and, thrusting its trunk under the fallen animal, lifts it to its feet again. Now the first elephant symbolizes Adam, who fell " through a tree," as an old English bestiary puts it, towards the fruit of which he had stretched out his hand. And all the

full of animal life and consciousness that they shriek when torn out of the earth, so " that living mortals, hearing them, run mad."

great prophets and the lesser prophets essayed in
vain to restore him to his first estate; but "the
new elephant, our Saviour," though accounted the
least of all the prophets, was able to accomplish it,
becoming a servant and abasing Himself that we
might be exalted.

Julius Cæsar, in his commentary on the Gallic
War (vi. 27), in speaking of the fauna of the
country, describes an animal something like the
unicorn as follows : "There is an ox having the
form of a deer, from the middle of whose forehead,
between the ears, there rises a single horn, longer
and straighter than the horns of any other animal
known to us, and spreading widely at the top in
palm-like branches. The appearance of the male
and the female is the same, and the shape and size
of the horns are similar." He then adds : "There
are also animals called *alces* [elks], like a deer in
form and colour, but larger in size. They shed
their horns, and their legs are without joints or
articulations. They do not lie down to rest, and
if they happen to fall to the ground they are
unable to rise. The trees serve them for beds,
against which they lean, and thus, slightly reclining,
take their repose. When the hunters discover these
places of resort, they either undermine the trees at
the roots or cut them so far that the trunk has
only the appearance of standing firmly, so that
when the animals lean against them, according to
their habit, the weakened trees give way and they
fall together to the earth." The stiff and stilty

manner in which the elk holds its legs in running and leaping, seems to have led Cæsar to infer that they were without joints, and from this queer mistake for such a sober and accurate observer to make the fabulous account of its method of sleeping could have easily arisen, especially as this was supposed to be the case with the elephant, the method of capturing which is also described in the Spanish *Poema de Alexandro* by Juan Lorenzo de Segura.

Mediæval poets use the statement that the elephant gives birth in the water as a symbol of baptismal regeneration, but the animal seldom figures metaphorically in madrigals or lays of love. The inditer of an amorous sonnet or soft ditty would hardly venture to compare himself or his sweetheart to the hugest and most unwieldy of pachyderms. It is rarely represented in sacred architecture, but is often found embroidered on sacerdotal vestments, and especially on chasubles, as a symbol of priestly chastity. Häufler (*Archiv für Kunde österreichischer Geschichtsquellen.*, 1850, ii. 593) mentions a chasuble of the eleventh century at Gös near Loeben adorned with various animals, and among them elephants with towers on their backs, which he thinks typify prudence and virtue equipped to resist the powers of evil. It may be, however, that, after the original symbolism was forgotten, the elephant continued to be used merely as a traditional decoration, in which case the howdah and other trappings would naturally be

I

added without attaching to them any special signification.

The serpent has four characteristics : (1) When it has grown old and its eyes are dim, it fasts forty days and forty nights until its skin shrivels and loosens. Thereupon it squeezes itself through a narrow crevice in the rocks, and thus casts its skin and renews its youth. And thou, O son of man, if thou desirest to put off the old Adam and be regenerated, must pass through the strait gate and walk in the narrow way, which leadeth unto life. (2) When the serpent goes to a spring to drink water, it leaves its venom in its hole; so he, who would refresh his soul with the waters of eternal life, must leave behind him every sin of his carnal heart. (3) The serpent fears a naked man and flees from him, but assails him when he is clothed. Those who are acquainted with this characteristic of the serpent throw off their garments, when pursued by it, and thus save their lives. So, too, when Adam was naked in the garden and had no desire for raiment, the serpent could do him no harm. In like manner, if we do not trouble ourselves about the vanities of this world, we need not fear the assaults of the wily serpent, the devil. According to this doctrine nudity is a sign of innocence and the sanctified should dispense with clothing, which originated in the fall of man and is a covering of sin, that may find a lurking-place even under the scanty vesture of a fig-leaf. The Adamites of the second, and the Picards of the fifteenth century held that those whom Christ had redeemed were restored to the original purity of our first parents in Eden, and should return to the primitive habits of the race, including nudity and sexual promiscuity. (4) When one seeks to kill the serpent, it exposes its whole body, in order to shield its head from the blows of its assailant. The application of this characteristic to Christians, who should endure every trial and affliction for the sake of Christ, their head, has already been noticed. The serpent shows its wisdom also in this, that it stops its ears to the charmer and refuses to listen to his spell, thus teaching us to shut our ears to Satanic suggestions. The notion that poisonous reptiles could be charmed so as to prevent them from stinging or to render their bite harmless, was based on such passages as Jer. viii. 17 and Ps. lviii. 5, and seemed to be confirmed by the wonderful feats of Oriental fakirs and magicians.

These imaginary attributes of the serpent are occasionally represented as religious symbols in churches among the wood-carvings of the chancel and the reliefs adorning the doorways or the capitals of columns, but more frequently in the illuminations of mediæval manuscripts. Still more common is the metaphorical use of them by the poets of the middle ages in illustration of both sacred and secular subjects. Thus in one of the mystic spiritual songs of the Minorite Jacopone da Todi, the reputed and probable author of the *Stabat Mater*, the first characteristic of the serpent

figures the love of Jesus, which purifies and renews
the soul. The third characteristic is applied in a
queer way by a troubadour, Bertolome Zorgi
(quoted by Lauchert, p. 186, from Diez: *Leben und
Werke der Troubadours*), who says of his lady-love
that, like the serpent, she flees from him when he
is naked, and is fearless in his presence only when
he is clothed, surely no unusual display of timidity
in a modest dame. It is also related in the *Poema
de Alexandro* already cited, that as the army of
the Macedonian monarch was passing through a
desert and suffering intensely from thirst, the
soldiers found a spring, which, however, was so surrounded by serpents that all who approached it
were in danger of being bitten. But Alexander,
who was not less distinguished for wisdom than for
valour, ordered the men to strip, so that they went
to the water unharmed by the serpents, which fled
from them as from moving pillars of fire. The
author tells many other marvellous stories of animals, and assures the reader that they are all true :
"esto es cosa vera." The serpent was likewise
revered by the Egyptians as a symbol of regeneration
and the renewal of life.

The *Physiologus* states that when the eagle has
grown old and its eyes have become dim and
darkened, it flies upward towards the sun until it
has scorched its wings and purged away the film
from its eyes ; then it descends to the earth and
plunges three times into a spring of pure water.
Thus it recovers its sight and renews its youth. In

like manner, when we have grown old in the sinful love of this world, and the eyes of the heart are obscured thereby, then should we seek the day-star of the divine word, and fly aloft on the wings of the spirit to the sun of righteous-ness, Christ, our Saviour, who will draw out of us the old man with all his works. And when we dip ourselves thrice in the new well-spring of sal-

Eagle renewing its youth.
(*Bestiary.*)

vation in the name of the Father, the Son, and the Holy Ghost, then will the old garment of the devil be taken away, and we shall be clothed in the new and shining raiment which God hath made ready for us.

The eagle can gaze at the bright sun without blinking, and is accustomed to carry its unfledged young on its wings upward and compel them to look upon the shining orb ; those which can do so with open and steadfast eyes it rears, but discards the others and lets them fall to the ground. Here the sun represents God the Father, upon whose face Christ can gaze undazzled by His glory, and to whom He presents the children of men who claim to have been born of Him ; those who are able to stand before God and to look upon the light of His countenance are accepted, while the others are rejected.

Again, we are told that the eagle looks from the

uppermost region of the air into the depths of the
sea, and when it perceives a fish swimming about,
plunges into the water and seizing the fish bears it
away to its aerie.   Here the eagle typifies Christ,
the sea the world, and the fish the elect whom He
saves and takes to Himself.

The eagle renewing its youth by plunging into a
fountain is the symbol of regeneration by baptism,
and is therefore sometimes sculptured on fonts and
baptisteries.   In ecclesiastical architecture the eagle
is often found perching alone, as, for example, in
the church at Alne ; in the miniatures of the manuscript bestiaries belonging to the Arsenal Library
and to the Royal Library of Brussels it is seen flying with its newly-fledged young up towards the
sun ; in a stained window in the cathedral at Lyons

Eaglets gazing at the sun.
(*Lyons Cathedral.*)

three eaglets are looking un-
flinchingly at the blazing sun,
while a fourth is falling to the
earth ; a mosaic in the baptistery
of Santa Maria di Capua represents an eagle taking a fish out
of the water, and the same scene
is carved on a Celtic cross at
St. Vigean's in Forfarshire, and
on the jamb of a Norman doorway at Ribbesford in Worcester-
shire ; it is also found on a metal plate in the British
Museum, and among the illuminations of a Celtic
manuscript of the *Book of Armagh* at Trinity
College, Dublin.

The fable of the rejuvenation of the eagle grew naturally enough out of the fact of the renewal of its plumage after moulting; but the Apostolic Fathers were not satisfied with this simple explanation of the words of the Psalmist (ciii. 5), and transformed an ordinary phenomenon into a supernatural and miraculous event, which would be more effective for exegetical purposes.

Aristotle (*Hist. Animal.*, cx. 32) relates that the upper beak of very old eagles grows so long as to prevent them from eating and to cause them to die of hunger. In the Greek version of the *Physiologus* of the twelfth century the author adds that in order to remedy this evil and to avert this danger the eagle breaks off the superfluity of its beak against a stone, a statement which is adduced by homilists and exegetists to prove that the rock of salvation is the only cure for the growth of carnal-mindedness, and the sole means of preventing spiritual starvation.

In Dante's *Divina Commedia* (Pt. I. 47-48) Beatrice is said to fix her eyes on the sun as steadfastly as never eagle did—

" Aquila si non gli s'affisse unquanco."

It was a test of Dante's fitness to visit the celestial spheres that he could do the same—

" E fissi gli occhi al sole oltre a nostr'uso."

Allusions to this notion occur in other parts of the poem. Ariosto uses the same imagery in one of his sonnets : " Although the young of the eagle may resemble the parent in its claws, head, breast, and plumage, but are not like it in keenness and strength of vision to endure the light, the eagle will not recognize them as its offspring. So the thoughts and desires of lovers should be in perfect conformity . . . Be not then different from me in any respect," he concludes, addressing his lady-love, " for you must accord with me wholly or not be mine at all "—

> " Non siete dunque in un da me difforme,
>   Perchè mi si confaccia il più di voi;
>   Che o nulla, o vi convien tutta esser mia."

A German poet, Wachsmut von Mühlhausen, declares that he will renew himself like the eagle and mount up joyously into the æther, " if thou, O lady, wilt console me in my sadness and my longing." Warriors, too, are praised or censured for possessing or not possessing the firm and unflinching eye of the eagle, when in the heat of battle. Thomasin von Zircläre says, in the *Welscher Gast*, that sovereigns should not be blinded by bribes, but should keep their sight unclouded, so as to be able to look clearly and fixedly at the truth in the light of justice, as eagles look at the sun, and that they should renew their strength for righteousness and ruling in equity by seeking communion with the Most High. They are likewise to imitate the eagle, which breaks off portions of its beak, when it has grown so long and crooked as to be an impediment, an admonition which might be taken as a warning against the circumlocutions of court etiquette and the trammels of red tape. In the literature of a later day one of the most splendidly rhetorical passages in the peroration of Milton's *Areopagitica* is borrowed from this superstition of the eaglet renewing its youth and purging its sight at the source of all life and illumination.

Strangely enough the fish is not especially mentioned by the *Physiologus*, although in sacred iconology it occurs most frequently as a symbol of Christ, the Greek word ΙΧΘΥΣ being the initial letters of the Greek phrase signifying Jesus Christ God's Son Saviour, Ἰησοῦς Χριστὸς Θεοῦ Υἱὸς Σωτήρ. But the fish, although proverbial among the Greeks for its stupidity, was carved on ancient tombs, because it was supposed to bear the soul of the deceased across the sea to the islands of the blest. This was especially the case with the dolphin, the strongest and swiftest of fishes, or, as Gregory of Nyssa calls it, the most royal of swimmers : ὁ δελφίς ἐστι των νηκτῶν ὁ βασιλικώτατος.   It is possible that the dolphin was at first, for the same reason, sculptured on Christian tombs, and that the fish was afterwards substituted for it on account of the monogrammatic meaning of the word.

The early Christians were accustomed to eat a roasted fish in commemoration of Christ's Passion, and a survival of this ceremony is the use of fish as an article of food on Friday. The fish was also sacred to Venus on account of its extraordinary fecundity ; for the same reason April, the opening (*aperilis*) or germinating month, was consecrated to this goddess, whose appropriate day (*dies Veneris, venerdi, vendredi*) was Friday, corresponding to Friatac, the day of Fria, the old German goddess of love. Patristic theologians were fond of seeking similitudes and discovering analogies between a baked fish and the suffering Christ: "inter piscem assum et Christum passum." Christian sepulchres are often adorned with frescoes or sculptures, in which the disciples are seated at a table furnished with a loaf of bread (the bread of life) and a baked fish. This is a sacramental or eucharistic meal.

Of sea-creatures only the whale and the fabulous remora and serra or winged saw-fish are discussed in the *Physiologus* and in the bestiaries. The whale has two characteristics. First, when he is hungry and lusts after food, he opens his wide mouth seaward and a pleasant odour issues from his maw, so that other fishes are deceived and swim eagerly towards the place whence the sweet odour comes. In heedless shoals they enter into his extended jaws; then suddenly the grim gums close and crush their prey. Thus the devil allures men to their destruction and closes upon them the barred gates of hell, from which they can no more escape than the fishes sporting in the ocean can return from the mouth of the whale.

Secondly, the mariners often mistake the whale, as it rests on the surface of the sea, for an island, on which they land and build a fire to cook their dinner, but when the whale begins to feel the heat through its thick hide, it plunges under the waves and engulphs all the brave seafarers with their high-prowed ships. In the old English bestiary this disaster is described in the succinct and graphic style of the old German epics. Here, too, the whale is the devil, the sea is the world, and the ship represents the human race.

Brunetto Latino states that the whale often remains stationary on the surface of the ocean, until it becomes incrusted with earth. From the seeds dropped by birds in this soil trees and shrubs spring up and grow to large forests, so that sailors are easily deceived and mistake the animal for an island. In the Book of Esdras (vi. 6) it is said that Behemoth and Leviathan, when they were created, covered each a seventh part of the earth. The Talmud adds that it would take a ship three days to sail from the head to the tail of one of these monsters; and some of the rabbis speak of whales fifteen stadia in length, which is a relatively sober estimate. An Arab writer maintains that the earth rests on the back of a whale, which performs the all-sustaining office of the turtle in Indian cosmogony, and that earthquakes and other convulsions of nature are caused by its occasional movements from one side to the other. The devil is constantly at work trying to persuade the whale to dive and thus destroy the world. Once the whale was just on the point of yielding to these Satanic solicitations, but was prevented by the merciful intervention of the Almighty, whereby the globe and its inhabitants were saved from such a catastrophe.

In architecture sometimes only the ship is represented, and the whale left to the imagination of the beholder, as for example in the old Norman church at Alne, or the whale is given and the ship omitted, one object being deemed sufficient to suggest the other.   In the miniatures of the bestiaries the whole scene is usually depicted in such a manner as to illustrate both characteristics : the ship lies at anchor, the mariners are cooking their dinner under the shadow of trees on the

Whale and ship.
(*Psalter of Isabella of France.*)

back of the whale, into whose extended jaws shoals of little fish are swimming.   A parchment codex of the Icelandic version of the *Physiologus*, dating from the thirteenth century, and now preserved in the Arna-Magnæan collection of the University Library of Copenhagen, has two crude drawings, in which these characteristics of the whale are portrayed.

The remora, called essinus (ἐχενηίς) in the bestiaries, and confounded with the sea-urchin, is a fish about a foot long and a native of the Indian Ocean, but so strong that it can keep a ship from moving by fastening itself to the keel.   In storms it holds the vessel steady, and prevents it from capsizing when tossed by the tempest, and is therefore a type of the Saviour, the sea symbolizing the world, and the ship man buffeted by the waves of temptation, which threaten to engulph him.

Pliny (ix. 25 ; xxxii. 1) extols the immense strength of this little fish, which, he says, decided the battle of Actium and the fate of the world by clinging to Anthony's galley and preventing it from going into action. Similar statements are made by Ælian (ii. 17) and Suetonius (*In Caio*, xlix.), from whom the authors of the bestiaries seem to have derived their information. Thus we are told that, when Caligula was returning from Astura to Antium, a remora sucked itself fast to the imperial five-decker, and neutralized the efforts of four hundred oarsmen. Again, as Periander was about to send a galley from Corinth to Corcyra to murder three hundred children, a great number of these fish fastened themselves to the vessel and kept it from sailing, although the wind was favourable. Out of gratitude for this good deed the echeneis (ship-detainer) was fostered and revered in the temple of Venus at Cnidus. Oppianus, in his didactic poem on fishing (τὰ Ἁλιευτικά), describes the astonishment and anger of the fishermen, when their boats are kept stationary by the force of these sea-creatures. The marvels of this sort recounted by ancient writers are repeated and magnified in German mediæval poems of heroic adventure and achievement, like *Graf Rudolf*, *Herzog Ernst*, and the *Alexander* of Pfaffen Lamprecht. The remora is sometimes called serra, but the latter is usually described as a sea-dragon, a fire-breathing monster with wings like a griffin, the tail of a goose, and the feet of a swan. When it sees a ship it

flies after it for thirty or forty leagues, but finally
grows weary and turns back to disport in the sea.
It symbolizes those who follow for a season in the
wake of the Church, but through lack of perseverance never reach the ark of safety.

According to the *Physiologus*, the phœnix is a
native of India and Arabia. When it is five
hundred years old, it flies to Lebanon, and fills its
wings with the fragrant gum of a tree growing
there, and thence hastens to Heliopolis in Egypt,
where it burns itself upon the high altar in the
temple of the sun. When the priest comes on the
next day to offer sacrifice, he removes the ashes
from the altar, and finds therein a small worm of
exceedingly sweet odour, which in three days
develops into a young bird, and on the fourth day
attains its full size and plumage, and greeting the
priest with reverence returns to its home. But if
the phœnix, adds the exegetist, is able to destroy
itself and to come to life again, why should the
Jews murmur at the words of our Saviour, when
He said: "I have power to lay down My life, and
I have power to take it again"?

The perfume which fills the two wings of the
phœnix symbolizes the sweetness of divine grace,
as diffused through the books of the Old and New
Testaments. Other expositors of Pelagian tendencies discern in these perfumes the good works
which the righteous man accumulates, and by
which he earns eternal life; and as the phœnix
kindles the fire which consumes it by the fanning

motion of its own wings, so the saint, mounting up on the wings of heavenly meditation, has his soul enkindled and renewed by the flames of the Holy Spirit.

Cremation as practised by the Romans would naturally serve to make the phœnix still more suitable and striking as a symbol of the Resurrection and of immortality; in this sense the bird in the act of burning itself was often sculptured on cinerary urns with the inscription D[is] M[anibus], and is also mentioned in Jewish writings as an emblem of the renewal of life and vigour. The Greek word for date-palm and phœnix is the same (φοῖνιξ), and the tree was fabled to die and then to spring up anew like the fowl. The passage in Psalm xcii. 12, "The righteous shall flourish like the palm-tree" (ὡς φοῖνιξ), may mean in the Septuagint like the phœnix, and was so understood by Tertullian and the *Physiologus*.

The phœnix, like so many other symbols, passed from the old to the new religion, and was transferred from the pagan urn to the Christian sarcophagus. Sometimes a date-palm is used to express the same idea; and very frequently the tree and the bird appear together. Mosaics in many early Christian churches, as for example in SS. Cosma e Damiano, St. Prassede, and St. Cecilia in Trastevere, represent the phœnix with a nimbus. Among the mosaics adorning the tribune of the Lateran is a large cross, and beneath it the New Jerusalem, out of the midst of which rises a stately palm-tree with a phœnix perched on its top.

A similar type of the atoning Christ is the pelican, tearing open its breast and feeding its young with its own blood.   When they are partly grown they smite their parents in the face and the old birds kill them; but no sooner do the parents perceive what they have done than they repent of their rashness and have compassion on their dead offspring, and, sprinkling them with their own blood, restore them to life.   In like manner, Christ was beaten and buffeted by the children of men, and yet shed His blood in order to give them eternal life.   St. Augustine refers to this fable in his commentary on Psalm cii. 5: "I am like a pelican in the wilderness," and says: "The males of these birds are wont to kill their young by blows of their beaks, and then to bewail their death for the space of three days.   At length, however, the female inflicts a severe wound on herself, and letting her blood flow over the dead ones, brings them to life again."   This supposed fact of natural history is often adduced by patristic theologians in illustration and confirmation of the doctrine of the Atonement.   In some old books of emblems, as well as in architecture, the same conduct is ascribed to the eagle and the vulture.   The Egyptian Horapollo says: "The vulture is the type of the merciful man, because, if food cannot be obtained for its

Pelican.   (*Bestiary.*)

young, it opens its own thigh and permits them to partake of its blood, so that they may not perish from want." The Hebrew word for vulture, *râchâm*, meaning a compassionate creature, was doubtless a recognition of this supposititious virtue. On a gold coin of the time of Hadrian the phœnix appears with the inscription *sæc. aur.*, as indicating the restoration of the golden age under his reign ; it occurs later on the coins and medals issued by Constantine and other Christian emperors.

On the principal door of St. Laurence in Nuremberg a burning phœnix is sculptured under the lintel on the right, and a pelican, in the act of piercing its breast to feed its young, under the lintel on the left. There are similar representations on the doorway, as well as on the

Phœnix. (*Bestiary.*)

capitals, of some columns in the Ernestine Chapel of Magdeburg Cathedral, and probably date from the thirteenth century. Phœnix and pelican are carved on the stalls of Bâle Minster, belonging to the latter half of the fifteenth century. In the northern transept of the cathedral at Lund in Sweden, over the window, is a pelican rending its breast with its beak, and on the western wall a phœnix burning in its nest; on the eastern wall is a crucifix, and over an arch to the south a lion tearing a man, showing how the devil deals with heretics. There are in the same church

K

some curious carvings of animals on the stalls of
the choir, symbolizing the conflict between Christianity and paganism. The phœnix and pelican
are frequently associated with other creatures having a like spiritual significance. Thus in a picture
with a Latin inscription in the church of St.
Laurence, and one with a German inscription in
St. Sebald's church in Nuremberg, the phœnix
and the unicorn are on one side, and the pelican
and the lion on the other side, emphasizing and
enforcing by an accumulation of types the doctrines of the incarnation, death, and resurrection of
Christ, and the redemption of mankind through
His sufferings. A painting of a similar character,
belonging to the Cologne school of the fourteenth
century, was formerly in the possession of Dr. Bessel,
president of the provincial court of Saarbrücken.

In the Florentine Galleria degli Uffizi, in the
cabinet of gems, is a shrine of mountain crystal
containing a golden casket adorned with a phœnix
in enamel, and bearing the inscription "sic moriendo
vita perennis." It is a masterpiece of one of the
most celebrated lithoglyphic artists of the sixteenth
century, Valerio Belli of Vicenza, better known as
Valerio Vicentino, who made it for Pope Clement
VII. (1523-34) as a pyx or receptacle for the host.
The outer case is of rock crystal, and embellished
with scenes from the life and Passion of Christ.

Both the phœnix and the pelican are used by
sacred and secular poets of the middle ages and
of modern times to illustrate the power of heavenly

and earthly love. Dante makes an original application of the fable in the *Inferno* (xxiv. 97-108),
where he describes the damned in the seventh
circle of hell as being burned and born again from
their ashes to suffer an endless repetition of their
torments, as the phœnix dies and renews its life
every five hundred years. Elsewhere (Pt. xxv.,
112) he speaks of Christ as "our pelican." The
Sicilian lyrical poet, Inghilfredi, who flourished in
the thirteenth century, confesses in one of his
canzoni that he is at once consumed and rejuvenated by the fires of love, like the phœnix; and
the Provençal poet, Aimeric de Pregulhan, is af-
fected by the tender passion in the same way, and
expresses himself in identical language. Giovanni
dall' Orto, in *La Notte Gioconda*, praises the breath
of the loved one as sweeter than the spices brought
by the phœnix from India and Sheba for its funeral
pyre. In another passage he entreats the fair dame,
who has slain him in her anger, to take pity on
him and, like the pelican, restore him to life by
the manifestations of her affection. Reinmar von
Zweter expresses the hope that the good may be
self-renewed like the phœnix, but that the bad may
remain without issue like the same mythical fowl.
Similes of this sort, in which diverse characteristics
of a single animal serve to illustrate opposite qualities, were deemed especially clever.

The otter is described as a small animal resembling a dog, and an enemy of the crocodile.
When the latter sleeps it keeps its mouth open;

but the otter wallows in the mire until it becomes thickly coated with mud, which dries and hardens and forms a sort of armour, thus enabling it to run securely into the jaws and down the throat of the sleeping crocodile, and to kill it by devouring its bowels. So our Saviour, after having put on flesh, descended into hell and carried away the souls dwelling therein; and as the otter comes forth unharmed from the belly of the crocodile, so our Lord rose from the grave on the third day, alive and uninjured. The ichneumon is fabled to slay the dragon in the same manner, and both animals are symbols of the triumph of the incarnate God over Satan.

Strabo states that the ichneumon attacks poisonous serpents, but never single-handed. It was therefore used in Egyptian hieroglyphics as an ideograph, signifying that union is strength. Ælian, Plutarch, and Pliny relate its feats of heroic audacity in entering the maw and eating the entrails of the crocodile; it was said to hunt up and destroy the eggs of this reptile, and was therefore cherished and revered as a public benefactor; hence, too, its name, the "tracker." As a matter of fact, however, it not only devours insects and small quadrupeds, but also destroys doves, domestic fowls and their eggs, and all kinds of fruits, and does immense harm to the husbandman. The fellahin have no greater foe. The Greek word for otter, ἔνυδρις, signifies also water-snake, and this ambiguity has caused it to be confounded with the hydra, whose

many heads, growing again as soon as they are
lopped off, symbolize the fearfully prolific and
ineradicable nature of original sin.   For this reason
the otter in the Waldensian *Physiologus* becomes
the type of the devil, who puts on cunning dis-
guises in order to insinuate himself into the heart
of man and to compass his destruction.   Owing to
this confusion of terms the otter most frequently
appears in the delineations of the artist as a serpent eating its way through the bowels of a
nondescript monster supposed to be a crocodile.

Otter and Water-snake.   (*Psalter of Isabella of France.*)

It is the nature of the panther to live in friendship with all animals except the dragon.   It has
a beautiful skin of many colours, like Joseph's coat,
and is an exceedingly beautiful beast, tame and
gentle.   When it has eaten a little it is satisfied,
and goes to sleep in its lair, and after three days
it awakes and roars with a loud voice, and out of
its mouth proceeds a sweet smell.   Then all the
beasts of the forest far and near follow after it,
attracted by this odour, which, according to an old
English bestiary, is

"A steam more grateful,
 Sweeter and stronger
 Than every perfume,
 Than blooms of plants

> And forest-leaves,
> Nobler than all
> Earth's ornaments."

This rare scent is offensive only to the dragon, which hastens to flee as soon as it gets a sniff of it. In like manner our Lord Jesus Christ arose out of the sleep of death, and drew all nations unto Him through His "sweet savour." As the Psalmist says: "The king's daughter is all glorious within; her clothing is of wrought gold;" so the adornment of our Saviour is variegated through chastity, purity, meekness, kindness, peace, temperance, and every excellence. Again, in the words of the wise man: "Because of the savour of thy good ointments, thy name is as an ointment poured forth, therefore do the virgins love thee." "Draw me, we will run after thee." "The smell of thine ointments" he declares to be "better than all spices." Also the passage in Hosea (v. 14), which reads in the Septuagint, " I will be unto Ephraim as a panther and as a lion to the house of Judah," is cited as pertinent. Finally Christ, like the panther, discomfits "the dragon, that old serpent, which is the devil."

A German poet of the twelfth century attributes the perfume of the panther's breath to its diet, consisting of aromatic roots and herbs that impart to it a balmy quality, which is not only grateful to the senses, but also healing to the beasts that inhale it. According to this view, the creature is a sort of peripatetic sanitarium, and is for this reason attended by a large concourse of animals which seek to be cured of their ailments. The attraction is not so much æsthetic and sentimental as medical or veterinary. The hygienic influence of the panther is prophylactic as well as remedial, so that, if one were disposed to carry the quibbling spirit of patristic theologians into the province of paranomasia, the beast might be called "an *ounce* of prevention." The breath of the panther is often likened to the virtue which went out of Christ and healed the woman who touched the hem of His garment.

In ecclesiastical architecture the panther is sometimes represented as facing the dragon, as, for example, on the doorway of the church at Alne, in Yorkshire. More frequently, however, the dragon is fleeing from the panther, which is followed by numerous beasts, usually divided into two groups, those nearest the panther typifying the Jews, and those farther off the Gentiles; as the Apostle Paul says of Christ, He "came and preached peace to you which were afar off, and to them that were nigh."

Panther and Dragon. (*Bestiary.*)

In Hugo von Langenstein's poem, *The Martyrdom of St. Martina*, written in 1293, a very elaborate allegory of the panther is introduced to illustrate the sufferings and virtues of his holy heroine. He characterizes Christ as the "heavenly panther," and the variegated skin of the animal is

minutely interpreted in a mystical sense as symbolizing the wisdom, love, humility, mercy, justice,
and other attributes of the Redeemer, about twenty
of which are specially mentioned.   Lauchert gives
numerous examples of rhetorical and metaphorical
allusions to this fable in profane literature.   Thus
an anonymous troubadour of the thirteenth century
compares the power of Amor to that of the panther,
whose sweet breath and beautiful colour attract all
beasts with so irresistible force that they would
rather die than not to follow in its footsteps.   The
Sicilian lyric poet Inghilfredi, already mentioned,
expresses the fascination he feels by the same
simile.   Guido delle Colonne and Messer Polo
celebrate the modesty of their mistresses, who are
as unconscious of their sweetness and beauty as
the panther.   The same imagery is employed by
poet laureates and royal panegyrists.   Frauenlob
likens the persuasive voice of Count Ludwig of
Oettingen to the sweet breath of the panther; and
another Meissen poet uses this comparison with
reference to Albrecht II. of Brandenburg, the
founder of Berlin.   Master Rumeland of Saxony,
a wandering minstrel, who sang the praises of
many princes, extols Duke Ludwig of Bavaria as
an eagle, a leopard, a panther, and indeed a whole
menagerie of typical beasts and birds.   Konrad
von Würzburg turns the point of the trope against
low - minded sovereigns, and says that a mean
prince shuns the society of the pure and noble
as the dragon flees from the panther.

In the *Lay of the Nibelungen*, Siegfrid bears a large quiver covered with panther's skin, which emits a pleasant odour, and emblematizes the irresistible charm of the youthful hero ; and in Pfaffen Lamprecht's *Alexander*, a curious work of the goldsmith's art belonging to Queen Candace is described, namely, an automatic panther, which not only howled, but also exhaled sweet perfumes. The account is too realistic to be a mere product of the fancy, and is probably the description of something which the poet had seen, and, if so, proves to what perfection this kind of artistic handicraft was carried in the twelfth century. The characteristics of the panther are likewise set forth in *Reinaert de Vos* (Martin's ed., pp. 54-55 *sqq.*).

The later bestiaries derive the word panther from πᾶν, signifying all, and implying that it was the whole world which Christ came to redeem. This idea of the universality of the Atonement is expressed by the Norman clerk in *Le Bestiaire Divin* as follows—

> " Pantiere dit, qui bien entent,
> Tant comme chose qui tot prent,
> Et senefie, sanz error,
> Jhesu Crist nostre Sauveor,
> Qui par sa grant humilité
> Vesti nostre charnalité,
> Et trest toz les siecles a sei."

In this connection it may be mentioned as a singular coincidence that, according to an ancient tradition, the real father of Jesus was a Roman soldier named Panthera.

The three beasts that obstructed Dante's path as
he found himself at the midway of life erring in a
dark and savage wood, were a panther, a lion, and
a wolf, supposed to be the types of luxury, pride,
and greed ; but they have nothing in common with
the animal symbolism of the *Physiologus*.

The testicles of the beaver, we are told, contain
a precious substance, which heals divers diseases,
and especially convulsions, once regarded as a sure
sign of diabolical possession.   When the animal is

Beaver. (*Bestiary*.)

pursued by the hunters, and
is in danger of being caught,
it bites off its private parts
and thus saves its life; for
it is a sagacious creature,
and knows why it is hunted.
Afterwards,   when   it   is
chased, it throws itself on its
back, so that the hunter may
see that what he seeks is no longer there, and go his
way.   But thou, O man, separate from thyself the
works of the flesh, which are adulteries, fornications,
revellings, and envyings, and throw them to the
devil, who hunteth after thy soul, saying : " I will
pursue my enemies and overtake them."   Then
canst thou exclaim with the Psalmist : " Our soul
is escaped as a bird out of the snare of the fowler ;
the snare is broken, and we are escaped."

It is well known that the beaver secretes in two
inguinal sacs a caseous substance with a pungent
perfume called castoreum.   The fable related by

the *Physiologus* is of very ancient date, and is recorded by the Egyptian priest Horapollo, as well as by Apuleius, Pliny, Ælian, and Juvenal, and was generally accepted as true by mediæval writers. Albertus Magnus, as we have seen, rejects it as " false, although frequently reported in parts of our land." In art, the beaver is commonly represented in the act of self-mutilation, which suffices to tell the whole story, the hunters being left to the imagination. Konrad von Würzburg chooses an odd and rather far-fetched comparison, when he commends to princes the prudence of the beaver, which saves its life by voluntarily depriving itself of what is dearest to it ; he thereby intends to inculcate the virtue of liberality freely exercised for the public weal, and without stint of self-sacrifice.

Still more marvellous is the account which the *Physiologus* gives of the hyena. This filthy beast, he says, haunts cemeteries and feeds on corpses. It has also the power of changing its sex, the same individual being sometimes male and sometimes female. This characteristic is used to illustrate the vice censured by Paul in his epistle to the Romans (i. 2, 27). In the Latin version of the *Physiologus* the hyena is made a type of the Jews, who at first had a knowledge of the true and living God, but now subsist on dry bones and dead ceremonials. They were the prophets of the Messiah and foretold His advent, but rejected Him when He appeared. As Jeremiah says (xii. 9, Septuagint): " The lair of the hyena has become my heritage."

In the bestiaries the words of James (i. 8, curiously enough attributed to Solomon), " A double-minded man is unstable in all his ways," and the saying of Christ, " No man can serve two masters," are cited as texts, the truth of which the habits of the hyena exemplify and establish.

In the apocryphal epistle of Barnabas (ix. 8) it is said : " Neither shalt thou eat of the hyena ; that is, again, be not an adulterer, nor a corrupter of others ; neither be like to such. And wherefore so ? Because that creature every year changes its kind, and is sometimes male and sometimes female." Philippe de Thaun, in his *Book of Creatures*, speaks of the hyena as "une beste mauvaise et orde," a foul and ugly beast, stinking and very fierce, digging into graves and devouring carrion. He begins his account of this animal with the following general observations—

> " Moult est a dire et a retraire
> Es essamples del Bestiaire,
> Qui sunt de bestes et de oiseaus,
> Moult profitables, boens et beaus.
> Et le livre si nos enseigne
> En quel guise le mal remaigne,
> Et la veie que deit tenir
> Cil qui a Deu veut revertir."

Sir Walter Raleigh, in his *History of the World* (London, 1614), excludes hybrids from Noah's ark, and mentions hyenas as belonging to this class. He asserts that only pure species were saved, and not mongrels. After the Deluge, hyenas, he says, were reproduced by a cross between the dog and the cat. This notion is about as correct as his belief that before the Deluge there were mountains thirty miles high, which were reduced to their present elevation by the abrasive action of the water.

The eyes of the hyena are fabled to turn into jewels when it dies; and the *Physiologus* asserts that it has in its eye a stone which, if it be placed under the tongue, enables a man to foretell future events. In the East the hyena is universally regarded as an incarnation of the sorcerer, and Arabian folk-lore is especially full of fearful stories of the doings of wizards and witches, who assume this form for diabolical purposes. The fact that the hyena is seldom seen by day, but begins to make night hideous with its cries as soon as it grows dark, tends to confirm the popular superstition that the creature is a man who has transformed himself into this filthy beast with the going down of the sun. For this reason a dread of the hyena as uncanny and capable of inflicting injury by malign and magical influences, prevails among all African and Asiatic peoples, where this animal has its habitat. Dogs, it is believed, lose their bark and scent if the shadow of a hyena falls upon them; he who tastes of its brain goes mad, and the hunter who kills it is sure to be pursued by its vindictive ghost.

In architecture the hyena is usually represented as preying upon the prostrate form of a man, probably a corpse, which it has dug out of a grave ; it symbolizes vice battening on corruption.

Hyena. (*Bestiary*.)

Sometimes, as among the sculptures on the church at Alne, we find the figure of the hyena standing alone, an embodiment of the evil principle in its most offensive form.

The salamander is a large lizard, which does not fear the fire, but puts it out by passing into it, and typifies the righteous man, who is not consumed by the fires of luxury and lust, but extinguishes them. As the Apostle Paul states : " Through faith they stopped the mouths of lions and quenched the violence of fire"; and the prophet Isaiah says of the just man : "When thou walkest through fire thou shalt not be burned." This was the case with the three Hebrew youths Ananias, Azarias, and Misael (Shadrach, Meshach, and Abednego), who were cast into the burning fiery furnace, and came forth unharmed, with no smell of fire on their garments.

The incombustible mineral substance known as amianthus was once supposed to be salamander's skin. In *Les Proprietez des Bestes* it is related that the Emperor of India had a full suit of clothes made of a thousand skins of salamanders, which he wore as a coat of mail in battle; and Vincent de Beauvais in his *Speculum Naturale* asserts that Pope Alexander III. had a tunic made of the same stuff, which was palish white in colour, and, when dirty, was cleansed by being thrown into the fire instead of being put into the wash-tub. There is no reason for regarding these stories as mere inventions, except in respect to the nature and origin of the material, since this method of cleaning asbestos garments by heating them red-hot is still practised by some tribes of Western China.

This fabulous and formidable lizard has been reduced by more careful observation to a small frog-like reptile with rows of tubercles on its sides, which secrete a milky poisonous fluid in sufficient quantities to extinguish a live coal and slightly to retard the action of fire.

Italian erotic poets are fond of referring to the salamander as typical of the lover, who either rejoices in the amorous fire ("il fuoco amoroso") as his native element, or regrets that he does not possess the nature of this reptile in order that he may not be utterly consumed by his passion.

"As the partridge gathereth young which she hath not brought forth, so he that getteth riches and not by right, shall leave them in the midst of his days, and at his end shall be as a fool." This passage from Jeremiah is quoted by the *Physiologus* as referring to the thievish propensity of the partridge in stealing the eggs of other birds and hatching them, but when the young are grown, they recognize their real parents and fly to them, leaving their self-constituted foster-mother standing alone like a fool. This bird is the type of the

devil, who seeks to gather to himself the children
of men, but when they grow in wisdom and are
come to a knowledge of the truth, they forsake
the devil and his works, and flee to their natural
mother, the Church.

The habit here ascribed to the partridge does
not seem to have been known to any Greek or
Roman naturalist; but in the *Institutes* of Manu
it is said that persons who steal raiment are
destined to be reborn as grey or speckled partridges, according to the colour of the vestments
stolen. The penalty thus inflicted by the strictly
retributive laws of metempsychosis would imply
certain pilfering propensities on the part of the bird,
and may be based upon a supposed tendency to steal
eggs originating in a desire for numerous offspring.

The partridge is monogamous in its domestic
habits, and has the feeling of conjugal attachment
and parental affection very strongly developed.
It possesses a remarkably benevolent disposition,
and is distinguished in a high
degree for the sentiment corresponding to philanthropy or
altruism in man, adopting the
orphans of other partridges and
treating them with the same tenderness as its own young; but
there is no evidence that its philo-
progenitiveness ever manifests
itself in thievery of any sort.

Partridge and her
Fosterlings.
(*Bestiary.*)

That such an exceptionally noble and virtuous fowl

should be condemned to figure the devil in Christian typology is only an additional proof of the perversions of hermeneutical theology.

Artistic delineations of this supposed characteristic in bestiaries, missals, and other books of devotion, as well as in sacred edifices, usually show the partridge sitting alone in her nest, while her fosterlings are hastening to join their real mother in the air above.

The charadrius (a species of plover) is a white bird without a dark spot on it ; and when a person is sick it is brought to his bedside in order to determine whether he will recover or not. If the sickness is unto death, then the bird turns away from him ; but if he is predestined to live, then the charadrius looks steadfastly into his face and draws the malady out of him, and, flying up towards the sun, causes the disease to be consumed by the solar heat, so that the sick man is restored to health. In like manner Jesus Christ, on whom there was neither spot nor wrinkle, came down from heaven and turned his face away from the Jews, but looked with favour upon the Gentiles and healed them of their spiritual infirmities. Only those upon whom the Lord lifts up the light of His countenance are sure of eternal life.

In architecture, and in the formative arts generally, the charadrius is represented as looking at the sick person or turning away its head, or quite frequently as flying up into the air. The last-mentioned movement of the bird is also a sign

L

of restoration to health, since it is carrying off the
malady or, more scientifically speaking, the bacteria
of disease to be burned and destroyed by the
intense heat of the sun.   This scene is carved in
stone on the doorway of the church at Alne; and
in the border of a lancet window in the apsis of
the cathedral at Lyons is the picture of a woman
half-reclining on a couch, while a bird is stretching
out its beak close to her left hand, which lies in
her lap, and another bird is flying towards her
with its head slightly averted.   Such delineations

Charadrius. (*Bestiary.*)

are often found in missals, prayer-books, and similar
aids to devotion, as, for example, in the profusely
and curiously illustrated manuscript psalter of
Isabella of France, now in the Royal Library at
Munich.

The marrow of the thigh-bone and the lungs of
this bird, which were believed to be a sure cure
for blindness, are compared to the chrism, and
signify the supernatural power that opens the eyes
of the spiritually blind and causes them to perceive
the truth, as in the case of Saul.

A minnesinger likens his lady-love to the charadrius, and declares that it is a question of life or

death whether her face is turned from or towards him. Another poet wishes that he possessed this fatal faculty in order that he might turn his eyes from mean and sordid mortals and thus destroy them, and insure long life to the noble and liberal-minded by looking benignantly upon them.

Both the crow and the turtle-dove are typical of Christian constancy and devotion. If either of these birds loses its mate, it never takes another, but lives a life of solitude. As our Lord went with only three disciples to the Mount of Olives, where He was transfigured before them and heard an approving voice from heaven, so His followers should withdraw from the world and devote themselves to religious meditation.

The turtle-dove is often referred to in poetry as a symbol of fidelity; thus Gottfried von Strasburg calls the Virgin Mary a turtle-dove in faithfulness. When it loses its mate it renounces all the pleasures of life, never again perches on a green bough, but sits disconsolate on a dry branch, and never drinks clear water, but first muddies the stream with its feet, and drinks the foul water as evidence of its sorrow.

A celebrated Spanish lyric poet and doctor of theology of the sixteenth century, Fray Luis Ponce de Leon, in his famous version of Solomon's Song, which caused him to be imprisoned for five years in the dungeons of the Inquisition, translates the eleventh verse of the first chapter thus : " We will make thee turtle-doves of gold with tips of silver."

The Hebrew word *thor* (necklace) meant in his opinion an ornament in the form of a turtle-dove, such as lovers were wont to present to their ladies in token of enduring affection, and the bridegroom in the Song of Songs promises his bride to give her one of gold, with its beak, tail, and claws tipped with silver.

In architectural decoration and works of art,

Turtle-doves.
(*Psalter of Isabella of France.*)

two turtle-doves are represented sitting together on a green bough, or a single one perched on a dead branch mourning its mate. The latter is a symbol of the man who is steadfast under tribulation, and of whom it is said, "he that endureth to the end shall be saved."

The fulica or heron is wise and discreet above all other birds. It never touches carrion, nor does it fly from place to place, but abides in one spot, dwelling there where it finds suitable food. So the righteous do not care for the corrupt things of this world and the offal of evil-mindedness, neither do they wander hither and thither after false doctrines, but abide in the simplicity of the faith in the bosom of the Church, where they are nourished with the pure bread of life. The ousel and the merl, on account of the sweetness of their song, are typical of the grace of God, and the hoopoe of filial affection.

The swallow, says the *Physiologus*, sleeps all winter, and wakes to new and vigorous life in the spring, as it is written : "Awake, thou that sleepest, and arise from the dead, and Christ shall give thee light." Luther, in his Latin commentary on the passage in Genesis (i. 20), in which it is said that the waters brought forth the fowl that fly above the earth and in the open firmament of heaven, states, in confirmation of the aqueous origin of birds, that even now swallows lie dormant all winter in the water, and issue from it in the vernal season, rising into the air and thus repeating annually the process of creation, and proving the truth of Holy Writ.

Ravens, according to the *Physiologus*, are hatched featherless, and remain callow for a long time, and are therefore not recognized by their parents, who take no care of them. In their distress they cry to God, who sends them manna in the form of dew for nourishment, as the Psalmist says : "He giveth food to the young ravens which cry." After twelve days, when the feathers begin to grow, the old birds recognize their offspring and feed them. Thus man, although made in the image of God, has lost all resemblance to his Creator; but when he has grown through grace into the divine like-ness, then God recognizes him as His child, and nurtures him through the sacraments of the Church, and does not let him perish. Another character-istic of the raven is that, when it finds a carcass, it first eats the eye. The great religious truth drawn from this fact of natural history is that "confession and penance are the ravens which pull out the eyes of covetousness from the soul dead in trespasses and sins." In our illustration both of these symbolisms of the raven are set forth.

Concerning the wolf, the bestiaries inform us that the word means ravisher, and this is, in fact, the signification of the Sanskrit name of the animal, *vṛika*, seizer. For this reason, they add, the term is applied to lewd women.[1] A peculiarity of the wolf is that it cannot turn its head, because there is no joint in its neck, but must turn its whole body when it wishes to look behind, thus symbolizing people stiff-necked and stubborn in sin. The female whelps in the month of May, when it thunders, and at no other time. She seeks food by night, approaching the sheepfold noiselessly and against the wind, in order that the dogs may not scent her; and if she steps on a dry twig, so that it breaks and crackles, she bites her foot severely as a punishment for her carelessness. Her nature is such that if she is seen by a man with her mouth shut, then she loses the power of opening

Raven. (*Bestiary.*)

---

[1] *Lupa* means she-wolf and prostitute, and *lupanar*, wolf's lair and brothel. *Ovis*, sheep, signifies ninny or simpleton, and the English word is used as a term of contempt. Plautus in his comedies ridicules the fast young men of his time as sheep that cannot keep away from the wolves and their dens.

it, but if a man is seen by her with his mouth open, then he loses his voice. When she is hungry, she fills her stomach with clay, but when she has taken prey, she puts her paw into her gullet and vomits the clay, and sates herself with flesh. Albertus Magnus, who gives this account of the wolf's method of stilling the pangs of hunger, states likewise that the wolf is in the habit of lubricating its paws with spittle in order to render its footsteps inaudible.[1] Brunetto Latino relates in his *Thesaurus*, that the wolf often presses its paw to its mouth in order to falsify or magnify its voice, and thus frighten the shepherds by making them think a whole pack is coming. In an engraving published by Cahier (*Mel. d'Arch.*, ii., pl. xxii., BM) a wolf is approaching a sheepcote, and holding its paw to its mouth. It may

Wolf. (*Bestiary*.)

be biting or lubricating its paw, keeping its mouth open, disgorging clay with the prospect of filling its maw with tender and succulent mutton, magnifying its voice, or practising any of the tricks which symbolize the many ruses of the devil in his dealings with mankind.

It is superfluous and would be tedious to make further citations from the *Physiologus*, since the specimens already given suffice to illustrate the

---

[1] "Vadens lupus per frondes lambit et lubricas facit pedes, ne incessus audiatur."—*De Animal.* xxii., Tract. II.

character and purpose of the work. It enjoyed a
high reputation among the early Christians, and, as
we have seen, has been translated into a score or
more of Oriental and Occidental languages. At
an early period in the history of the Church it
was condemned as heretical, and forbidden to the
faithful by the apocryphal decree of Gelasius, but
found not long afterwards a powerful patron in
Gregory the Great, who made very free use of it
in scriptural exposition. From the seventh to the
twelfth century it was universally esteemed as a
Christian compendium of natural history, and a
popular epitome of moral and theological instruction. During this period most of the translations
and paraphrases of it were made, now kept as
curiosities in old libraries, to which they have been
transmitted as the musty heirlooms of mediæval
monasteries, secularized and suppressed by the
progress of modern civilization.

The invention of printing naturally gave the
work a wider diffusion as a folk-book; but long
before the birth of Gutenberg and the age of
movable types, it was cited by preachers and
theologians, and used by artists for the illustration
of sacred themes, as may be seen in illuminated
manuscripts of the Bible, and in mediæval missals
and similar books of devotion. Thus, in a codex
of the Vulgate of the seventh century, the initials
and capitals are composed of doves, fishes, eagles,
and other symbolical creatures; and an Evangeliarium, once the property of Charlemagne, and now

belonging to the National Library of Paris, contains a miniature representing the gospel fountain in the form of a Byzantine baptistery, to which all beasts and birds are flocking for refreshment. The beautifully-illuminated parchment psalter of Isabella of France, dating from the middle of the fourteenth century, and already mentioned as one of the treasures of the Royal Library of Munich, has the margins adorned with drawings of animals, which have no direct relation to the text, but only a far-fetched symbological significance, inasmuch as they elucidate the teachings of the *Physiologus*, and represent scenes from Jewish history and mythology supposed to have a prefigurative character.

Virtues and vices are often figured by women contending for victory, and bearing shields on which are inscribed their names or emblems, as, for example, the twelve virtues and twelve vices in the cathedral at Amiens ; sometimes they are riding on animals, as in the miniatures of a manuscript in the Musée de Cluny dating from the fourteenth century. Here Humility is mounted on a panther, Chastity on a unicorn ; Patience or Christian Resignation wears a helmet adorned with a swan, because this fowl sings with its dying breath like the martyrs ; Love bears a pelican on her shield ; Devotion rides an ibex, the symbol of aspiration and perseverance, owing to its fondness for high altitudes and its climbing power, and has a phœnix on her shield to signify the renewing

virtue of fervid piety; Pride has an eagle on her
shield, because this bird discards those of her
young which cannot endure the fierce light of the
sun, as a haughty spirit despises the meek and
lowly; on the shield of Lust is a siren, whose sweet
song allures men to their destruction.

In the cloister connected with the cathedral of
Le-Puy-en-Velay are mural paintings personifying
Grammar, Logic, Rhetoric (the trivium), and Music.
Logic is a female figure in a stately cathedra, and
at her feet is Aristotle sitting on a stool and
earnestly carrying on a discussion, and noting the
points of his argument on his fingers.   Underneath
is the motto : " Me sine doctores frustra coluere
sorores;" implying that the sister arts cultivate
dialectics in vain without the aid of the doctors
or men of learning.   Logic has a rather amused
expression, and holds in her hands a lizard and
a scorpion engaged in fierce combat, a parody of
scholastic disputations and the proverbial venom of
odium theologicum.

In the Bibles of the tenth century the evangelists
are pictured as men with the heads of beasts; and
the four gospels are summed up symbolically in
the form of the so-called "Tetramorph," a four-
bodied and four-headed monster composed of man,
ox, eagle, and lion, with wings covered with eyes
like a peacock's tail, a combination of incongruities
surpassing in whimsicalness the famous Florentine
bronze of the Etruscan chimera, or the marvellous
creations of Indian and Egyptian mythology.   A

mosaic of the thirteenth century in the monastery
of Vatopedi on Mt. Athos shows the four heads
enveloped by six wings, and the feet of the man
resting on two-winged wheels, as described in the
visions of Ezekiel and of St. John the Divine. A
tetramorph sculptured out of stone, ridden by a

The Gospel and the Law. (*Hortus Deliciarum.*)

woman with a crown on her head, and dating from
the year 1300, adorns the south portal of the
cathedral at Worms, and is exhibited in a plaster
cast in the Germanic Museum at Nuremberg. It
typifies the rapid triumph of the gospel. A miniature in the *Hortus Deliciarum*, formerly in the

Strasburg Library, represents a similar monster, on
which is seated a woman wearing a crown, bearing
a banner, holding a goblet in her hand, and
catching the blood from the side of the crucified
Saviour; another woman mounted on an ass, and
partially blindfolded, holds in her right hand a
knife, and in her left hand the tables of the law
and a ram for sacrifice.   They signify respectively
the New and the Old Dispensation. Above the cross
on the gospel side is a radiant sun, and on the
opposite side a waning moon.   The standard of
Judaism, instead of floating in the breeze, has
fallen to the ground; the attitude of the ass and
the noose at its feet are intended to illustrate the
passage referring to the cross as "a snare, and a
trap, and a stumbling-block" to Israel.

On the cover of an Evangeliarium in the cathedral
library of Trier is a plate of copper enamel engraved with biblical scenes; in the centre is the
Crucifixion, and standing round the cross are Mary
and John and the symbolical figures of the Church
and the Synagogue; above are the sun and moon
in eclipse, indicating that "there was darkness over
all the earth."

The church of Saint-Nizier at Troyes has a
stained window of the sixteenth century with a
representation of the apocalyptic beast which rose
out of the sea having seven heads and ten horns, as
well as of the other beast, which came up out of
the earth and had two horns like a lamb; the
artist appears, however, to have been over-liberal in

endowing the monster with eleven horns, counting that of the snail.

Beasts of the Apocalypse. (*Saint-Nizier of Troyes.*)

In the church of St. Nicholas at Göttingen is a picture dating from 1424, and symbolizing the origin and formation, or rather the fabrication, of Christian theology. God the Father appears in the sky with the four evangelists as man, ox, eagle, and lion, hovering like angels beneath Him and holding Him up. Each has in his hand a vessel from which he pours the contents of his gospel, indicated by a label containing the first words of it, into two mills turned by the twelve apostles by means of long bars. The several gospels, thus reduced to homogeneous pulp by passing through the mills of the epistles, run out into a large goblet held by a pope, an archbishop, a bishop, and a cardinal. It is designed to show that the evangelists were inspired by God to write the gospels, which were then elaborated by the apostles into doctrinal consistency as the expressed juice of Scripture or essence of theology, and that this product is in the keeping of the Church and to be dispensed by the sacerdotal order. On two labels issuing from the lower part of the mill are inscribed the words *et deus erat vbm* ("and the Word was God") and *et vbm caro ftm. c.* ("and the Word was made flesh"). Here we have the crude symbolism of the divine Incarnation, as it is ground out of Holy Writ by apostolic theologians and presented in potable form to believers by ecclesiastical dignitaries. We may add, as an interesting coincidence, that this conception of our sacred writings corresponds to that entertained by the Brahmans, who speak of the magical and supernatural virtue inherent in the Vedic hymns or mantras as the juice (*rasa*) of the metres, which is expressed and utilized by the ritual machinery of song and sacrifice. This essence is the wonder-working *brahma*, the monopoly of which by the priests is the chief source of their power.

On the capital of a column in the abbey of Vézelai in Burgundy is a relief representing two men working at a mill, one pouring corn into the hopper, and the other turning the crank and holding a sack to receive the flour. St. Jerome, in his exposition of Matthew xxiv. 41, says the two women, there said to be grinding at the mill, signify

Gospel-mill. (*Abbey of Vézelai in Burgundy.*)

the Synagogue and the Church; the former brings the wheat of the law, and the latter separates from it the fine flour of the gospel, leaving only the bran of empty ceremonialism as the portion of Judaism. This forced interpretation was not original with the learned and ingenious anchorite, but seems to have been traditional in the primitive Church, and is frequently met with in patristic theology.

The two men in the relief just mentioned are a
Hebrew prophet and the Apostle Paul.   The latter,
who was educated as a disciple of Gamaliel and
became the first systematic theologist of the Church
and the real founder of dogmatic and historical
Christianity, dwells in his epistles with peculiar
emphasis on the relations of Judaic rites and
ceremonies to the New Dispensation, and might
therefore be fitly portrayed as an assiduous toiler
at the typological mill, by which, in the words of a
Father, the precious grain of the Old Testament
Scriptures is ground and bolted and converted into
the flour of gospel truth.   In a mediæval Latin
verse descriptive of this process the apostle of the
Gentiles is expressly mentioned—

' Tollis, agendo molam, de furfure Paule farinam ;
  Mosaicæ legis intima nota facis.
  Fit de tot granis verus sine furfure panis
  Perpetuusque cibus noster et angelicus."

" Turning the mill, O Paul, thou takest the flour from the
        bran ;
  The hidden things of the Mosaic law thou makest known.
  Of so many grains is made true bread without bran,
  Eternal food for us and food for the angels."

The symbolism of the mill is often delineated
on painted windows, as, for example, in the cathedral of St. Etienne in Bourges and in Canterbury
Cathedral.   According to a description of the
Benedictine Abbey of Saint-Denis written by the
celebrated Abbot Suger in the twelfth century
(de rebus administratione sua gestis), one of the

stained windows contained a representation of the prophets pouring grain into the hopper of a mill, while Paul turns the crank and bags the grist.   The same idea of the propædeutic and prefigurative relation of Judaism to Christianity is expressed on another gorgeously-stained window in the cathedral of Bourges by the ark of the covenant surmounted by a crucifix and drawn by a man, an ox, an eagle, and a lion, the four beasts of the evangelists, thus transforming the sacred repository of the tables of the law into the triumphal chariot of the cross, as intimated in the accompanying inscription—

" Fœderis ex arca cruce Christi sistitur ara,
    Fœdere majori vult ibi Vita mori . . ."

In a window of the church at Bron in France, belonging to the sixteenth century, there is a painting of Christ seated on a globe in a four-wheeled chariot drawn by an angel, an ox, a lion, and an eagle, and attended by a pope and a cardinal at the fore wheels and two bishops at the hind wheels, pushing it along.   An ivory carving of the eleventh century in the Bodleian Library, Oxford, shows the Virgin with a cross on her shoulder, a book in her hand, and her feet on a lion, a dragon, a crocodile, and wolf, and in a manuscript of the same period in the National Library at Paris the Virgin holds a palm branch and tramples on a skeleton and a dragon, signifying the victory of the gospel over death and the powers of darkness.

It is rather strange that the cock, which is so

M

frequently mentioned in the Scriptures, and which plays so important and honourable a part as the monitor and reprover of the cowardly and recreant Peter, should be entirely passed over by the *Physiologus* and the bestiaries.   On ancient pagan and early Christian sarcophagi two fighting-cocks are often sculptured, one of which has already succumbed to the onsets of its adversary, and were probably intended to represent the battle of life. The cock typifies both vigilance and liberality,

Cock calling hens.
(*Psalter of Isabella of France.*)

because it is always on the watch, and when it finds anything, it does not eat it, but calls the hens together and divides it among them.   In like manner the preacher should distribute among his flock the kernels of divine truth which he discovers in Holy Writ, picking them into pieces in order that they may be more readily taken in and digested, as a mediæval poet declares—

> " Gallus granum reperit, convocat uxores
> Et illud distribuit inter cariores.
> Tales discant clerici pietatis mores,
> Dando suis subditis scriptuarum flores ;
> Sic sua distribuere cunctis derelictis,
> Atque curam gerere nudis stafflictis."

It might be added that the preacher should not be a weather-cock, blown about by every wind of doctrine.   In the Musée de Cluny is a manuscript of roundelays addressed to Louise of Savoy,

Countess of Angoulême and mother of Francis I. of France, with illustrations of the seven Virtues subduing their opposite Vices; among them is Liberality mounted on a cock pouring gold coins out of a vessel with one hand and holding a large platter or salver in the other; at her feet is Avarice bestriding an ape.

The cockatrice or basilisk, on the other hand, holds a prominent place in mediæval symbology and ecclesiastical architecture. This little king (βασιλίσκος) of reptiles, so called because the wart

Liberality and Avarice.
(*Manuscript in Musée de Cluny.*)

on its head resembles a crown, had the reputation of being a terror to all its subjects, the most venemous serpents fleeing affrighted when they hear its hiss. It is hatched from the egg laid by a cock in the seventh year of its age, and it happens in this wise. When the egg has grown large, it produces an intense griping in the bowels of the cock, which seeks a warm place in a stable or on a dung-heap, and there lays the egg. A serpent or toad then comes and sits on it, and hatches a creature with the head of a cock and the body of a reptile. No

sooner is it born than it hides itself in a crevice or
cistern, or in the rafters of a house, so as not to be
seen by any one ; for such is its nature that if a man
sees it before it sees him, it will die, but if it sees
him first, he will fall down dead.   It has also the
power of darting poison from its eyes, so deadly
that it kills birds flying over the spot where it lies
hidden ; even herbs and shrubs, which it touches
in passing, wither away.   This baneful reptile is
beautiful in form and colour, having a skin of
variegated hues spotted with white ; but, adds the
author in a moralizing strain, beauty is often associated with badness.   Whoever wishes to slay the
basilisk, holds before his face a vessel of crystal
through which he looks at the beast; and the
crystal not only arrests the venom issuing from its
eyes, but even causes it to be reflected and hurled
back upon the animal, which is killed by the fatal
recoil.

The basilisk signifies the devil, who entered into
Paradise and enticed our first parents to eat of the
forbidden fruit.   For this transgression they were
driven forth from Eden, and when they had passed
away from the earth, which they had corrupted,
they were cast into the burning pit with the basilisk.
Then the merciful Son of the King of Heaven took
pity on the many people poisoned by this old serpent, which no one had been able to destroy ; and
He chose a vessel clearer than crystal, the blessed
body of our Lady, the purest of virgins, in which to
encounter the direful foe.   And when the basilisk

darted the venom from its eyes, the vessel caught it
and threw it back upon the reptile, which languished
during the thirty years of Christ's incarnation, until
the victory was fully won by the crucifixion. And
after He had been placed in the tomb, He rose
again on the third day and descended into the pit,
where the basilisk had concealed itself, and rescued
all those who had been infected with its poison
from the time of Adam, and restored them to
everlasting life.

Fighting the Basilisk. (*Abbey of Vézelai.*)

Jacopo da Lentino in his erotics makes the fable
illustrate the perils of love; and a Provençal poet,
Aimeric de Pregulhan, compares himself to a
basilisk and his mistress to a mirror, which he
cannot look upon without being smitten to death.

The basilisk figures frequently in illustrations of
devotional works and in sacred architecture, as, for

example, on the capital of a column in the church
of the Abbey of Vézelai, where a man approaches
the hissing reptile, holding a conical vessel as a
shield before his face; near him is an enormous
locust with a human head. This sculpture symbolizes the redemption of the Gentile world from the
thralls of Satan by the atonement of Christ. Beda,
in his commentary on the thirtieth chapter of Proverbs, says : " Locusts refer to the nations formerly
without Christ for their king, without prophets,
without teachers; but now gathered together in
the unity of the faith, they hasten to the spiritual
combat against the devil." This is a spiritualization of the passage : " The locusts have no king,
yet they go forth all of them in bands " (xxx. 27),
or, as it reads in the Vulgate : " Regem locusta non
habet, et egreditur universa per suas turmas," a
rendering which facilitates the symbolical interpretation given by the venerable Anglo-Saxon
presbyter.

Gregory the Great, in his exposition of Job
(*Moralia, sive Expositiones in Jobum*), states, in
explanation of the verse " Canst thou make him
afraid as a grasshopper?" that grasshopper or locust
signifies converted paganism ("conversa gentilitas").
This, he adds, is what Solomon means when he
says, " The almond tree shall flourish, the locust
shall grow fat, and the caper bush shall waste
away."[1] " Now the almond flowers before all other

---

[1] This is the Vulgate version of Eccl. xii. 5 : " Florebit
amygdalus, impinguabitur locusta, dissipabitur capparis."

trees; and what is meant by the flowering almond, unless it be the beginning of the holy Church, which put forth in its preachers the first blossoms of virtue and bore the earliest fruits of holiness? 'The locust shall grow fat' signifies that the unction and richness of heavenly grace shall be infused into the leanness and barrenness of heathenism. 'The caper bush shall waste away,' because, when the Gentiles are called and attain the gift of faith, the Jews shall be left desolate, and shall remain sterile." In this connection Gregory quotes the passage from Proverbs (xxx. 27), already mentioned, and interprets it as referring to the Gentiles, who, when they were left to themselves, were alien to the Divine law, but, when they were gathered and arrayed together, went forward to fight the fight of faith against spiritual adversaries.

The locust with a human head signifies the Gentile nations united under Christ as their head to war against Satan. "The basilisk is the king of serpents," says Gregory, "but who is the head of the reprobates, unless it be Antichrist?" Essentially the same exegesis is given by St. Hilarius in his commentary on Matthew iii. 4, where locusts are mentioned as the principal articles of food of John the Baptist, the forerunner of Him who was to gather in the Gentiles, and also by St. Ambrosius in his remarks on the third chapter of Luke, so that Gregory cannot claim to be the originator of this brilliant feat of hermeneutics. Odo, the second Abbot of Cluny, in the fourth decade of the tenth century, abridged the *Moralia* of Gregory, and it was probably to this work that the sculpture in the church at Vézelai owes its origin, since Vézelai stood for a long time in intimate relations to Cluny, and, indeed, seems at this time to have been to some extent under the jurisdiction of the rich and powerful Benedictine abbey on the Grône.

Another capital in the abbey of Vézelai represents in relief a man in a Phrygian cap mounted on a basilisk and holding a round missile in his

Sphinx and Basilisk.   (*Abbey of Vézelai.*)

right hand.   His arm is drawn back as if in the act of hurling this weapon at a sphinx-like creature, that has the head of a woman and the feet of an ox, and wards off the attack by means of a crystal vessel, as already described.   The basilisk begins to show signs of succumbing to the retroflex action of its own venom.   The sphinx, if we may regard the cloven-hoofed monster as such, wears a crown, and is partially clad in armour, and is probably a symbol of spiritual knowledge and strength overcoming evil.

Albertus Magnus, the most circumspect and critical of mediæval scholars touching the marvellous tales which constituted the natural history of his day, remarks : " What is related about an old cock ('decrepitum gallum') laying an egg, and putting it in the dung, and about a basilisk being hatched out of it, and looking like a cock in all respects except that it has the long tail of a serpent, I do not think is true ; yet it is reported as a fact by Hermes, and is accepted by many persons " (*De Animal.*, xxiii.).

In the same treatise (xxv.) he adds : " It is said that the weasel kills the basilisk, and that the troglodytes of Nubia send weasels into their caves for this purpose before entering these habitations themselves. And if this be true, it seems indeed wonderful. . . . Hermes also asserts that if silver be rubbed with its ashes, it receives the splendour, weight, and solidity of gold. Some aver, furthermore, that there is a sort of basilisk that flies, but I have not read of this kind in the books of sages and philosophers."

Evidently the basilisk was a riddle to the great Dominican, Aristotelian, and Doctor Universalis, of which he could find no satisfactory solution—a creature which excited his wonder, and made excessive demands on his credulity, but which he could not dismiss as a mere figment of superstitious fancy, owing to the weight of testimony in its favour, and especially on account of the deference due to the almost supernatural and semi-divine

authority of Hermes Trismegistus. The mythical
cock's egg, however, continued during the middle
ages, and even into modern times, to furnish the
principal ingredient for the fabrication of witches'
ointment, the devil's chrism, with which he anointed his elect, and thereby enabled old hags to
transform themselves into beasts, ride through the
air on broomsticks, and work divers kinds of
fiendish mischief. How this belief compromised
our innocent but ostentatious knight of the barn-
yard, and led to his criminal prosecution and
punishment as a satellite of Satan and phar-
maceutical purveyor to his infernal majesty, has
been shown by the author in a work entitled *The
Criminal Prosecution and Capital Punishment of
Animals.*

Modern science, which, in its mission of abolish-
ing mysteries, has relegated so many ancient fables
and venerable traditions to that

> " limbo large and broad, since called
> The paradise of fools,"

and which tends more and more to circumscribe
and gradually eliminate the sphere of the miraculous in nature, has now stripped the dread basilisk
of its fatal qualities. The sole residuum which
sober research has left us is a harmless species
of hooded lizard, whose only peculiarity is the
power of blowing up its conical crest with wind.
The cockatrice, with its "death-darting" eye, has
been curtailed of its formidable proportions and

degraded to a funny little saurian, which might serve to amuse children, but has lost all the terrors with which mythical zoölogy once invested it even in the minds of the most intelligent men and greatest thinkers of their day. The transformation, too, which scholarly opinion and popular belief have undergone on this point is typical of the functions and efficiency of science in subverting superstition.

Besides its value as a key to zoölogical symbolism as expressed in art and literature, and especially in hermeneutical theology and ecclesiastical architecture, the *Physiologus* is psychologically interesting as an index to the intellectual condition of an age which could accept its absurd statements as scientific facts, and seriously apply them to biblical exegesis and Christian dogmatics.

In addition to the Scriptural expositions already cited, the following may serve as specimens of the wretched twaddle which men now revered as the lights of the Church, and quoted as infallible authorities in questions of divinity, were capable of uttering. "David said : ' As the hart panteth after the water-brooks, so panteth my soul after thee, O God.' The *Physiologus* tells us that the hart is the foe of the dragon, which, when it sees its enemy, runs away and creeps into a cleft of the rocks. Then the hart goes to a stream and fills his belly with water, and spews it into the cleft, and, having thus drowned out the dragon, tramples it under his feet and kills it; as the prophet Isaiah predicts that at the coming of Christ a man shall

'go into the clefts of the rocks, and into the tops of the ragged rocks, for fear of the Lord.' Thus our Saviour slew with the water and blood flowing from His side the great dragon that was once a partaker of Divine wisdom in heaven, and redeemed

Hart and Dragon. (*Bestiary.*)

us thereby, and taught us to contend against the hidden designs of the devil. Hearken then to the voice within thee, which bids thee not to commit whoredom, nor to steal, nor to go after another man's wife; but, when thou hast drunken of the water of the New Law, kill all idle words and vain works. The hart loves to dwell in hilly regions; hills are types of the contemplative life of prophets and saints, and the sources of spiritual strength; as the Psalmist says: 'I will lift up mine eyes unto the hills, from whence cometh my help.'" According to the exegetist the hart longs for water not in order to quench thirst, but for the purpose of expelling dragons from their holes. Others assert that the hart, in killing the dragon, inhales its poisonous breath, which produces intense thirst and consequent longing for the water-brooks. Either interpretation shows the tendency of the expositor to seek extravagant and far-fetched explanations of the simplest texts, thus violating one of the most elementary principles of scientific investigation.

The hart was also fabled to renew its antlers and become rejuvenated by eating serpents and drinking from a pure spring, and this characteristic is used by Æmilius Dracontius in his poem *De Deo* to symbolize the regeneration of the human soul and its purification from evil by the waters of salvation. Representations of the hostility of the hart to the dragon occur occasionally in ecclesiastical architecture, but very frequently in illustrated bestiaries, breviaries, psalters, and other devotional works.

Again, we are informed that " the antelope is a wild animal with two powerful horns, with which it saws trees asunder and fells them. When it is thirsty it goes down to the Euphrates to drink. Growing on the banks of this river are certain shrubs of pleasant savour, which the antelope attempts

Antelope. (*Bestiary.*)

to eat, and thereby gets its horns entangled in the branches, so that it cannot free itself again. Then it cries out with a loud voice, and the hunters hearing it hasten to take it, or it is killed by beasts of prey. The two horns are the Books of the Old and New Testaments, with which the believer can resist the adversary and push him to the ground, and can cut down all growing sins and vices ; but he who allows himself to be drawn aside from the waters of salvation by the pleasures of the world,

and gets entangled in the thickets of lust and pride
and evil passions, falls an easy prey to the devil."
The author then quotes as a passage from Holy
Writ the words " Wine and women separate a
man from God," evidently an inference from the
admonitions contained in Prov. xxxi. 3-5.

The fiction of the antelope is alluded to by
minnesingers in illustration of the fate of malicious
and meddlesome courtiers, who are finally taken
and destroyed in the web of their own devices.   A
Venetian marble relief of the tenth century, now
in the Berlin Museum, represents a lion attacking
an antelope ; it symbolizes Satan assaulting the
soul, and is based upon the fable of the *Physiologus*.

Antelope on the Euphrates.   (*Psalter of Isabella of France.*)

The mishap of the antelope was a favourite
theme of mediæval artists, who usually gave only the
final scene, in which the entangled beast is killed ;
in the engraving, taken from the illuminated
psalter of Isabella of France, the whole story is
told.   It is also one of the beasts on the arch of
the doorway at Alne.

In the bestiaries barnacle geese are described as
growing on trees by the sea-side, and hanging from
the boughs by their beaks until they are covered

with feathers and fall like ripe fruit. If they reach the water they swim and live, but if they remain on the dry ground they perish. They illustrate the saving efficacy of baptism. Gerard of Wales [1] cites this legend as a fact designed to prove the doctrine of the Immaculate Conception, as these birds are born without procreation.

Barnacle Geese. (*Bestiary*.)

It must be remembered that the men who wrote such hermeneutical stuff as this, and took such childish tales seriously as the testimony of nature to the truth of revelation, were not obscure and ignorant persons, but the most learned divines and eminent representatives of the early Church, the creators of patristic theology, the great exegetists and eloquent apologists, who were deemed worthy of canonization and adoration as saints. But what preacher of to-day, if we except perhaps an American backwoods evangelist, or illiterate Capuchin discoursing to rude peasants in the remote districts of Southern Italy, would risk his reputation for sanity by expatiating from the pulpit or expounding the Bible in this style? And yet it was by this credulous and utterly uncritical class

[1] Gerald. Top. Hibern. v. 47. Cf. Jacobs: *The Jews of Angeviy, England*, p. 54.

of minds that the foundations of historical and dogmatic Christianity were laid, and the constitution and canonicity of our sacred Scriptures determined. It was they who framed the accepted creed of Christendom, and settled *ex cathedrâ* what doctrines were to be received as orthodox, and what opinions were to be rejected as heretical. Persons more incompetent to decide any of the difficult and delicate questions thus submitted to their judgment can hardly be imagined. Their belief in any event was in direct proportion to its marvellousness and incredibility, and the highest law of evidence which they recognized and applied as the test of divine truth was Tertullian's famous criterion: "Credo quia absurdum." The queer and often comical irrelevancy of their citations of biblical texts to the matter under discussion betrays their lack of logical faculty, and their incapacity for close and consecutive thinking. They do not show the slightest ability to sift testimony and to separate the true from the false in any statement; on the principle of *omne mirabile pro probabili* they were ready to accept as indubitable whatever was sufficiently wonderful, and to regard as conclusive demonstration a *petitio principii* which a modern school-boy of ordinary acumen would easily detect. It is evident that minds so implicitly credulous could have had no proper appreciation of the problems which the rise and growth of Christianity during the early period of its dogmatic evolution presented for solution, nor is it hardly possible that they should not have been deceived in any investigations they undertook, or in any conclusions they reached concerning the authenticity of the events recorded in the gospels and other scriptures of the New Testament, and the genuineness of these records. Under such circumstances it is not surprising that our sacred canon should begin with an astrological legend related as an historical fact in connection with the birth of Jesus, and end with a wild and weird apocalyptic vision, giving an autoptic description of the Last Judgment and the glories of the heavenly Jerusalem. In the same mental category to-day are the men and women who receive the Book of Mormon as a revelation from on high, who believe in the immaculate conception of Anna Lee, and accept George Jacob Schweinfurth as the incarnation of the Son of God, who listen to the sounds produced by the voluntary dislocation of the toe-joints of two tricksy girls as rappings from the spirit-world, and who put their faith in the healing waters of the grotto of Lourdes and the panacea of " Christian science " as expounded by Mrs. Eddy.

N

CHAPTER IV

SYMBOLISM SUPERSEDED BY SATIRE

Excess of animal symbolism in sacred edifices of the eleventh and twelfth centuries—Earnest but fruitless protest of St. Bernard—Image-worship authorized and enjoined by the Council held at Nice in 787—Images not to be inventions of artists, but to be fashioned according to ecclesiastical traditions and ecclesiological prescriptions— Views of St. Nilus—Paintings and sculptures for the instruction of the ignorant—Gautier de Coinsi renews the protest against "wild cats and lions" in the house of God—Angelus Rumpler makes the same complaint— Warnings by the Councils of Milan and Bordeaux—Introductions of episodes from the beast-epos with satirical tendencies—Secular guilds supplant religious orders as architects—Caricature of sacred rites—Fox preaching to geese in St. Martin's Church in Leicester—Sculptures in Strasburg Minster—Reliefs of the wolf's novitiate in Freiburg Minster—Poem by Marie de France—Samson and the lion—Provost's cushion in St. Michael's at Pforzheim—Burlesque of Calvin in St. Sernin at Toulouse—Luther satirized in St. Victor's Church at Xanten—Foolscap paper—Origin and character of the Papstesel—Monstrosities as portents—Bishop-fish—The Papal Ass in religious polemics—The Monk-calf of Freiburg and its interpretation—Miniatures illustrating the "Woes of France"—The fox of the *Physiologus* and of the beast-epos—Reliefs of the wiles of the fox and the woes of drunkenness in St. Fiacre—Execution of the cat in the cathedral at Tarragona—Significance of the crane extracting a bone from the fox's throat in Autun Cathedral—Burrowing foxes types of devils in Worcester

Cathedral—Scenes from the Reynardine and other poems
in the church of the Templars, St. Denis, Amiens Cathedral, Sherborne Minster, and other sacred edifices, but
most fully represented in Bristol Cathedral and Beverly
Minster—Heraldic rebuses and canting devices—Satire
on the election of a pope in Lincoln Cathedral—Mendicant friars caricatured as foxes in Ely, Gloucester,
Winchester, and other cathedrals—Odo of Sherington's
opinion of these orders—Similar delineations in the
churches and cloisters of continental Europe : Kempen,
Emmerick, Calcar, and Cleves—The *Lay of Aristotle*
and Vergil's affair of gallantry—The *Vision of Piers
Plowman* — Animals as musicians — Grotesques, bur-
lesques, and riddles—Funeral banquet at the burial of the
fox at Marienhafen—The frog as a symbol of regeneration—Carvings of individual fancies and conceits and
illustrations of proverbs—Episodes from the *Roman de
Renart*—Many of these sculptures, especially in Northern
France and the Netherlands, destroyed by iconoclasts
and revolutionists.

IT was in the eleventh and especially in the twelfth
century that symbolical animals played a most
conspicuous and very peculiar part in the ornamentation of church furniture and in ecclesiastical
architecture. Lamps, censers, pyxes, aspergills,
chrismatories, reliquaries, and sacramental vessels
were wrought in the form of griffins, ostriches,
pelicans, cranes, dolphins, doves, dragons, lions, or
some other real or fabulous creature, or had these
animals carved on them. It was deemed a hard
hit at the devil, and a masterly stroke of pious policy,
to press beasts of evil omen and Satanic significance
into the service of the Church, and force them to
assist at the celebration of holy offices. They were
therefore embroidered on sacerdotal vestments and
sculptured in the chancel and the chapels and

around the altars of the sanctuary, where religious rites were usually performed. Later, towards the close of the twelfth century, they began to take possession of the windows, portals, arches, and pinnacles, and finally extended to the whole exterior of the edifice, no part of which was safe from their encroachments. It was especially in cloisters that these beasts ran riot, but not without provoking the indignation and opposition of many ecclesiastics.

One of the earliest of these protests was that of St. Bernard of Clairvaux, who about the year 1125 wrote a letter on the subject to William, Abbot of St. Thierry, sharply censuring what he regarded as a profanation of sacred places. "What business," he exclaims, "have those ridiculous monstrosities, those creatures of wonderfully deformed beauty and beautiful deformity, before the eyes of studious friars in the courts of cloisters? What mean those filthy apes, those fierce lions, those monstrous centaurs, those half-men, those spotted tigers, those fighting soldiers and horn-blowing hunters? Thou seest many bodies under one head, and again many heads on one body. Here is a serpent's tail attached to a quadruped, there a quadruped's head on a fish. There a beast presents the fore-parts of a horse and drags after it the rear of a goat; here a horned animal has the hind parts of a horse. In short, there is seen everywhere such a marvellous diversity of forms, that one reads with more pleasure what is carved in stones than what is written in books, and would rather gaze all day upon these singular creations than to meditate on the divine word. O God! if one is not ashamed of these puerilities, why does one not at least spare the expense ? "

That the famous " doctor mellifluus " should have been ignorant of the meaning of the artistic representations he condemns is scarcely credible ; naturally enough, however, the coarse symbolism which they sought to express could hardly fail of being offensive to the refined and subtile mysticism of the saintly Cistercian, who rejected the dogma of the Immaculate Conception of the Virgin Mary as a too gross and sensual suggestion and emblematic expression of her spiritual purity. He was indignant that the Christian mysteries should be degraded and vulgarized by being clothed in what he deemed the foul and tattered vesture of pagan allegory. This attitude was perfectly consistent with his character as a reformer of the Church, and especially of the cloisters, and a zealous promoter of stricter monastic discipline. As ecclesiastical architecture was at that time still in the hands of the religious orders and the secular clergy, he held them responsible for these exhibitions, which he regarded as an evidence of their frivolity and dissoluteness.

Suger, the celebrated abbot of St. Denis and minister of state of Louis VII., was less fastidious and austere than St. Bernard, and in rebuilding the famous Benedictine abbey in 1144 did not hesitate to have the stained windows adorned with symbolical animals, which he appears to have prized both as decorations and sources of edification.

The seventh Œcumenical Council, which was held at Nice in 787, and which authorized icon-olatry and enjoined this cult as a religious duty upon believers, decided that the images were not to be the invention of the artist, but were to be fashioned according to the traditions and prescriptions of the Catholic Church. The artist was not permitted to follow his own fancies or to work out his own devices, but his sole function was to execute the intentions and embody the ideas and suggestions of the official ecclesiologists as derived from the writings of the Fathers : " Non est imaginum structura pictorum inventio, sed ecclesiæ catholicæ probata legislatio atque traditio." In the fifth century St. Nilus wrote to Olympiodorus : " You ask me whether it is proper to burden the walls of the sanctuary with representations of divers animals, hares, goats, and other beasts seeking safety in flight from the snares which cover the ground, and from the hunters, who with their dogs are eagerly pursuing them. Elsewhere, on the shore, we see all sorts of fish gathered by fishermen. I reply that it is puerile to amuse the eyes of the faithful in this manner." [1]

Evidently the censorious saint did not take the symbolical significance of such pictures into consideration, but looked upon them as purely orna-

---

[1] *Maxima Bibliotheca Patrum*, xxvii. 325.

mental and designed to please the eye. As a matter of fact, there was a large class of persons in the early and mediæval Church who relied upon such paintings and sculptures for their religious instruction and edification, like the old woman into whose mouth François Villon puts these words—

> " Femme je suis, pauverette et ancienne,
> Qui riens ne sçay, onques lettres ne leuz,
> Au moustier voy, dont je suis paroissienne,
> Paradis painct où sont harpes et luz
> Et un enfer où dampnés sont boulluz,
> Lung me fait pour, l'autre joye et liesse."

Symbolical representations of beasts and other delineations of this kind, however grotesque, are the records of human thoughts and beliefs in certain stages of civilization, and deserve to be deciphered with as much care as Runic signs or hieroglyphic and cuneiform inscriptions.

A hundred years after St. Bernard, Gautier de Coinsi, Prior of Vic sur Aisne, found it necessary again to censure the clergy for permitting "wild cats and lions" to rank with saints in the house of God, and for preferring to adorn their chambers with the lewd exploits of Isegrim and his spouse rather than to decorate the minsters with the miracles of the Virgin—

> " En leur moustiers ne font pas faire
> Sitost l'image Nostre Dame,
> Com font Isangrin et sa fame
> En leurs chambres où ils reponnent."

Again, in the beginning of the sixteenth century the pious abbot of Formbach, Angelus Rumpler,

renewed St. Bernard's query as to the purpose and
fitness of putting lions, dragons, and the like in
the churches, which ought, he says, to be simply
and suitably adorned, and not so conspicuously as
to furnish occasion for gazing instead of praying.
" Not that I censure proper ornament," he adds,
"but only what is fantastical and superfluous.   For
pictures are the books of the laity or unlearned;
but by pictures I mean such as portray the
Passion of Christ and the sufferings of the saints."
He wishes to have representations that will incite
to devotion, and not merely gratify curiosity or
engender evil propensities.   What he expressly
reprehends are scenes which a young girl cannot
look at without having her mind corrupted and
lascivious desires excited in her heart; and the
manner in which he refers to them proves that
they must have existed in places of worship.
What we should expend for the relief of the poor,
he concludes, we squander on sumptuous and
needless edifices; but enough of this: *sed de hac
re hactenus.*

The first Council of Milan in 1565 warned the
bishops not to permit in the churches any paintings or sculptures opposed to the truth of Scripture,
or of tradition or ecclesiastical history: "Caveant
episcopi, ne quid pingatur aut sculpatur, quod
veritati scripturarum, traditionum aut ecclesiasti-
carum historiarum adversetur."   Twenty years later
(1585) the Council of Bordeaux forbade preachers
to introduce fables into their sermons, and thus

move their hearers to laughter, instead of drawing
tears of contrition from their eyes, as they ought
to do : " Concionatoris enim est, non risum movere,
sed lacrymas auditoribus excutere."

The symbolical meaning which Clemens Alexandrinus, Augustine, Origen, Chrysostom, Epiphanius,
Jerome, Bonaventura, Ambrosius, Isidorus, and
other great interpreters of Holy Writ had discovered in these real or fabulous creatures was
now forgotten or discarded.   The gross and beastly
types had been superseded by the finer mysticism
of expositors like the abbot of Clairvaux, whose
æsthetic sense as well as religious feeling was deeply
offended by these crude and whimsical illustrations
of spiritual truths.

Meanwhile other fables, derived partly from
hagiological sources and partly from old Germanic
sagas and the marvels related of foreign lands by
mediæval travellers, had become gradually mixed
up with the *Physiologus*, and under its shelter and
sanction as a precedent succeeded in creeping into
holy places.   Scenes from the beast-epos, especially the adventures of the fox and the wolf,
carved on wood, cut in stone, painted in fresco,
or more frequently pictured in glass, began to
make themselves conspicuous on the stalls of the
chancel, and on the pulpits and portals and stained
windows of cathedrals.   At first they were designed to enforce moral precepts and to illustrate
ethical principles, but in seeking these ends they
found it necessary to satirize the vices of the clergy,

and to censure with deserved severity the greed
and gluttony and general dissoluteness of the
monastic orders.

During the thirteenth and fourteenth centuries
the religious fraternities were in a great degree
supplanted as builders by associations of secular
architects, and, as the influence of the laity became
predominant in church ornamentation, and the
spirit which resulted in the Reformation grew
bolder and more aggressive, this satirical tendency
increased, and did not confine itself to the exposure of religious hypocrisy and pseudo-sanctity,
but soon delighted in ridiculing and caricaturing
sacramental rites and sacred observances. Apes
in choristers' robes, swine in monks' hoods, asses
in cowls chanting and playing the organ, sirens in
the costume of nuns with their faces carefully
veiled and the rest of their persons exposed, stags
in chasubles ministering at the altar, and wolves
in the confessional giving absolution to lambs,
were some of the means employed to burlesque
the principal ceremonies and fundamental institutions of the Church, and to turn them into ridicule.
On one of the painted windows of St. Martin's
Church, in Leicester, was the picture of a fox in
surplice preaching to a flock of geese from the
text: "Testis est mihi Deus quam cupiam vos
omnes visceribus meis" ("God is my witness how
I long for you all in my bowels"). One of the
wood-carvings in Ely Cathedral represents the fox
arrayed in episcopal robes, with almuce and stole

and crosier, discoursing to a similar audience from the same passage of Scripture; in the next scene he has made a practical application of the text by throwing off his holy vestments and hurrying away with a goose, pursued by an old woman with a distaff.[1] Here we have not merely an exposure of the begging friars, but a hard hit at the highest dignitaries of the Church.

The obscenity of many of these delineations resulted naturally and inevitably from the fact that they satirized obscene things. Thus the abbot Grandidier, in describing the grotesque figures sculptured on the pulpit staircase in Strasburg Minster, says: "On y remarquait entr' autres celle d'un moine couché au dessous et aux pieds d'une béguine, dont il soulevait les juppes." This pulpit was constructed in 1486 under the supervision of the famous preacher, Johannes Geiler von Kaisersberg, in whose sermons the licentiousness of the monks and particularly the unchastity of the vagabond béguines were severely scourged. Indeed, béguinage came to be synonymous with spurious piety or lust in the disguise of sanctity. But however coarsely such scenes may have been depicted, they originated in a high moral purpose, and had a pure aim, which, as the old *plattdeutsch* poet Lauremberg, in his *Schertzgedichte*, says of the hidden wisdom in Reincke Vos, shone forth like a glowing coal in the ashes, or a gold penny in a greasy pocket—

[1] Herrig's *Archiv*, lviii. 255.

" Glyck als dat Führ schulet in der Asche,
  Un güldne Penninge in eener schmierigen Tasche."

With the progress of the Reformation these
representations were drawn into the great religious
movement and put to polemical uses, and proved
to be more effective in influencing the mass of
public opinion than any doctrinal discussion. Thus
Fischart published woodcuts of the sculptures near
the choir of Strasburg Minster with explanatory
doggerels, in which he interpreted them as an
allegorical derision of the Romish clergy; and this
view seems to have been accepted by the Catholics
themselves, although a zealous Protestant, Oscar
Schad, in his description of the cathedral, printed
in 1617, vents his indignation against the Franciscan, Friedrich Johann Nass, who, he says, " had
the effrontery to thrust his nose into this matter,
beslavering with his venom the sound expositions
of Fischart, and absurdly affirming these beasts to
be types of pious and faithful evangelical preachers
and godly servants of the Word."   As these sculptures date from the end of the thirteenth century,
and are therefore much older than Protestantism,
which dates from the Diet held by the evangelical
estates at Spire, in 1529, the interpretation of them
given by Nass is grossly anachronistic. Besides,
they caricature, not a Protestant, but a Catholic
rite, namely, the burial of the fox, as prescribed by
the Romish ceremonial.   First comes the bear
with an aspergill and a vessel of holy water; the
wolf carries a crucifix, and the hare holds a burning

taper; the bier, on which lies the fox simulating
death and plotting revenge, is borne by a sow and
a he-goat. An ape is seated on the ground near
the bier, apparently as spectator. A stag is chanting the office at an altar, while a cat serves as
lectern to support the epistles, which are read by
an ass. At the feet of the bear is a globe with a

Burial of the Fox. (*Choir of Strasburg Minster.*)

cross on it forming a reichsapfel or tut, and indicating, perhaps, that the officiating priests are Car-
thusians, since the tut was the badge of their order
(Herrig's *Archiv*, lxvi. 269-70). It is possible, however, that the cross is intended to indicate a grave
in the cemetery, to which the fox is being borne.

The fact that the chapter of the cathedral caused
these sculptures to be chiseled off in 1685 is a confession that they were thought to be directed, or
might, at least, be easily turned, against the papal
hierarchy. Also a Lutheran bookseller, who kept
woodcuts of them on sale, was condemned to stand
in his shirt and do penance for his offence in front
of the minster, and was then banished from the city.

Again, in Freiburg Minster (Breisgau), in a narrow passage leading from the south transept to
the choir, are reliefs belonging to the first half of

the twelfth century, and representing the wolf's
novitiate.   The lupine candidate for a cloistral life
or for the clerical office is learning his letters from
a monk, who is seated on a faldstool with a peda-
gogue's baton consisting of a bundle of rods in his
hand.   The dull pupil, who holds a pointer awkwardly in his right paw, has already reached the
third letter of the alphabet in his pursuit of knowledge, when the longing for lamb gets the better of
his love of learning, and he seizes a sheep of the

Novitiate of the Wolf. (*Freiburg Minster.*)

pastoral flock and endeavours to devour it.   The
tonsured teacher applies the rod vigorously to the
back of the recreant novice, whose natural appetites
assert themselves and are not to be extinguished by
the capoch.   These works of art delineate episodes
of the beast-epos, and correspond to the description
given by Marie de France of the wolf's attempt to
become a monk, being drawn to this pious vocation
by merry thoughts of fat living.   Her poem might
be rendered into English as follows—

" There was once a priest whc wished to see
If he could teach the wolf his A B C.
' A,' said the priest ; the wolf said ' A,'
And grinned in a grim and guileful way.
' B,' said the priest, 'and say it with me.'
' B,' said the wolf, 'the letter I see.'
' C,' said the priest, ' keep on just so.'
' C,' said the wolf.   ' Don't be so slow,'
Remarked the priest ; 'come, go on now.'
And the wolf replied : ' I don't know how.'
' Then see how it looks and spell it out.'
' Lamb, lamb, it means without a doubt.'
' Beware,' said the priest, 'or you'll get a blow,
For your mouth with your thoughts doth overflow.'
And thus it haps ofttimes to each,
That his secret thought is by his speech
Revealed, and, ere he is aware,
Is out of his lips and in the air." [1]

Near the wolf seizing the lamb is Samson in the
act of tearing open the jaws of a lion.   The long

[1] " FABLE 80.—*D'un prestre et d'un lou.*

" Une prestres volt jadis aprendre
I lou a letres fere entendre.
A dist li prestres.—A dist li leus
Qui mult est fel et engingneux.
B dist li prestres, di o moi.
B dist li leux, la letre voi.
C dist li prestres, di avant.
C dist li leus.   Ail dont tant,
Respont li prestres, or di par toi.
Li leu respont : je ne sai coi.
Di que te semble, si espel.
Respont li leus : Aignel, aignel.
Li prestres dist : que verte touche;
Tel on penser, tel en la bouche.
De pensons, le voit l'en souvent;
Ce dont il pensent durement,
Est par la bouche conneu.
Ainçois que d'autre soit seu,
La bouche monstre le penser;
Tout doit ele de li parler."

hair of the Hebrew solar hero, which in the myth
is said to be the source of his strength, as the force
of the sun is in its rays, has caused this figure to
be mistaken for a woman, and interpreted as a
symbol of spiritual power overcoming brute force.
A similar sculpture adorns a console in the Stiftskirche at Stuttgart, a capital in the church of
Remagen in the Rhineland, and the outside of the
apsis of the old Romanic church at Schöngrabern
in Lower Austria.   Here Samson wears his hair in
a long braid.   It may be found also on the portal
of the cathedral of St. Stephen's in Vienna, on an
altar in the monastery Klosterneuberg, on a stall
in the cathedral of Amiens, and on the capital of
a column in the church of St. Sauveur-de-Nevres,
where it bears the inscription: "Samson adest,
heros fortis."   Indeed, it is very common in
mediæval church edifices and on consecrated
vessels, and is sometimes associated with representations of Christ's deliverance of the captive
spirits from hell, as in a painting in the vestibule
of Freiburg Minster.   Another sculpture in this
minster shows a man contending against a griffin,
which signifies the effort to overcome carnal
passion.   So, too, the centaur, which will be more
fully considered hereafter, is the symbol of what
Paul calls the natural man, or *homo animal*, as it is
rendered in the Vulgate.

Flögel (*Geschichte der komischen Literatur*, iii.
358) mentions a beautifully-embroidered cushion
of the provost's chair in the collegiate church of

St. Michael at Pforzheim.   The embroidery represents a wolf in monastic garb standing in a pulpit
and discoursing from an open book to a flock of
geese, which are devoutly listening and holding
each a rosary in its beak.   The sacristan, who performs the duties of goose-herd, is dressed in motley.
Out of the hood of the preacher projects the head
of a goose.   A fox is lying in wait under the pulpit,
and round the wolf is embroidered the verse—

> " Ich will euch wohl viel Fabeln sagen,
>   Bis ich fühle alln [1] mein Kragen."
> " Of fables to you I'll tell a deal,
> · Till in my maw I all may feel."

This cushion was purchased in 1540 by Jacob Heer-
brand, Chancellor of the University of Tübingen,
when he was sent with other theologians to promote
the cause of the Reformation in the Margravate
of Baden-Durlach, and was used by him against
the papacy in his polemical treatise, *Refutatio
defensionis assertionum Jesuiticarum.*

In this manner the whole beast-epos was diverted
from its original course, as a purely narrative poem,
into the turbulent and more or less filthy channel
of religious controversy.   Thus a zealous champion
of Protestantism, John Bale, published at Zurich
in 1542, under the pseudonym of John Harryson,
a book entitled : " Yet a Course at the Romysche
foxe, a dysclosynge or openynge of the Manne of
Synne."   Catholic defenders of the faith, too, were

---

[1] *Alln = alle in.*   The sense is the same whether we read
Kragen (craw) or *Magen* (maw).

O

not slow in filling their quivers with arrows drawn
from the same exhaustless source.   Not only the
printing-press, but also the walls and other parts
of sacred edifices were put to polemical purposes,
as, for example, in the chancel of St. Sernin at
Toulouse, where a fat hog in gown and bands discoursing from a pulpit is styled *Calvin le porc
preschant* ("Calvin the pig preaching").   This is the
interpretation given to the carving and its legend
by M. de Montalembert; but the clerical animal
is not cloven-hoofed, and resembles an ass rather
than a pig, and the inscription may read *Calvin
le père*, since a nail driven into the second letter
of the third word has so defaced it as to render it
difficult to decipher.   This work of art may, therefore, portray "Father Calvin" in the form of an
ass preaching heresies to his deluded disciples, one
of whom is kneeling before the sacred desk with
eyes devout and the palm of his hand on an open
book, as if appealing to Holy Writ in confirmation
of the doctrines proclaimed from the sacred desk.
In St. Victor's Church at Xanten on the Rhine is
an *Ecce Homo*, dating from 1536, representing
Christ followed by a great rabble crying, "Crucify
Him!"   The leader of this bloodthirsty mob is
Martin Luther, who wears a pilgrim's scrip, on
which the head of a beast of prey takes the place
of the conventional cross and shell.   Near him is
a man making grimaces by thrusting his finger into
his cheek, while another is throwing filth.
    The reformers of the sixteenth century indulged

very freely in coarse caricatures of this sort, and often outdid their adversaries in such expressions of scorn. Thus Henry VIII. showed his contempt of the Roman See by using for official purposes a paper with the water-mark of a hog wearing a tiara, just as the Republican parliament substituted a fool's cap and bells for the King's arms on the official paper of the realm; hence the name which the large folio paper used in law-offices and courts of justice still bears.

One of the most noted of this class of productions was the so-called Papstesel, or Papal Ass. This monster has the form of a woman with the head of an ass; the left hand is that of a human being, the right hand is an elephant's trunk, the rump is the mask-like face of a man with long beard and horns, and a serpentine neck ending in a dragon's head; one of the feet is an eagle's claw, and the other an ox's hoof, and the body is covered with scales like a fish.

This drawing has been commonly, but erroneously, attributed to the elder Lucas Cranach, who may have copied, but certainly did not create it. It is also a mistake to suppose that it was intended originally to ridicule the papacy. In December 1445 the city of Rome was devastated by an inundation of the Tiber, followed by famine and pestilence. After the waters had subsided, this strange carcass is said to have been found in the deposit of the flood on the banks of the river, and a full description of it is given in Malipiero's

Venetian annals.[1] No contemporary writer seems
to have entertained the slightest doubt that the
remains of such an abnormal creature were actually
discovered ; the only difference of opinion that
could possibly arise would be in regard to its origin
and significance, whether it was a work of God or
of Satan, and what it might forebode.

In the middle ages monstrosities and freaks of
nature were looked upon as dire portents, and
every marvellous phenomenon was deemed a sure
sign of the impending wrath of God. Not only
comets, eclipses, and other remarkable appearances
in the sky, but even any uncommon occurrence on
the earth, such as a fall of red snow, sufficed to fill
the hearts of men with chilling fear, and to freeze
the blood in their veins ; and the birth of a double-
headed calf or a deformed pig was a source of
terror to whole nations. The intellectual awaken-
ing, known as the revival of letters, tended to
confirm rather than to undermine the belief in the
existence of monstrosities, inasmuch as it cultivated
and diffused a literature all alive with centaurs,
fauns, satyrs, hippocamps, tritons, sirens, nereids,
sphinxes, griffins, dragons, minotaurs, and chimeras,
the reality of which no true humanist would think

[1] *Archivo Storico*, vii. 422. Cf. *Der Papstesel, ein Beitrag
zur Kultur- und Kunstgeschichte des Reformationszeitalters*,
von Konrad Lange, Göttingen, 1891. This monograph contains the most thorough discussion of the subject hitherto
published, including a clear and consistent account of the
origin and character of this monstrous figment of the
imagination, and the symbolical and satirical purposes
which it was made to subserve.

of calling in question, and the renascence of which
soon exerted a marked influence upon the decorative
arts. With a like faith begotten of enthusiasm,
scholars accepted the reports of Herodotus, the
father of history, and of Ktesias, the Münchausen
of classical antiquity, concerning goat-hoofed and
dog-headed men, one-legged giants, men with one
eye (*monoculi*—perhaps a primitive race of dudes),
men with eyes in their breasts, and others with
their heads beneath their shoulders, or without any
heads at all. It is not surprising, therefore, that
the sixteenth century, notwithstanding its superior
enlightenment and reputation for learning, should
have produced numerous and ponderous tomes devoted to the description and exposition of marvels
and monstrosities. Perhaps the most exhaustive
repertory of this kind is the *Prodigiorum ac
ostentorum Chronicon* of Lycosthenes (Wolfhart),
published at Bâle in 1557. The author begins
with the serpent in Eden, " ante Christum 3959,"
and gives a brief account, with rough woodcuts,
of every wonderful thing he had ever heard or
read of down to A.D. 1557, in a volume of six
hundred and seventy pages. In the Royal Library
of Munich there are two copies of this work, one
of which has a manuscript continuation of more
than fifty pages, bringing it down to 1677, with
many drawings in the style of the illustrations
contained in the printed book. To this is added
by a third chronicler, in French, the queer description of a spectral battle between three armies, said

to have been fought in the clouds on February 25,
1696, and witnessed by more than two hundred
persons.   In accordance with the current opinion
of their time, both Lycosthenes and the author
of the continuation interpret these phenomena as
tokens of the divine anger, and endeavour to
connect them with great physical disasters and
noteworthy historical events.

Shakespeare indicates the fascination which such
vulgar superstitions and tales of prodigies had for
the most refined and sensitive persons of an earlier
day, when he makes Othello beguile the gentle
Desdemona of her tears and win her heart by
discoursing about them.   Not only the outlying
and unexplored regions of the
earth, but the sea also was prolific of wonders, the most remarkable of which was the so-
called bishop-fish (*Episcopus
marinus*) or sea-bishop (*Meer-
bischof*), a specimen of which is
said to have been caught in the
Baltic in 1433.   It had a mitre
on its head, a crosier in its hand,
and wore a dalmatica.   The
king of Poland wished to confine it in a tower, but it stub-
bornly resisted this attempt on
its freedom, and by mute ges-
tures entreated its fellow-prelates,
the bishops of the realm, to whom it showed

Sea-bishop.
(*Gessner's Fischbuch.*)

special reverence, to let it return to its native element. This request was finally granted, and, in token of joy and gratitude, it made the sign of the cross, and gave the episcopal benediction with its fin, as it disappeared under the waves. Engravings of this marine marvel were published in Gessner's *Fischbuch* in 1575, in Schott's *Physica Curiosa*, and in other works of the sixteenth and seventeenth centuries. In 1531, according to Dutch chroniclers, another bishop-fish was taken in the German Ocean, and sent to the king of Poland, but it obstinately refused to eat anything, and died on the third day of its captivity. Gessner describes also the merman (*Homus marinus*) and the mermonk (*Monachus marinus*), said to have been taken in the Baltic, the British Channel, in the Red Sea, and on the coast of Dalmatia. Evidently we have here to do with some of the numerous species of seals seen through the magnifying and distorting medium of religious superstition. The Jesuit Gaspar Schott, in the above-mentioned work, a volume of nearly fourteen hundred pages, discusses all sorts of monsters and marvels real and imaginary, demons, spooks, deformed men, energumens, birds, abnormities of land and sea, and portents of earth and sky, showing the material, efficient, and final causes of such phenomena. All these strange forms were supposed to be special creations or manifestations having a profound spiritual significance, and bearing peculiar relations to the Church, which drew them into its pale, and put them to decorative and

didactic uses in ecclesiastical architecture, as, for
example, in the rose-window of the south transept
of the cathedral of Lausanne, dating from the
thirteenth century.

Whatever may have been the origin of the
Roman monster, whether the story arose from the
fortuitous concurrence of parts of men and of
beasts that had perished in the flood, or was the
trick of some wag, whose love of a joke could not
be repressed by the horrors of the situation, or was
a mere invention of the imagination excited by
fear, there is no doubt that drawings of it were
made soon after its supposed discovery. The
earliest known representation of it in art is a relief
on the north door of the cathedral of Como,
sculptured by the brothers Jacob and Thomas
Rodari about the year 1497.[1] As a satire on the
see of Rome it would certainly not have found a
place in a Catholic church at that time ; but as a
divine admonition and warning, and especially as
a symbol of the woes of inundation, foreign in-
vasion, famine, and pestilence, by which the States
of the Church and Italy were then sorely afflicted,
such a carving, however offensive to the taste of
the present day, would have been considered
perfectly appropriate and even highly edifying.

If, as Lange assumes, the strange figure was

---

[1] This door is popularly known as *porta della rana*, from
the carving of a frog snapping at an insect. The frog,
according to the *Physiologus*, is a type of those who snatch
at the fleeting pleasures of this world.

simply an allegory of the city of Rome, it would
naturally be portrayed as a female; the ass's head
would signify subjugation and servitude; the
elephant's proboscis would indicate the pest of
syphilis, then confounded with elephantiasis, which

Papal Ass. (*Cathedral of Como.*)

the Spaniards had introduced into Naples from
the New World, and the French troops had brought
with them to Rome; the eagle's claw would represent the rapacity of Charles VIII.; the ox's hoof
would refer to Alexander VI., whose coat-of-arms
was an ox, and who kept his footing in the Vatican

only by sharing his power with the French king,
while the scaly skin would suggest the devastating
overflow of the Tiber.

About this time, however, the dissoluteness of
the Roman pontiff, and the scandalous conduct of
his mistresses and his children, began to excite the
attention and to provoke the censure of the public
to such a degree, that there would be a general
tendency to interpret the monster, not perhaps as
a symbol of the institution of the papacy, but as a
satire on the licentious occupant of the apostolic
see, and a warning from God against the evil
doings of the Vicar of Christ.

Somewhat later, probably about the year 1500, it
was engraved on copper by the goldsmith Wenzel
of Olmutz, and seems to have been accepted by
the Moravians as emblematic of the Romish hierarchy, and used as a means of anti-papal agitation.
It next appears as a woodcut in Melanchthon's
*Figur des Antichristlichen Bapsts vnd seiner
Synagog*, published in 1523, and again in the same
year in his and Luther's joint work entitled, *Deutung
der czwo grewlichen Figuren Bapstesels czu Rom,
vnd Munckkalbs zu Freyberg ynn Meysszen funden*.
A new and improved edition of Melanchthon's
exposition of the Papstesel was printed at Wittenberg in 1535, and endorsed with Luther's "Amen."
It also appears as Plate II. in Luther's *Abbildung
des Bapstum* (Wittenberg, 1545), a series of coarse
and positively indecent woodcuts, probably the
work of Lucas Cranach, with explanatory doggerel

verses. In a letter of June 3, 1545, to Nicholas
von Amsdorf, first Protestant bishop of Raumburg,
the Reformer writes : " Your nephew George showed
me a picture of the pope," adding by way of
comment, and evidently with a chuckle of delight,
" but Master Lucas is *ein grober Maler ;* " and in a
letter of June 15 to the same friend he remarks :
" I shall endeavour to have Lucas the painter
exchange this foul picture for a more proper one."
The reference here is not to the Papstesel, but to
Plate I., entitled, *Ortus et origo Papæ* (" Rise and
Origin of the Pope "), and representing his Holiness
as the excrements of a ghastly, grinning monster.
The infant pontiff, thus born in corruption, is reared
by the Furies, Alecto rocking his cradle, Megæra
acting as his wet-nurse, and Tisiphone holding him
in leading strings. It is evident from the descriptive
rhymes accompanying these drawings that Luther
fully entered into the spirit of the artist's conceptions, and heartily enjoyed their coarse humour.
His seeming censure of the " gross painter" and
the "foul picture," and the expression of his intention
of having a more decent delineation substituted
for it, must be taken ironically, and may have been
called forth by some criticism of his correspondent.

The " Münchkalb " (monk-calf), the second of the
monsters delineated and discussed in the *Interpretation of two grewsome Figures* already cited, was
reported to have been taken from a cow in a public
slaughter-house at Freiburg, December 12, 1522,
and to have had a round, flabby, and mis-shapen

head with a tonsure, on which were two large warts
or wens. The chin was that of a man; the nose,
ears, and upper jaw were those of a calf; the hide
hung in folds between the shoulders, like a monk's
cowl, and had slits in the hind legs, like the slashes
in old costumes. This hideous creature was interpreted by Luther as a symbol of the stupidity
and beastliness of the monastic orders, although
Melanchthon afterwards discovered in it a different
signification, explaining it as portending the excesses of the reformatory movement that revealed
themselves in iconoclastic outrages and the horrors
of the Peasants' War, which broke out three years
later. It is an interesting fact that one of the
earliest explications of it was given by a Bohemian
astrologer in Prague, who saw in it a condemnation
of the heresy and apostasy of Luther, the renegade
monk. A similar view is taken by Cochlæus,
Emser, and other Catholic controversialists, and in
a treatise on monsters from the time of Constantine
to the year 1570 by the French theologian Sorbinus,[1]
the causal connection between the birth of such
creatures and some form of schism in the body of
Christ, or some sacrilegious assault upon the orthodox faith, is shown to the satisfaction of every true
believer.

In the City Library of Lyons is the manuscript
of a poem entitled *De Tristibus Galliæ* ("Woes
of France"), with miniature paintings of a satirical

---

[1] *Arnoldi Sorbini Tholosanorum theologi et regii ecclesi-
astæ Tractatus de monstris*, etc. Paris, 1570.

character directed against the sectaries and schis-
matics, who are represented as abasing and pillaging
the land.   A lion, the symbol of France, is ridden
by an ape, which bears a sack full of spoils, probably taken from churches and cloisters; another
ape has tied a priest's vestment to the lion's hind
leg; a third holds the king of beasts ignominiously
by the tail, while a fourth confronts the lion with a
halberd.   Several apes are listening to a sermon
delivered by a field-preacher; others are evidently
applying the teachings of the itinerant evangelist
by plundering consecrated places and insulting a
crucifix.

The woes of France, resulting from Panama scandals, which in our day are the sensational theme of
the journalist's pen, would have been delineated in
the middle ages quite as vividly and truthfully, and
far more pleasingly, by the artist's pencil.

As the fox not only holds a prominent place in
the *Physiologus*, but is also
the protagonist of the beast-
epos, it is natural that this
animal should figure con-
spicuously in pictorial and
plastic art, and become, from
the very nature of its characteristics, a favourite vehicle

The wiles of the Fox.
(*Bestiary.*)

of satire.   The oldest of these representations are
based upon the *Physiologus*, in which it is stated
that "when the fox is hungry, it lies down in a
furrow of the field and covers itself partly with

earth, as though it had been long dead. Then the ravens and other rapacious birds come to devour it, when it suddenly leaps up and tears them in pieces. Thus the devil deceives those who love the corrupt things of this world and obey the lusts of the flesh, and entices them to their own destruction." "He who tells idle tales and indulges in carnal pleasures," adds an old English bestiary, "pecks at the skin of the fox and tears its flesh, but the devil requites the sinner by seizing him and dragging him down to murky hell. The devil and the reprobate are crafty like the fox, and deserve shame. He who speaks fair words and meditates evil is a fox; such a one was Herod, for he said that he would believe on Christ, when he really meant to kill Him."

In the church of St. Fiacre, near Le Faouet, in the department of Morbihan, formerly a portion of Brittany, are wood-carvings on the richly-ornamented rood-loft portraying these wiles of the fox, which in the first scene is lying on its back with protruding tongue and apparently dead; instead of carrion-crows, as elsewhere, a cock and several inquisitive hens are pecking at different parts of its body. In the second scene the fox has sprung up and caught one of them by the neck.

There are similar reliefs on the abacus of a column in the cathedral of Tarragona in Spain. On the opposite side of the abacus are sculptures of what Meissner (Herrig's *Archiv*, lxv. 214) calls the burial of the cat, but which would seem rather

to represent the carrying of the cat to execution.
Tabby lies on a litter, which might be mistaken for
a bier, but is really a stretcher used instead of a
hangman's cart, borne by rats and mice, and preceded by a long procession of these rodents with
banners, vessels of holy water, aspergills, crosiers,
censers. The executioner, a rat bearing an axe,
marches with the full consciousness of his official
dignity under the litter. This stately pageant is

Execution of the Cat.   (*Cathedral of Tarragona, Spain.*)

followed by a more lively spectacle : the cat springs
up and catches a rat, while the rest of the solemn
assembly disperse in all directions, leaving the
sacred utensils and the pompous paraphernalia of
the panic-stricken procession scattered on the
ground. The presence of the rat as headsman indicates that the execution is about to take place ;
if it had already occurred and the "master of high
works" (*maître des hautes-œuvres*, as the French
were wont to style this important functionary) had

done his duty, it would be hard to imagine the decapitated culprit coming to life again.[1]

Returning to St. Fiacre, we find in that quaint church a third relief of a fox lurking behind some bushes, from which a cock and three hens are picking snails. Still farther in the background is a second fox wearing a cowl and standing in a sort of framework or enclosure, which Champfleury calls a donjon, but Meissner with greater proba-

Fox ensnaring Fowls. (*Church of St. Fiacre, Le Faouet.*)

bility assumes to be a pulpit. Here we have, instead of the fox of the *Physiologus*, the chicken-stealing and sanctimonious Reynard of the mediæval epic.

Another relief in the same church represents a man seated on a bench and steadying with his left hand a wine-cask, which rests on his knee. In his teeth he holds a fox by the tip of the tail, the half-flayed body of which hangs between his legs. Champfleury explains this sculpture as a figurative illustration of the phrase *écorcher le renard* ("flay the fox"), *i. e.* suffer from what the Germans call

[1] Vide article on "Odo de Ceringtonia" in Herrig's *Archiv*, lxiv. In a work entitled *Gothic Architecture in Spain*, by George Edmond Street, is an engraving of this piece of sculpture. Odo of Sherington's *Book of Fables* was translated into Spanish under the title of *Libro de los Gatos*, of which a German version by Kunst has been published in Lemcke's *Jahrbuch*, vi. Cf. Voight's *Kleinere Denkmäler der Thiersage*.

Katzenjammer, or the after-effects of a drunken debauch. In a word, it teaches a moral lesson by a drastic exhibition of the woes of inebriety. Rabelais describes Gargantua as a person who was wont to " flay the fox," and the common people of France still use the phrase *piquer un renard* (" prick a fox ") in the same sense. Pepys records in his Diary on one occasion : " I drank so much wine that I was even almost foxed." Wine or beer that sours in fermenting is said " to fox " or to be " foxy,"

Flaying the Fox.
(*St. Fiacre, Le Faouet.*)

because it goes to the head, and by deranging the stomach acts as an emetic.

On the capital of a column in the cathedral at Autun is chiselled the scene in which the crane extracts a bone from the fox's throat. Here the artist clothes the fable with a symbolical significance derived from the *Physiologus* and the bestiaries, in which the fox typifies the devil, and the crane is an emblem of Christian care and vigilance, ever active in saving souls from the jaws of hell. In this case, the crane must be imagined as coming to the rescue, not of the fox, but of the bone.

" The fox," says the *Physiologus*, " injures the earth by burrowing in it; the earth signifies man, who should bring forth the fruits of righteousness; sin is the hole, which the devil digs and thereby

P

causes these fruits to wither away. As the wise
king saith : ' Take us the foxes, the little foxes that
spoil the vines ; for our vines have tender grapes.'
David also spoke of becoming ' a portion of foxes ';
and our Saviour bore the same testimony when He
said : ' The foxes have holes.' "

This teaching is embodied in a carving on a
miserere in the celebrated Worcester Cathedral,
which shows foxes running in and out of holes ;
opposite this populous kennel stands John the
Evangelist with his gospel in his hand and an
eagle at his feet. Here the foxes are types of the
devil, and the beholder is called upon to choose
between the wily adversary and the herald of
divine truth. Sometimes all four evangelists, or
Christ alone, are thus set in opposition to the
vulpine devils. Foxes in cowls are the itinerant
friars, who were feared and hated by the secular
clergy on account of their restless and innovating
spirit and propensity to religious agitation, which
disturbed the peace of the Church, and the comfort
of the holders of high dignities, and the incumbents
of fat benefices. The privileges conferred upon
the mendicant orders by Innocent III. and his
successors, the reputation which many of their
members justly acquired for scholarship, and the
eminence they attained as professors at the uni-
versities, excited the envy of the great body of
ecclesiastics. It was their severely reformatory
aim and exposure of established abuses, not less
than their arrogance in the garb of poverty, that

made them the objects of hatred and the subjects
of satire.

The following may serve as fair specimens of the
manner in which the exploits of the fox are
delineated in various European churches, and the
spiritual or satirical uses to which they are put.[1]
In the Maison des Templiers, formerly connected
with the neighbouring church of the Templars
in Metz, and probably used as a refectory, are
traces of a painting of the thirteenth century portraying about thirty animals, to which the fox
is preaching from a pulpit. Among Reynard's
auditors are the bear, the ape, the he-goat, the
griffin, the cock, the hare, the stork, the sow, and
the cat, which are either holding prayer-books or
psalters, or singing hymns from sheets of music,
while the unicorn plays the bagpipe, and the ass
performs on the harp. A little apart, with its
back turned towards these worshippers, is another
fox, in the act of receiving the chalice from a stag,
while a third fox, dressed as a pilgrim, greets a
leopard in passing. In the background stands a
tent, in which a dead animal, probably a calf, is
lying.

In the church of St. Denis at Amboise, two
foxes with pilgrim's staff and scrip are witnessing
the slaughter of the innocents, doubtless in allusion
to Herod, whom Christ called " that fox." The
frequency with which the fox appears in the garb

[1] Cf. Meissner's contributions to Herrig's *Archiv*, lxv., *et
alias.*

of a pilgrim is a satire on the craftiness and deceitfulness of this class of pious vagrants, who were morally about on a level with the modern tramp. This is especially true of the professional pilgrim or palmer, who passed his life in perpetual vagabondage, and was to all intents and purposes a mediæval tramp. It is not merely an accidental coincidence that palmer became a synonym for swindler, and that the most voracious and devastating of caterpillars was called palmer-worm, but showed the popular appreciation of the " votarist in palmer's weed."

On a stall in the cathedral of Amiens is carved a fox preaching to a flock of domestic fowls. The pulpit is in the form of a tray, and the preacher is reaching over the edge, as if zealously expounding the Scriptures, but really for the purpose of seizing a hen, whose devout interest in the sermon has brought her into dangerous proximity to the eager-eyed and rapacious gospeller. Again, on the exterior of Canterbury Cathedral are bas-reliefs representing a fox in monastic habit discoursing to a solemn assembly of geese.

On the underside of the seat of a faldstool in the choir of Sherborne Minster is a carving of the fox on the gallows, with four geese acting as hangmen, and a monk standing on either side of it with a book in his hand. Also on the church of St. Michael in Bruges is a stone sculpture, formerly the tympanum or facing of a pediment over the portal of the collegiate church of St. Ursin, repre-

senting a cock and hen hauling a fox on a cart to
the place of execution, and preceded by a bear
with a ball or globe at his feet, evidently the priest
who is to minister spiritual comfort to the culprit
in his last moments. The fox has anything but a
penitent air; on the contrary, he seems to take

Cock and Hen drawing Fox to execution. (*St. Ursin, Bruges.*)

quite a cheerful view of the situation, and his sly
look implies an intention to play his executioners
some trick before reaching the scaffold. He tries
to assume a long face as he journeys towards his
long home, but the real state of his mind is betrayed
by the merry twinkle of his eye. It is the incident
so humorously described by the poet of Champagne—

> " Renard s'en allait tristement
> S'emparer de son dernier gîte ;
> Canteclair s'en allait gaiement
> Enterrer son mort au plus vite.
> Notre défunt etait en carrosse porté,
> Bien et dument empaqueté
> Et vêtu d'une robe, helas ! qu'on nomme biere :
> Robe d'hiver, robe d'été,
> Que les morts ne dépouillent guère."

The stalls of Bristol Cathedral are adorned with
a series of grotesques, which depict the trial of

the fox as described in the beast-epos. First we
have a man riding on a bear towards the fox, who
is peeping from behind a tree; this is Bruin, the
royal messenger, coming to summon Reynard to
appear before the king and answer for his crimes.
In the next scene Bruin is caught in the cleft of
the log through his greediness for honey, and
severely beaten by boors with cudgels. Thirdly,
Reynard is sentenced to be hanged, and the
necessary preparations are made for the imposing
execution of the death-warrant. King Noble and
his royal spouse are seated on their respective
thrones; the bear, the wolf, and the goose are
helping the condemned up the fatal ladder with
undisguised pleasure, while the squirrel sits on the
top of the gallows-tree and pulls a rope attached
to the poor sinner's neck. Then follows the
mousing adventure of Tybert, the cat in the house
of the priest, in portraying which the artist has
adhered quite closely to the description of the
exciting incident given by the poet, so that his
work bears a striking resemblance to Kaulbach's
well-known sketch. The cat, in desperate self-
defence, scratches the priest in a very sensitive part
of his body, to the great horror of his housekeeper,
or, maybe, his wife (for at that time sacerdotal
celibacy had not become imperative, and was by
no means universal in the Catholic Church), who
pulls the sacrilegious depredator violently by the
tail, while the malicious instigator of all this
trouble stands in a corner and laughs. Reynard

appears next in a monk's hood, standing in a
pulpit and preaching to several geese, that stretch
out their long necks and listen with a peculiar
expression of mingled solemnity and sentimentality
to the seductive orator. Again the irrepressible
proclivity of the hypocritical homilist to overreach
some tender member of his flock brings him from
the sacred desk to the scaffold, where he is seen
dangling from the cross-beam of a gallows, a
number of his former auditors holding the rope,
and one of them tugging at the scoundrel's tail in
order to hasten the process of strangulation, while
another is perched on the top of the gallows,
cackling for joy and flapping her wings in triumph.
A woman, doubtless Reynard's wife, Dame Her-
melin, riding on a mule and probably returning
from her husband's trial, is the subject of the
seventh carving ; on one side is a house, evidently
Malepartus, with Reynard looking warily out of
the door, and a dove-cot with several doves in it.
In the eighth scene the bear and the wolf are
dancing to the music of a drum beaten by an ape,
thus showing their gladness at the condemnation
of their common enemy. There were originally
other carvings of incidents mentioned in the
poem, but they have been partially destroyed, and
those still preserved have been renovated and re-ar-
ranged without the slightest regard to their logical
or chronological sequence. The general resemblance to Kaulbach's illustrations of *Reineke Fuchs*
is due, as already intimated, to the fact that

they both faithfully depict episodes of the same epos.

In this cathedral are also comical carvings of incidents derived from other poems and popular tales, as, for example, that of an abbot riding backward on an ass and holding the tail of his steed in his hand in the manner described in Bürger's ballad, where the emperor says to the round, fat, oily abbot of St. Gall—

"So lass' ich Euch führen zu Esel durch's Land,
Verkehrt, statt des Zaumes den Schwanz in der Hand."
"Bestriding an ass you shall ride through the land,
With the tail instead of the reins in your hand."

Another series of wood-carvings are the following more or less fanciful delineations of the artist, although some represent scenes from the French versions of the beast-epos :—

I. A chained and muzzled bear with a ring in its nose ; on either side a fox looking out slyly from behind a tree, and two labourers with wheel-barrows.

II. A naked man armed with a sword, and attacked by two animals resembling a bear and a wolf; on the right side the nude buttocks of a man, recalling the episode in the fourteenth branch of the *Roman de Renart*: "De l'ours et du lou et du Vilains, qui monstrerent lor cus"—

"Trestuit trois nos cus mostrerrons,
Et cil qui graignor cul aura
Le bacon tout emportera."—(xiv. 7087 *sqq.*)

III. A snail creeping up a mountain and driven

by a monk; at a little distance a knight watching the performance.   In the *Roman de Renart* the snail holds the responsible office of gonfalonier, and bears the royal standard—

> "Le Rois Tardins le limaçon
> Bailla le roial gonfanon,
> Et li commanda l'avant-garde,
> Et le lupart l'arrière-garde."—(3511-14.)

But there is no such incident in the Reynardine poems as that portrayed here; Gautier de Coinsi, however, mentions the snail as one of the animals which served to adorn consecrated edifices—

> "Plus delitont sont si fait conte
> As bones gens par Saint-Omer,
> Que de Renart ne de Roumer,
> Ne de Tardin le limaçon."

In *Renart le Nouvel* it is the snail, as chief ensign bearer, that scales the walls of Malepartus, after Reynard has escaped by a secret passage, and plants the banner of the king upon the battlements—

> "Es-vous Tardins le limaçon
> Ki dist que par tans le sara,
> As Murs s'ahiert, amont rampa
> Nului n'i vit, jus descendi,
> A le porte vint, si l'ouvri ;
> Mais ains mist le roial baniere
> Ens en le maistre tour de piere
> En signe pris est li castiaus.
> Au Roi Noble est cis signes briaus."—(4214-22.)

In a Roman Catholic prayer-book (*Livre d'Heures*) of the thirteenth century there is a

miniature painting of a man in the act of shooting
a snail with an arbalist or cross-bow.   The snail is
sitting erect on an arabesque resembling a vine.
M. de Bastard thinks the snail is a symbol of Christ
and the resurrection; but if this interpretation be
correct, it is difficult to understand the signification
of the cross-bowman.   In another large picture of
the fifteenth century we see a crowd of people,
among them one woman, attacking a snail with
swords and staves, and crying out in the words of
the inscription—

> "Vuide ce lieu, tres orde beste,
>   Qui des vignes les bourgeons mange."

> "Quit this place, you filthy beast,
>   That eats the fresh buds of the vine."

The Church, as we have shown in a volume
entitled *The Criminal Prosecution and Capital
Punishment of Animals*, claimed and exercised the
power of expelling bugs and slugs and noxious
insects from the vineyards and cultivated fields by
anathematizing them, after they had been formally
tried and condemned; and it is this function of the
papal hierarchy that the two delineations above-
mentioned are intended to illustrate.   It is not
necessary to seek in them a more recondite symbolism or theological meaning.

IV. Two men mounted, one on a goose and the
other on a hog, and each armed with a spear;
probably the caricature of a tournament.

V. A pedlar thrown down and plundered by
apes, which are taking the wares out of his pack.

VI. An ape as doctor examining a bottle of urine.

VII. An ape playing on a lute, an instrument whose "lascivious pleasing" was associated with amorous delights and gallant intrigues.

VIII. An ape sitting astride an ass, which a boor is holding by the tail and belabouring with a cudgel.

These carvings belong probably to the end of the fifteenth century. The stone sculptures in the "Elder Lady Chapel" are much older, and date from the early part of the thirteenth century; the fox, as was its wont, is running off with a goose; an ape and a ram are performing on sylvan pipes; another ape is playing on a syrinx and carrying a hare on its back.

Although such representations may have been inventions of the artist, it is hardly possible that they should have been placed in the church without the will and consent of the ecclesiastical authorities, whose intention was evidently to censure by burlesquing the vices and foibles of their day. But what must be regarded as most curious and characteristic is, that satirical and often necessarily obscene delineations of this kind, although designed for moral reproof and correction, should have been deemed suitable decorations of sacred architecture. That they sometimes made "the judicious grieve" we have already seen; but it is plain that they must have been sanctioned by the majority of the clergy and generally approved by the devout laity.

In Beverly Minster the misereres of the stalls in the choir are adorned with carvings of animals, in which the adventures of the fox as an itinerant preacher are more fully delineated than in any other ecclesiastical edifice. During the middle ages, Beverly or Inderawood, as it was originally called, was a popular place of pilgrimage, where the bones of St. John of Beverly, who was Archbishop of York in the eighth century, and canonized by Benedict IX. in 1037, were revered by pious multitudes of all classes, that thronged to this shrine from every part of England. Even after the Reformation Beverly remained a stronghold of Catholicism, and the chief centre of reactionary movements.

The carvings in question were the work of "Johannes Wake clericus," whose escutcheon was a crowing cock (Wake!); this chanticleer may have been, however, a pictorial pun or heraldic rebus, a mere canting device, and not necessarily a family coat-of-arms. They were made in the very year (1520) in which Luther burned the papal bull at Wittenberg, and were directed, not against the secular clergy, to which Wake himself belonged, but against the mendicant orders, and especially against the Black Friars (Dominicans) and Gray Friars (Franciscans), then exceedingly active as predicants in Beverly. These restless and irritating elements in the sleek and comfortable sacerdotal body were perpetual thorns in the flesh to the conservative dignitaries of the Church, who regarded

them with quite as deep aversion as they did the
heretical Protestants themselves.   The following
are the subjects of the carvings :—

I. A fox running away with a goose and pursued
by a man.

II. A fox in a monk's habit preaching to a flock
of geese; behind the exhorter is an ape that seizes
every goose within his reach, throwing it over his
shoulder and holding it by the neck; several of
them are already hanging in this position.

III. The fox is being hanged by geese, six of
them tugging at the rope as executioners, and two
standing by as spectators.   To this carving there
are two pendants or side-views; in one the fox is
lying apparently dead under the gallows, and an
ape is removing the noose from the culprit's neck;
in the other the resuscitated rascal has fallen upon
the sleeping geese and carried off two of them.

IV. The fox steals a goose; the cries of the
other geese attract the attention of an old woman,
who rushes out of the house, but comes too late to
prevent the robbery.

V. A man pursues a fox with dogs, but the wily
quarry is already safe in its hole and peeping out
with a crafty look.   A side-scene shows Reynard
in bed, suffering doubtless from indigestion caused
by over-indulgence in fat poultry.

VI. A fox-hunt with hounds.

VII. Three peasants are hauling a cart with a
fox lying on it, evidently a representation of
Reynard's trick of pretending to be dead, and being

picked up and thrown on the cart, where the fish, with which it is laden, can be eaten at leisure.

Besides these episodes from the beast-epos, there are many purely grotesque carvings or scenes intended to enforce moral lessons or to illustrate the wisdom of homely proverbs; a cat playing the fiddle for dancing mice, which she sports with and finally eats; an elephant with a howdah; a dance of death with two men in motley; a man putting his cart before the horse, and another threshing eggs with a flail; a woman pulling a man by the hair; an animal eating out of a narrow-necked vessel, in which its head is stuck fast; a boar-hunt; a stag-hunt; an owl surrounded by small birds; a lion with its paw on a woman's head; a boar playing the bagpipe and another the harp, young pigs dancing, and an ape on horseback leading three muzzled bears by chains; a pedlar plundered by apes; an ape as doctor examining a flask of urine; an ape dandling an infant; a miser hoarding his money, while the devil seizes him from behind; a drunkard holding a goblet and clutched by a demon, and finally several canting arms of canons, such as cocks fighting on a tun (Cockton), persons placing weights on scales (Witton, *i. e.* Weight on), a crowing cock (Wake), and other equally far-fetched rebuses.

In the church of St. Mary in Beverly are still older carvings of a like character: two capoched foxes at a lectern reading scripture-lessons; a fox as friar preaching; a fox engaged in a medical diagnosis as above; foxes with crosiers, and each with a goose in its hood; and a man riding a goat with a rabbit under his arm. The dress of the foxes shows them to be Cistercians.

On the stalls of the choir in Lincoln Cathedral are somewhat similar wood-carvings dating from the fourteenth century: two apes bearing a young ape on a bier, and stopping to pray before a chapel or shrine; a crane dropping stones into a bottle in order to make the water rise within reach; and the devil blowing a fire with a bellows and boiling a kettle, out of which emerges a man wearing a tiara. This is probably a satire on the election of a pope.

In Ely Cathedral we find a fox preaching to geese; the vulpine divine wears an almuce and stole, and holds a bishop's crook in the left hand; in the right hand is a scroll, with the words already quoted from a similar representation on the window of St. Martin's Church in Leicester: "Testis est mihi Deus quam cupiam vos visceribus meis." Another fox is running off with a goose, and is pursued by an old woman with a distaff. There are also carvings of squirrels, symbols of the constant strivings of the Holy Spirit; apes; a hunt; a hart trampling on a serpent, typifying Christ subduing Satan by the waters of salvation; two men playing dice and drinking, and a woman standing near and weeping over a broken bee-hive fallen to the ground, a moral discourse on drunkenness as subversive of domestic happiness and thrift.

Carvings of a like character decorate the

cathedrals of Gloucester and Winchester, and
satirize the same religious fraternities. Indeed
they existed formerly in nearly all the principal
English churches and priories, adorning usually the
stalls of the choir, the lectern, or the organ-loft.
At a later period, when the Reformation began to
be an earnest movement intensively and extensively,
and interpreted these works as deriding the offices
of the Church and scoffing at the clergy, the very
persons to whom they owed their origin, they were
in many cases destroyed, as, for example, in the
fine old Gothic cathedral at Chester.

In the collegiate church of St. Victor, at Xanten
on the Rhine, are carvings on the backs of the stalls
of the choir, in which the begging friars are figured
as a monster with the body and feet of a pig, the
tail of a fox, and the head of a cowled monk. It
is a piece of symbolism recalling the portentous
porco sacerdos mentioned by Lycosthenes (p. 529),
and embodying in plastic form the opinion expressed by Innocent III., who, as a man of learning and lover of the nicer elegancies of life, at first
refused to confirm the rules of the order of St.
Francis, saying that they were more fit for swine
than for human beings.

The Benedictine Odo of Sherington, who lived
in the twelfth century, in his fable of the wolf in
sheep's clothing denounces the rapacity and hypocrisy of the Cistercians, stigmatizing them as rene-
gades and legacy-hunters, and declaring that he
would rather associate with a pagan or a Jew than

with such a monk. Many of the carvings already described derive their inspiration directly from Odo's fables, and inculcate his teachings.

An American bishop and High-Churchman was wont to call out to his servant, whenever a dissenting orthodox minister visited him : " John, count the spoons ; there is an evangelical in the house ! " This warning, although not intended by the corpulent and otherwise good-humoured prelate to be taken seriously, expresses the real antipathy of mediæval bishops and other secular clergy towards the mendicant and predicant orders.

The embodiment of this feeling in works of art was by no means confined to the ecclesiastical edifices of England, although more frequently met with there than on the Continent, especially in the churches and monasteries belonging to the Benedictines. Foxes in the disguise of begging friars are found in the cathedral of St. Etienne at Limoges, in St. Jaurin of Evreux, in the cathedral of Le Mans, and were formerly on the arms of the seats in the chancel of the cathedral Notre Dame at Rouen, but were hewn off by an over-zealous iconoclastic canon.

On the frieze of a column in St. Peter's Church at Aulnay is the sculpture of an ass standing on its hind legs and invested with a dalmatica. It is evidently " Bernard li arciprestres," as the ass is called in the *Roman de Renart*, and may be regarded as a scoffing allusion to the noble and saintly reformer of the Bernardines and Cistercians.

In the magnificent cathedral of Toledo in Spain
are reliefs carved towards the close of the fifteenth
century, and representing a bear near a beehive in
search of honey; a fox strangling a cock; a woman
riding on a mule to market with two geese in a
basket, and a fox creeping up behind her in order
to steal them; an ape feeding a duck with a spoon,
and a young ape catching hold of the old one and
evidently soliciting a share of the food; a pig with
a girdle and a knife (the pig turned butcher); the
story of Aristotle as related in the *Lai d'Aristote;*
a man in motley approaching a tent, where he is
received by a naked woman, who draws aside the
curtain in order to admit him.

The *Lay of Aristotle* is a satire on the power
of love and the irresistible fascination of female
beauty, against which neither philosophic wisdom
nor old age is proof. The poem, based upon an
old tradition, was written by Henri d'Andely, a
canon of the cathedral of Notre-Dame of Rouen
at the end of the twelfth century, and is contained
in Etienne Barbazan's collection of *Fabliaux et
Contes François des XIIe.—XVe. Siècles* (Paris,
1756). The fable is briefly as follows. Whilst
Alexander was pursuing his career of conquest in
the Orient, he became so deeply enamoured of an
East Indian girl as, in the opinion of his soldiers,
to imperil the success of the campaign by giving
to dalliance too much rein. Aristotle was thereupon deputed by the army to remonstrate with
the young monarch, who confessed his fault and

promised to have no further intercourse with the dangerous beauty. Naturally the young lady was quick to observe the change, and on reproaching her lover with neglect and learning the cause of it, vowed to avenge herself on the officious philosopher. Accordingly the next day she went into the orchard wearing only a long chemise of finest muslin, and walked to and fro under Aristotle's windows, singing to herself and culling flowers. Aristotle looked out and at first feigned indifference, but soon had his wise head turned, and descending to the orchard made an ardent declaration of love, and expressed his willingness to do anything to win her favour. As a test of the sincerity of his affection she demanded that he should condescend to be her palfrey. After some hesitation he acceded to this humiliating proposal, permitted himself to be saddled and bridled, and began to creep over the grass on all fours with the exultant girl seated on his back, holding the reins in one hand and a riding-whip in the other. Alexander, who had watched the progress of this gallant adventure from a window of the palace, now drew near and derided the absurd infatuation of his grave preceptor, who candidly confessed his folly, but could not refrain from the pedagogical habit of drawing a moral lesson from it for the benefit of others. " Beware," he said, " for if love can make such a fool of an old man, how much more dangerous must it be to youth!"

The *Lay of Aristotle* seems to have been often

delineated in Christian art, especially in cloisters, where it was designed to glorify asceticism and celibacy.   One of the finest representations of it is a bas-relief underneath a console on the façade of the cathedral church of Saint-Jean in Lyons, dating from the fifteenth century.   Behind the philosopher, degraded to a lady's palfrey, is a hare, the symbol of libidinousness; in the two corners above are persons generally supposed to be Alexander and his mistress; it is probable, however, that the scene on the right,

The "Lay of Aristotle."
(*Saint-Jean, Lyons.*)

slightly mutilated, represents Aristotle declaring his love, and the one on the left the young lady imposing the conditions on which her favour may be secured.   There is also a sculpture of the story of Aristotle on a capital in the church of Saint-Pierre in Caen, as well as one in the apex of an arch and another on the base of a column in the cloister of Cadouin.   They used to be interpreted as portraying the conjugal relations of Samson and Delilah, but really have a broader application in illustration of the concluding lines of Henri d'Andely's poem—

" Veritez est, et je le di,
　　Qu' amors vainc tout et tout vaincra
　　Tant com cis siècles durera."

Mediæval legend makes Vergil the hero of an equally farcical affair of gallantry with the daughter of the Emperor of Rome, who invited him to a rendezvous at the foot of a tower in which she dwelt. She then ordered her attendants to let down from her window a basket by a rope, for the ostensible purpose of drawing him up; but instead of being lifted to the goal of his lofty hopes he was left suspended in the midway air, and became an object of scoffing to every passer-by. This episode was also sculptured on a pillar in the cloister of Cadouin, but has been gradually destroyed, so that only few traces of it are now left. It was commonly supposed to represent the manner in which Saul of Tarsus after his conversion escaped the fury of the Jews by being let down in a basket from the wall of Damascus. The monks were extremely fond of selecting the wisest and most illustrious men of pagan antiquity, and thus satirizing their frailty in their relations to women in order to exalt their own cloistered virtue and saintly chastity.

These cynical, satirical, moral, and sometimes perhaps purely fanciful delineations, with the description of which it would be easy to fill a large volume, were derived almost exclusively from the cycle of Reynard's adventures, as recorded in different versions of the beast-epos, and have rarely any relation to the *Physiologus*. But it is not probable that they would have ever found admis-

which they drew many keen-pointed darts to hurl
against the hated hierarchy. As is well known,
the writings of Chaucer and Petrarch were used
very effectively in the same way. The author of
Piers Plowman is extremely severe in his stric-
tures on the "foure ordres" of begging friars,
namely, Franciscans, Dominicans, Carmelites, and
Augustines; especially the first two seem to have
been the peculiar objects of his aversion. The
Benedictines hated these orders, and not only
warned the people against them in sermons, but
also burlesqued them in the carvings, paintings,
and sculptures of their cloisters and churches,
portraying them as wily foxes, ravenous wolves,
asses, hogs, and stinking and salacious goats; and
there is no doubt that the obnoxious *frères*, however worthy may have been the original objects
of the brotherhoods, soon degenerated into persons
who made a profession of poverty, but practised
all sorts of fraud to enrich their convents, which
became in a short time the grandest and wealthiest
in England. They succeeded in acquiring immense
influence over the masses, and thereby excited the
envy and jealousy of the secular clergy, and made
themselves odious to the better classes by reason
of their intrigues and arrogance, and their success
in extorting rich bequests from the dying. They
were the sensational preachers of their day, and
sought to attract crowds by novel doctrines, eccen-
tric manners, coarse wit, funny stories, rhetorical
pyrotechnics, and other astounding feats of pulpit

prestidigitation, so that Langland was wholly
justified in denouncing them as

> " but jugulers and iapers, of kynde,
> Lorels and lechures and lemmans holden,"

who

> " ryht as Robertes men raken aboute
> At feires and at ful ales and fyllen the cuppe,
> And precheth all of pardon to plesen the puple."

In the frequent representations of animals performing on musical instruments and like whimsical
conceits the artist did not take his subjects either
from the *Physiologus* or the beast-epos, but was
permitted to give line and scope to the sarcastic
suggestions of his own fancy in censure of public
folly and iniquity. On the stalls of the choir in
Boston Minster, St. Botolph's in Lincolnshire, and
on a churchwarden's pew now in the Hôtel de
Cluny, are carvings of pigs playing on the organ
or on the harp. The hog and also the dog as
harpist occur in St. Peter's Cathedral, Poitiers,
and date from the first half of the thirteenth
century. In the cathedral of Burgos, a splendid
monument of pure Gothic style erected by German
architects in the thirteenth century, are carvings
of a bishop carried off by a bull-headed devil; two
knights and their ladies dancing to the dulcet
tones of a lute; pigs seated on stools and eating
pap out of pots; wine-skins as knights on horseback, with lances in the rest and ready to tilt,
evidently a caricature of tournaments and persi-
flage of theological polemics; a sow spinning

while giving suck to her farrow, and a boar causing the organ to peal for the entertainment and
edification of his family; a sow playing on the
bagpipe, and her pigs dancing round an over-
turned trough; a man assailed and knocked down
by apes, whose young he had captured; a fox
as hunter riding on a dog, and carrying on his
shoulders another dog tied by its hind legs to a
stick, showing how the tables may be turned.   As
it was the assumed and generally acknowledged
function of the Church to correct and reprove all
forms of vice and folly, and to do what Hamlet
asserted to be "the purpose of playing," namely,
"to show virtue her own feature, scorn her own
image, and the very age and body of the time
his form and pressure," perhaps we have in these
beastly musicians a satire on the numerous wandering minstrels, mediæval Bohemians, and vagabond
Beghards, whose morals were not of the best.
Some such motive would explain their admission
into the Church more satisfactorily than to regard
them as mere caprices of the artist, which the
ecclesiastical authorities tolerated simply because
they amused the public.   Besides, the repetition
of them in so many churches in different countries would imply a general scheme of reform
and systematic crusade against the prevailing
iniquities.

The collegiate church at Manchester, in which
many grotesque designs of this sort are found,
contains also hunting-scenes with tuns, evidently

allusions in rebus to Huntington, the first warden.
In numerous instances it is impossible to solve
these artistic puzzles, as neither history nor local
tradition has preserved the key to them.   An eagle
flying away with a child to its aerie is the memorial
of an incident said to have occurred in the house
of Stanley, one of whose members, James Stanley,
was the warden of Manchester College from 1506
to 1515.[1]   The same family tradition is carved on
a stool in the chancel of Salisbury Cathedral, and
might easily be mistaken for an eagle mounting up
with an eaglet to the sun.

Rats hanging a cat in the presence of owls, that
are looking on with judicial gravity and an air of
profound legal wisdom, are depicted in Great Mal-
vern Abbey, and may illustrate the doctrine of final
retribution.

Beside excellent specimens of the commoner
symbols founded on the *Physiologus*, such as the
unicorn asleep in the lap of a virgin, the pelican
feeding her young with blood from her breast, and
others of a similar character, there is, on one of
the stalls in the chancel of Boston Minster, the
carving of an armed knight on a steed in harness.
While the horse is in full gallop one of its shoes
is flung off, but the rider, without stopping, turns
round in his saddle and catches the shoe in his
hand as it flies through the air.   Meissner suggests
that this may be mythological, and celebrate the

---

[1] Cf. Herrig's *Archiv*, lxv. 217-222.

exploit of some Scandinavian god or hero. More probably, however, it immortalizes the marvellous feat of some Lincolnshire chevalier, and has only a local importance.

On the old church of Marienhafen, in East Friesland, were numerous animals cut in stone, which adorned the portal and extended on the frieze entirely round the building. The edifice was demolished in 1829, but the city architect of Emden, Marten, made drawings of the sculptures as they lay scattered about in the churchyard, and they were subsequently published by the " Gesellschaft für bildende Kunst und vaterländische Alterthümer zu Emden."[1] One series of these works of art tells the story of the wolf at school, and does not differ essentially from the reliefs at Freiburg already described. Another series portrays the burial of the fox, and follows quite closely the text of the last branch of the *Roman de Renart.* An animal in a cowl is reading the Gospel, another is celebrating mass at an altar, while an ape, as acolyte, rings the sacring-bell; a fourth animal is standing on its hind legs and reading the lections.

The next scene is a funeral banquet : one of the animals is sweeping the dining-hall, another drawing wine, a third carrying a bowl or pitcher, and others bringing food into the hall, where numerous animals are feasting. At the table three apes are carving a joint, a fourth is eating a piece of bread,

[1] Cf. *Das Ostfriesische Monatsblatt,* June, 1878.

and a fifth is holding an empty glass to be filled.
Then comes the funeral procession : one animal
with a censer, another with a cross, a hog with
an aspergill and a basin of holy water, an ass in
priestly robes, a horse as sexton with a spade,
a camel with a tabor, a goat with a bell, a wolf
bearing a crucifix, a pig with a shovel, and a fox
lying on a bier.   In another scene at the grave two
horned animals seize the deceased by the head and
feet and lay him in the pit.   These are the under-
takers, Brichemer the stag and Belin the ram, as
described in the French poem—

> " Li Cors ont iluec descendu
>   Qui covert iert d'un paile vert,
>   Et quant il l'orent descovert
>   Brichemer par le chief le prist,
>   Ainsi con Bernart li aprist,
>   Qui maint mis en terre en avoit ;
>   A Belin que devant lui voit
>   A fet Renart par les piez prendre.
>   En la fosse sanz plus attendre
>   L'ont mis et couchie doucement,
>   Et l'Arciprestre innelement
>   Geta sus l'eue beneoite."

In the sculptures a priest, standing behind the stag,
gives the benediction, an animal resembling a pig
sprinkles holy water with an aspergill, and an ape
gazes sorrowfully into the grave, by which two
shovels are lying.   The animals are much defaced,
so that it is impossible sometimes to determine
what kind of creatures they are intended to represent.   Another group tells the story of the goat in
the well.

The western portal of the cathedral of Brandenburg on the Havel is adorned with reliefs similar to those already described. In the first scene a fox as friar is reading scripture-lessons to some geese; in the second he is preaching to them from a pulpit, but before the sermon is ended rushes into the devout flock and seizes a plump auditress by the neck. Then follows the trial, with geese as witnesses, the judge sitting on a chair and an executioner at his side with a drawn sword; finally the culprit makes confession and saves his life. Among the sculptures, all of which are seriously injured, is one of a man fighting a basilisk with a venom-repelling cone of crystal as described in the *Physiologus*.

The cornice of the cathedral of Paderborn is decorated with delineations of scenes from the fables. In the first, the fox and the crane are dining together, the latter eating with relish out of a tall and narrow-necked vase in which the food is contained, while the former must be content with what can be got by licking the outside of the vessel; in the second, a crane is extracting a bone from the throat of a fox, doubtless in this connection simply a representation of the incident described in the fable, without any reference to the symbolism of saving souls from the jaws of hell, as is elsewhere the case. Thirdly, an old woman sitting on a bench and spinning strikes with her distaff an ape, which is trying to steal a dish of food. Finally, there are sculptures of a frog and a swan, whose

aquatic habits may have some relation to the re-
viving and transforming virtue of the baptismal
rite and the waters of salvation.   Perhaps the
change of the batrachian from tadpole to frog may
furnish the basis of this symbolism of regeneration.
In the Egyptian Museum at Turin is a lamp of
terra-cotta in the shape of a frog, with the inscription ΕΓΩ ΕΙΜΙ ΑΝΑΤΑϹΙϹ: "I am the resurrection." The Vedic poet Vasishtha (*Rigveda*, vii. 103)
invokes the frogs as deities, and compares their
croaking to the chanting of Brahmans, who are
performing sacrificial rites, and praying to the
cloud-compelling Parjaňya for rain in time of
drought.   The frog that lows like a cow, and bleats
like a goat, the speckled and the green frog are
entreated jointly and severally to refresh and enrich and renew the earth.   In the *Liber de Hæri-
sibus* (xi.) of Philaster, Bishop of Brescia, the frog-
worshippers (*ranarum cultores*) are mentioned as
an heretical Christian sect ; and a law of the year
428 forbade Arians, Macedonians, and Batrachi-
tians to reside within the limits of the Roman
Empire.   It may have been due to this tendency
to worship frogs that their entrails were used as
charms in ancient times (Juvenal, iii. 44), and prescribed as a potent medicament by mediæval
quacksalvers.   Although the swan is not mentioned in the *Physiologus*, the melancholy musical
tones which it is supposed to utter when dying,
and especially after having been mortally wounded,
are often compared by early Christian poets to

the last utterances of the crucified Saviour and the sweet resignation of the blessed martyrs. This figurative application of the fabled characteristic of the bird would account for its presence in ecclesiastical architecture.

In the window-frame of an outside corridor of the same church are three hares hewn in stone, and having altogether only three ears, but so arranged that each hare seems to have two ears. This sculpture may have symbolized originally the doctrine of the Trinity, but in the present instance has no religious significance, since it was placed there probably as a votive offering by the travelling handicraftsmen of Paderborn as the badge or ensign of their guild. In the cloister of the Franciscan nuns at Muotta, in Switzerland, is a woodcarving of three hares similarly arranged; in this case it was doubtless intended to be an emblem of Trinitarianism.

In the parish church of Kempen on the Rhine the misericords are adorned with nearly thirty

Carvings on Stalls in Parish Church of Kempen.

carvings illustrating fables and proverbs. Here we have not only the crane eating out of a tall and

slender vessel, as at Paderborn, but also the counter-
plot of the fox who turns the tables on the crane
by inviting the latter to dinner and serving the
food as thin soup in a shallow dish, from which he
easily and eagerly laps it up, while his long-billed
guest gets scarcely a drop.   A man threshing eggs
with a flail would be interpreted in general as an
example of energy misapplied ; but in this case it
has a special censorious significance not commonly
understood.   It was one of the privileges of the

Carvings on Stalls in Parish Church of Kempen.

clergy to collect eggs from parishioners during
Lent, and the exercise of this right was popularly
known as *Eierdreschen* (egg-threshing), owing to
the diligence and zeal with which these ovarious
contributions were levied.   The man beating eggs
with a flail satirizes this odious exaction, and is
carved on the stalls of many churches in the Rhinelands, as, for example, at Calcar, Cleves, and Emmerich.[1]   Other carvings at Kempen refer to the

[1] In connection with this form of tribute it may be mentioned
as a parody on trial by ordeal, that if any person's contribution amounted to half an egg and he refused to give a
whole one, it was customary to lay the egg on the threshold of
the house and strike it in two with a knife ; if the yolk flowed

same custom, and are evidently intended to deride the egg-hunting parson; such as a man holding an egg up to the light to see if it is fresh, a man feeling of a hen in order to ascertain the prospect of eggs, so as not to be deceived by any excusatory

Carvings on Stalls in Parish Church of Kempen.

plea of the peasant that the hens don't lay, a man sitting on eggs to hatch them, and a man weeping over a basket full of eggs fallen to the ground. Of the other representations, more or less sarcastic

Carvings on Stalls in Parish Church of Kempen.

in their purpose, are a fisherman drawing an eel-pot out of the water; another hauling in a net; a fox preaching to fowls, while a cowled confederate lies

towards the house, the tributary was declared to be free, but if it flowed outwards, he was condemned to pay a fine.

R

in wait for them behind the pulpit ; two dogs fighting over a bone ; a fox swimming after ducks in a
pond ; an ass kneeling with a pack on its back and
a rosary in its mouth ; a man casting daisies before
swine (*margaritas ante porcos*), a confusion of the

Carvings on Stalls in Parish Church of Kempen.

pearl (margarite) with the flower (marguerite) ; an
ass playing the lyre (*asinus ad lyram*) ; a pig playing the bagpipe ; a fox confessing a bird, as it is
usually explained, but more probably a delineation

Carvings on Stalls in Parish Church of Kempen.

of the incident related in the *Roman de Renart*, in
which Hubert the kite officiates as confessor to
Reynard and is suddenly seized and eaten by the
crafty confessant ; a bear getting honey out of a
hive ; a cat sitting near a bell, to which a strap is
attached, and surrounded by four mice, who are

evidently trying to devise the best means of putting it round her neck. Ernst aus'm Weerth thinks the cat rings the bell to entice the mice, perhaps to a supper, " not where they eat, but where they are eaten," as Hamlet would say ; this interpretation is far-fetched and absurd ; the intention of the artist was simply to illustrate the phrase " to bell the cat." The ass with a rosary is also carved on a stall in the Minorite cloister of Cleves, and dates from the year 1474 ; it was designed to throw ridicule on the Dominicans, whose founder, in the second decade of the thirteenth century, introduced the rosary as a means of keeping a proper tale of prayers, and who were held in derision on this account, especially by their rivals the Franciscans. The idea of performing devotions by counting beads was not original with Domingo de Guzman, but was borrowed from the Mohammedans. The pack is the heavy burden of sin, which the new and im-proved system of supplication by machinery is expected to lighten. At Kempen there are also carvings of a man shearing swine, great cry and little wool, a general illustration of the proverb, and perhaps a special satire on preaching friars ; a mer-maid with comb and mirror, probably the German siren of the Lorelei ; a pig putting on trousers ; an ape carrying a young donkey in a dosser, or maybe one of her own young, although the creature in the pannier has a decidedly asinine look ; an owl view-ing its face in a mirror, a rebus of the typical medi-æval wag Tyll Eulenspiegel ; a pelican feeding her brood with her blood, and other more common or less striking delineations, all of which are remarkable for their fidelity to nature, and show in the main, a wonderful degree of technical skill in their execution.   This realistic and individualizing tendency reveals itself in the care and exactness with which the minutest characteristics are observed and reproduced.   They are the works of the Flemish school of wood-carving, which flourished during the fifteenth century at many places in the Rhinelands, and especially at Calcar.

As has been already stated, the same subjects with some additions and slight variations are treated in St. Martin's Church at Emmerich, in the church of St. Nicholas at Calcar, and in the Minorite cloister of Cleves, although the carvings are inferior in

Jolly Friar and Tinker.
(*Minorite Cloister in Cleves.*)

artistic execution to those of Kempen.   At Cleves are also representations of a man riding backwards on a pig; a man stroking a cat; two mendicant monks, one holding a fire-pot and the other a bellows; the same monks fighting; a friar and a tinker having a jollification together; and a cloven-hoofed animal reading a breviary and supposed to be the devil; unfortunately for this interpretation the German devil is not cloven-footed, but solipedous, having a hoof like that of a horse. The creature is evidently meant to be a stag, which in the beast-epos discharges the grave functions of an ecclesiastic. At Calcar the hare plays the bagpipe, and on the back of one of the stalls reclines a queer man-monster with the breasts of a woman, the feet of a goat, fins on his legs, faces on his shoulders and knees, and eyes in his hips, reading a book. At Emmerich a goat nibbling a grape vine exemplifies the fable of the goat as gardener, and a man sitting between two stools illustrates the vice of indecision and the danger of playing fast and loose with principles.

It may be added, in concluding this portion of the subject, that the church edifices of the Netherlands were formerly richly adorned with paintings and sculptures of a symbolical, satirical, and didactic character, but that they have been nearly all destroyed. The work of demolition, begun by Catholic iconoclasts, was continued by Calvinistic reformers, and completed by French radicals and revolutionists.

CHAPTER V

WHIMSEYS OF ECCLESIOLOGY AND SYMBOLOGY

Universality of the symbolism of the cross—Cruciform phenomena in nature—The sign of the cross in the Old Testament, and its prefigurative significance—Wonder-working power of the cross in Jewish history — Its presence in the Garden of Eden and in the Hebrew alphabet—The cosmos has the form of a cross—Influence of the doctrine of the Trinity upon art—Trinitarian suggestions in the material creation—Mystic meanings in sacred architecture—Symbolism of bells and significance of orientation—Superstitious regard for the points of the compass—Transition from christolatry to hagiolatry —Subtilities of ecclesiology— Meagreness of Hebrew mythology—Exercise of the mythopœic faculty by the Rabbis — Early Christian opposition to the theatre— Theatrical rites and indecent amusements in churches and cloisters—Feast of Fools, etc.—Analogy between the anatomy of the ass and the architecture of a cathedral —Jewish and Christian reverence for the ass—Feast of the Ass—Symbolism swallowed up in buffoonery—Traffic in holy relics—Satirized in Heywood's play of *The Four P.P.*—Anatomical peculiarities of saints—Queer freaks in sacred osteology—Specimens of relics in Catholic churches — Miraculous power of self-multiplication— Choice collection of Frederic the Wise—Anti-Semitic sculptures in Christian churches—Coarse relief ridiculing the Jews at Wittenberg, and its interpretation by Luther —Similar carvings in other cities—Decrees of John the Good and Frederic the Hohenstaufe concerning usury —Classical myths in Christian art—Orpheus a prototype of Christ—Bacchus and the Lord's vineyard—Greek comic poets adored as Christian saints — Isis as the Virgin Mary—Crude symbolism of early Christian art—Influence of Pagan antiquity—The peacock as a Christian emblem—Moralization of the myth of Argus and Io—Sirens and centaurs in architecture—The Sigurd Saga —Weighing of souls—Recording angels and devils—Woman as an emissary of Satan—The devil in Christian art—Dance of death—Oldest representation of it—Its democratic character and popularity—Manuscripts with miniatures—Holbein's drawings — Sensational sermons of Honoré de Sainte Marie—Modern delineations of the theme by Rethel, Seitz, Lührig, and others.

As the cross was the symbol of human redemption, and the whole creation since the Fall was supposed to have been groaning and travailing together in longing for the advent of the Messiah and the consummation of the Atonement, the Fathers of the Church and the later defendants of the faith, Tertullian, Justin Martyr, Jerome, Origen, Jacobus de Voragine, and Hrabanus Maurus, imagined they discovered cruciform and cruciferous phenomena everywhere in animate and inanimate nature, and laid great stress upon this fancy as an incontestable proof of the divine origin of Christianity. Furthermore, as the Jewish people was the special channel through which this salvation was to be received, the literary and historical records of the Jews were assumed to be full of allusions to the cross, and their religious rites were interpreted as having no purpose or validity except as prophecies and prefigurations of it. We are told that man was created in the form of a cross, a curious and characteristic example of what logicians call hysteron-proteron,

or what in common parlance is said to be putting
the cart before the horse, since the cross took this
shape because, as an instrument of human punishment and torture, it was made to fit the man.
Again, as a primitive physico-psychology resolved
man into seven elements, four of the body and
three of the soul, so the cross is composed of four
notches and three pieces of wood. Three multiplied
by four makes twelve, and this number corresponds
to the sum of the commandments of the Old (ten)
and New (two) Testaments. Four and three form
respectively the basis of the quadrivium and the
trivium, which together constitute the seven liberal
arts, and comprise the whole cycle of human
knowledge. The cross was made of wood, because
it was through a tree that man fell, and by a tree
he must be raised up and redeemed. Indeed some
typologists are sufficiently strenuous to maintain
that the cross was originally a tree in the Garden
of Eden, where it grew in the form of the Hebrew
letter Tau (T), that Adam and Eve hid themselves
behind it, after they had sinned and when they
heard the voice of God, and that the blood of the
murdered Abel cried out from under it, thus
prefiguring the expiatory blood of Christ. It was
a branch of this tree that Moses cast into the
waters of Marah to make them sweet, and the great
lawgiver's wonder-working wand was a piece of
the same wood. The world itself is constructed in
the shape of a cross, whose four points correspond
to the four cardinal points or intersections of the

horizon with the meridian. Birds cannot rise in
the air and fly unless their wings are extended in
the form of a cross; men assume this attitude in
prayer and in swimming; a ship cannot sail without making the sign of the cross with the mast
and the yard-arms; and the spade with which man
tills the ground, toiling in the sweat of his brow as
the penalty of his transgression, is cruciform. A
poet and divine of the seventeenth century has put
these forced conceits into a verse quite worthy of
the theme—

> "Who can blot out the cross, which th' instrument
> Of God dewed on me in the sacrament?
> Who can deny me power and liberty
> To stretch mine arms, and mine own cross to be?
> Swim, and at every stroke thou art thy cross!
> The mast and yard make one when seas do toss.
> Look down, thou spy'st ever crosses in small things;
> Look up, thou seest birds raised on crossed wings.
> All the globe's frame and sphere is nothing else
> But the meridian's crossing parallels."

In the twelfth chapter of the Epistle of Barnabas,
the act of Moses in stretching out his hands, in
order that Israel might overcome Amalek in battle,
is said to signify the power of the cross. The
same interpretation is given to the words of Isaiah:
"I have spread out my hands all the day unto
a rebellious people," which mystic christology
explains as the rejection of the crucified Saviour
by the Jews. The youthful David prevailed over
Goliath because he had a cross-shaped staff in his
hand, to which alone he owed his victory. The

two sticks which the widow of Zarephath gathered
to cook a cake with, she held in the form of a
cross, and it was the wonder-working virtue of this
sign that caused the barrel of meal to waste not,
and the cruse of oil not to fail; afterwards the
prophet Elijah restored her son to life by stretching
himself three times upon the child in the form of
a cross and in adoration of the Trinity. The
faggot which Isaac bore on his shoulders to the
place of sacrifice took the same shape, and it was
for this reason that God sent an angel to arrest
the hand of Abraham, and accepted a ram for a
burnt-offering instead of his son. That the brazen
serpent which Moses put upon a pole prefigured
the Crucifixion is not a matter of the slightest
doubt, even to the most enlightened orthodox
hermeneutician of the present day. St. Jerome
was so sure of this that he did not scruple to
translate "in cruce" the phrase which means
simply "upon a pole," and is so rendered in the
Septuagint (ἐν δοκῷ); and an eminent American
divine recently declared that the efficacy of the
brazen serpent in healing the children of Israel
was due solely to its typical connection with the
atoning death of Christ. The fact that Tau, the
imaginary symbol of the cross, is the last letter of
the Hebrew alphabet, was adduced as conclusive
proof that Judaism, in reality the most intensely
tribal of all religions, and reflecting more fully
than any other the life and character of the race
that originated it, existed merely as a system of

shadowy types, having for its whole end and aim
the gospel of the cross.[1] The same sort of reasoning has discovered a profound significance in the
accidental resemblance of the Roman numeral X
to St. Andrew's cross (*crux decussata*), which must
therefore bear some mystic relation to the decalogue.

The pascha, according to Justin Martyr, was a
symbolic adumbration of the Crucifixion. " For
the lamb which was roasted was so placed as to
resemble the figure of a cross ; with one spit it
was pierced longitudinally, from the tail to the
head ; with another it was transfixed through the
shoulders, so that the fore legs became extended."
However natural it may have been for Paul, as a
Jew, to speak of Christ metaphorically as " our
Passover," it is little creditable to the critical
acumen and logical perception of later theologians
that they should have taken this figure of speech
literally, and reared an imposing christological
superstructure on the unsubstantial basis of a
trope. The smearing of the door-posts with blood
in the celebration of the Jewish feast, says Justin
Martyr, has direct reference to the death of the
Redeemer, " because the Greek word to smear,
χρίεσθαι, and the word Christ are the same." As
smearing is only another term for anointing, and
Christ means anointed, and is the Greek synonym

---

[1] " Unde non inconvenienter reor quod sicut omnium
elementorum finis est, ita totidem librorum veteris Testa-
menti finis est crux."—Paschasius Radbert, *In Lam. Jer.
Bibl. Patrum*, xiv. 773.

of the Hebrew Messiah (*mâshiah*), there is nothing very startling in such an etymological coincidence.

Before the twelfth century Christ was represented as fastened to the cross with four nails, one in each hand and foot; but out of deference to the doctrine of the Trinity it was deemed necessary to use only three nails; the feet were therefore made to rest upon a wooden support, held to the upright beam by a single nail. Soon afterwards the simpler method was devised of placing one foot upon the other with a spike driven through both of them. Cimabue was the first to adopt this mode of arranging the feet in painting; and it was in the twentieth year of his age that the celebration of the Feast of the Holy Trinity in the Romish Church was authorized and enjoined by the Synod of Arles (1260). This is but one example of the far-reaching and permanent influence of ecclesiastical decrees and the promulgation of dogmas upon art.

The legends of the Holy Rood surpass in extravagance and absurdity all that pagan Germans ever fabled of the sacred ash Yggdrasil, or Brahmans of their sacrificial post, the Yupa, or Buddhists of the Bôdhitree. With what persistence and apparent pleasure the theological mind still continues to run in this old and abandoned rut, is startlingly and depressingly revealed in a paper on " Vestiges of the Blessed Trinity in the Material Creation," published in *The Dublin Review* for January 1893 by the Rev. John S. Vaughan, who finds traces of

this doctrine "written large across the whole face
of nature," and everywhere suggested by "such
familiar things as rocks, mountains, seas, and
lakes." He discovers "the mystery of the Trinity"
in the fact that every object has three dimensions,
that a plant is composed of seed, stalk, and flower;
that life is "vegetative, sensitive, and rational";
that matter is solid, fluid, and gaseous; that time is
past, present, and future; and above all, that there
are "three fundamental colours," which "dissolve
in the unity of white light." Red, he says, is the
caloric ray, and corresponds to the Father, the
source of vital warmth and energy; the yellow is
the luminous ray, and corresponds to the Son,
"the Light of the world"; the blue is the chemical
or actinic ray, and corresponds to the Holy Spirit.
If cucumbers or melons, he adds, be placed under
glass absorbing the blue ray, they will grow rapidly
and put forth luxuriant blossoms, but soon fade
away without bearing fruit, and this phenomenon
he calls "a physical reflection of the Christian
precept, 'Quench not the Spirit.'" Only an intellect that had been wont to feed upon the husks
of hermeneutic theology, to the exclusion of all
wholesomer nutriment, could conceive of such
twaddle, and offer it to an enlightened public as
an argument from analogy. The wonder is that
he did not go more deeply into the exact and
natural sciences, and make the triangle, the trefoil,
and the trilobite a three-fold confirmation of Trinitarianism. The investigator who puts Nature to

the rack, and questions her like an inquisitor with
the boot and the thumbkin, can easily extort from
her a confession of the truth of any whimsey he
may choose to entertain.

William Durand, in his *Rationale Divinorum
Officiorum*, printed in 1459 by Gutenberg and Fust
at Mayence, makes every portion of the church
edifice full of symbolic significance. The erudite
and ingenious ecclesiologist gives free rein to his
fancy, and discovers mystic meanings in the structure, of which the architect had not the faintest
presentiment. The latter seems, therefore, to have
"builded better than he knew," and to have put
unconsciously into his work more things than he
ever dreamed of in draughting his designs, just as
the great poets, Dante, Shakespeare, and Goethe,
have embodied in their writings many deep
thoughts of which they themselves were utterly
ignorant, and which would have been wholly lost to
the world if some learned and acute commentator
had not taken pains to point them out. Thus,
according to Durand, the stones represent the
faithful; the lime, which binds the stones together,
is fervent love and charity; its mixture with sand
refers to "actions performed for the temporal good
of our brethren"; the water, that serves to mix the
lime and sand, is an emblem of the Holy Spirit;
and "as stones cannot adhere without mortar, so
man without charity cannot enter as an element
into the construction of the heavenly Jerusalem."

Also bells, being made of brass, are shriller and

louder than the trumpets of the law, and denote that God, who under the old dispensation was known only to the Jews, is now proclaimed to the whole world; the durable material out of which they are formed indicates that the truths of the Gospel are not to be superseded, but will endure to the end of time; the hardness of this material signifies the fortitude of the Christian apostle, to whom it is said: " I have given thee a forehead more hard than their forehead." Paul's assertion: " I am become as sounding brass," proves that the bell typifies the mouth of the preacher, whose tongue, like that of the bell, strikes both sides, expounding and proclaiming both Testaments; it shows also that the preacher should, on one side, correct vice in himself, and, on the other side, reprove it in his hearers. The wooden frame on which the bell is suspended stands for the cross; the iron fastening it to the wood is the binding force of moral duty, which is inseparable from the cross. The wheel by which the bell is rung is the preacher's mind, through which the knowledge of the divine law passes into the understanding of the people; and the three cords or strands of the bell-rope denote the threefold character of Scripture, consisting of history, allegory, and morality. As the rope descends from the wooden trestle to the hand, so the mystery of the cross descends to the hand and produces good works; while the upward and downward motion of the rope shows that Scripture speaks of high things and low things, or, in other words, is to be interpreted literally and mystically.

Curiously enough, there are still educated persons who earnestly pursue researches and fondly indulge in speculations of this sort, and seem to be edified thereby. In a book on *Symbolisms in the Churches of the Middle Ages*, written by J. Mason Neable and Benjamin Webb, and translated into French with an introduction by the Abbé Bourassée (Tours, 1857), the authors, as staunch Catholics, regard the use of the ogive in Protestant churches as a desecration of this symbol of the Holy Trinity. No Catholic architect, they declare, should design a triple window for a dissenting or heretical sect (including the Established Church of England), or introduce the trefoil into such building, since this use of them would be a " sacrilegious prostitution of sacred architecture, which is the voice of the Church." The only wonder is, from this point of view, that the Creator should permit clover and other trifoliate plants to grow in Protestant cemeteries or tricuspid molars in a heretic's mouth, and that an angry and outraged Deity does not strike the impious Unitarian dead who dares to sit on a three-legged stool, or presumes to steep his tea on a tripod.

Touching the signification of orientation in ecclesiastical architecture, Gregory the Great, in his exposition of Ezekiel xl. 6, says the east gate of the temple in the prophet's vision designates Jesus Christ. "Who else can be meant by this gate

but our Lord and Redeemer, who is to us the gate
of heaven, as it is written, ' No man cometh unto
the Father but by Me'; and again, ' He that
entereth not in by the door . . . the same is a
thief and a robber'; and then soon afterwards, ' I
am the door.' He it is of whom Zechariah said,
' Behold the man, whose name is the East.' [1] The
gate looking toward the East refers, therefore,
to Him who has shown us the way to the source of
light." One cannot but admire the cogency of the
illustrious pope's reasoning, and the peculiar perti-
nence of his scriptural citations.

According to the Talmud, the manifestations of
God are revealed in the West in distinction from
the East, toward which the heathen and the heretics
(Essenes) turn their faces in their devotions.
Patristic superstition, on the contrary, looked upon
the West as the seat of darkness, and the abode of
demons; for this reason, the rose-window was
placed high up in the western wall of the church,
as the light of the Gospel that is thus made visible
to those sitting in darkness, and "turneth the
shadow of death into the morning." [2] The towers
at the western end of the edifice, with their
bells, were intended to terrify and discomfit the
demons, and, at the same time, to summon the

---

[1] The passage (Zech. vi. 12) reads in the Vulgate : "Ecce
vir, oriens nomen ejus." In the original, the word here
translated "oriens" means "springing up," and in our
English version is rendered "the Branch."

[2] Cf. Lactantius, *Divin. Instit.*, ii. 10 ; Hieronym, *In Amos*
and *In Ezech.*

nations to Christ, who in the earliest churches
was seated over the western entrance to receive
them. After the twelfth century, when the dread
of the last judgment, which it was supposed
would take place at the end of the eleventh
century and introduce the millennium, had completely passed away, the space above the doorway was usually occupied by the image of the
saint to whom the church was dedicated, thus
marking a transition from christolatry to hagiolatry. The sculptures of the doorway plane,
and the paintings of the Catharine-wheel windows,
very frequently represented the revolt of the
angels, as may be seen in Freiburg Minster, and
in the cathedral of St. John in Lyons. The
North is the region of meteorological devils,
which, under the dominion and leadership of the
" Prince of the power of the air," produce storms
and convulsions in nature, and foster unruly
passions and deeds of violence in man. The evil
principle, as embodied in unclean beasts and
exhibited in obscene and lascivious actions, was
properly portrayed in the sculptures and paintings
on the north side of the church, which was assigned
to Satan and his satellites, and known as "the
black side." On the other hand, the South shared
the sacred character of the East, and was consecrated to saints and martyrs and the famous
doctors of theology and sturdy defenders of the
faith. On the walls and in the windows toward
the south are depicted the triumphs of Christianity,

the millennial reign of Christ, the worship of the
Lamb, and similar scenes.   Does not the prophet
Habakkuk say that God came from Teman, and
does not Teman mean South ?   What more conclusive proof could any rational and not utterly
carnal mind desire ?

In the first half of the fifth century, Eucherius,
Bishop of Lyons, wrote a book of formulas of
spiritual knowledge (*Liber Formularum Spiritualis
Intelligentiæ*), modelled after the *Clavis* of Melito,
in which this symbolism of the points of the compass is elaborately amplified and explained.   The
south signifies the " fervour of faith "; " the
streams in the south," spoken of by the Psalmist
(cxxvi. 4), refer to the effluence of the Holy Spirit ;
the ardently erotic and highly poetic passage in
Solomon's Song (iv. 16), " Awake, O north wind ;
and come, thou south," is interpreted as equivalent
to the words, " Get thee behind me, Satan ; and
draw near to me, O divine Spirit."

Durand finds some esoteric meaning, known
only to ecclesiologists, in every part and proportion
of the sacred structure.   " Its length indicates
long-suffering, which patiently endures adversity
and affliction, waiting to reach the heavenly home.
Its breadth is the largeness of Christian charity,
which embraces friends and foes.   Its height is
the measure of the lofty hope of eternal happiness."
Every joist and buttress, every stone and timber
from the crypt to the corona of the cornice, every
arch and pinnacle, the lantern of the dome, and the

weather-cock on the steeple, is made to yield some
mystic quality, or convey some moral lesson.
" The panes of the windows," according to Claude
Villette (*Raisons de l'Office*, Paris, 1601), " are the
Scriptures, which communicate the light of truth
coming from above and ward off the wind, snow,
and hail of heresies, false doctrines, and schisms,
sent by the father of lies. The frames, in which
the panes of glass are firmly set, signify the
Œcumenical Councils by which the Scriptures are
interpreted and upheld, and the doctrines they
teach made manifest. The size of the windows
shows the depth and magnitude of Holy Writ,
incomprehensible to the natural man ; their circular
form denotes that the Church is complete in herself,
and consistent in all her doctrines."

Such are a few specimens of the subtilties and
trivialities of mediæval and modern symbologists,
which suffice to illustrate the general tendency of
their speculations, and the excess of abstrusity
and absurdity to which they carried their queer
conceits.

Hebrew literature has only a very meagre
mythology, compared with the literature of India
or Greece or any ancient people of Aryan blood.
The jealously vindictive and supreme ascendency
of the Jewish tribal god did not favour the growth
and exercise of the mythopœic faculty, but made
every attempt to foster it fatal alike to the safety
and comfort of the individual, and to the consoli-
dation and continuity of the national life. But the

Hebrew imagination, although debarred from the populous regions of Olympus and Tartarus by the stern command of Jehovah, " Thou shalt have no other gods before Me," would not be cheated of its rights, and mythologized in less inviting but unforbidden directions, grazing and ruminating on the stubbled fields of scholia, and getting what nutriment could be extracted from such dry and sapless fodder. In this wise, the Rabbis succeeded in evolving a whole system of myths and fables out of their sacred books and ceremonial institutions. Noah's dove, which returned to the ark with an olive branch, had received it, according to the Talmudists, from the hand of God ; and out of this assumption was developed a most luxuriant and wide-spreading banyan forest of allegory. The Sabbath was also personified and made to appear before the seat of God, like Schiller's poet before the throne of Zeus, and to complain of its isolation in being set apart as a holy day. Jehovah regretted that he could not change this condition of things without destroying the consecrated character of the seventh day, but he conferred upon it, in compensation for its loneliness, the privilege of being for ever united with the chosen people in nuptial ties, and of fostering as the fruit of this union the so-called Sabbath-soul of Israel. And the Lord blessed this marriage, and declared it to be sacred and indissoluble, and absolutely essential to the happiness and prosperity of the Jewish nation. When the Roman government forbade the observance of the Sabbath by severe penalties, Rabbi Simon Ben Jochai went to Rome and succeeded in having the prohibition removed, using this fable in his interview with the emperor in order to enforce the claims of the Sabbath as a divine institution, indispensable to the welfare of Israel. There is an apologue by Rabbi Jehuda Bar Shalom, in which the rite of circumcision is the chief actor, and the Sabbath plays a subordinate and less commendable part, being too much given up to convivial pleasures.

The Rabbis mythologized even with the letters of the alphabet, all of which, from Aleph to Tau, appear in person before Jehovah to present their respective claims to consideration, and indulge in the most wearisome and nonsensical harangues. This sort of apologue arose from the peculiar sacredness attached to the text of the law or Thora, which was identified with the wisdom personified in the eighth chapter of Proverbs, and with the uncreated Word, which was with God before the creation of the world, and afterwards became the incarnate Logos of the Gnostics and the synonym of Christ.[1]

This superstitious reverence for the letter of the law was transmitted to the early Christians, who naturally applied it to their own sacred records, declaring them to be theopneustic, or " given by

[1] Cf. *Die Fabel im Talmud und Midrasch*, von Dr. Samuel Back, in *Monatsschrift für Geschichte und Wissenschaft des Judenthums*. Krotoschin, 1880-81.

inspiration of God." Out of this feeling, dogmatic theology easily developed the doctrine of plenary inspiration, which the Reformers and later Protestants used as an effective weapon, opposing the infallible authority of Holy Writ to the infallible authority of the Holy See, and which was finally carried to that extreme of fetichistic bibliolatry that has been such a serious obstacle to the spread of knowledge and to the progress of the race, and is now just beginning to be set aside by scientific research and sound criticism.

At the beginning of the Christian era the theatre had fallen into decay, and hardly anything remained of it except the brutal butcheries of the amphitheatre, and the noisy and turbulent diversions of the circus. It was natural enough that the early Christians should have detested and denounced such performances. Actors as a class were anathematized and declared accursed by ecclesiastical authorities. A capitulary of Charlemagne, inspired and dictated by the Church, declared all players (*histriones*) to be infamous and incompetent to testify in courts of justice. The Provincial Councils of Mayence, Tours, and Chalons in 813 decreed the histrionic profession ignominious, and excommunicated all clergymen who countenanced theatrical representations. In 1186, Philippe Auguste issued an edict banishing actors from his realm.

But the passion for the theatre is too deeply rooted in human nature to be easily eradicated;

and the Church, finding all efforts to suppress it
unavailing, determined to direct and utilize it.
Accordingly theatrical elements were introduced
into the celebration of Christian festivals, which
were mostly of pagan origin. The old Roman
Lupercalia became the feast of the Purification;
the Saturnalia survived in the Carnival; the Robi-
galia, consisting of offerings in the fields to the
god Robigus (or according to Ovid, *Fast.*, iv. 905-35,
the goddess Robigo) to avert mildew, gave rise to
the processions of Rogation week; the pagan feast
of the dead is celebrated as All Souls' Day; and
St. John's Day and Christmas are relics of sol-
stitial worship and fulfilments of the Baptist's
prophecy : " He must increase, but I must decrease."

At a very early period the Church began to
invest her solemn rites with a theatrical character.
At Christmas, children robed as angels sang songs
in differents parts of the sacred edifice above the
choir, a group of shepherds passed through the
transept towards a stable built behind the altar,
and were met by two priests costumed as midwives,
who inquired : " What seek ye ? " The shepherds
replied : " Our Saviour, the Christ." " The child
is here," was the response, and all knelt before the
crib in the presence of the mother, and chanted the
Salve Virgo. On the feast of the Epiphany the
three kings entered through the chief portal and
advanced in gorgeous array to the place where the
infant lay and worshipped Him, presenting their
gifts. They then went out through the door of

the transept in accordance with the statement that
the wise men "departed into their own country
another way." Priests in albs mounted up on
towers to represent the Ascension ; and at Pentecost
a dove descended from the arched ceiling of the
church to denote the Holy Spirit coming down
from heaven. On Palm Sunday an immense crowd
of people approached the city from the country,
strewing branches in the way of a man riding on
an ass ; as the procession drew near, the priests
and choristers sang : " Lift up your heads, O ye
gates."

Such are a few examples of the childish and
clumsy manner in which the Church sought to
render her ceremonies more vivid and impressive
as well as more entertaining. This rude dramatiz-
ation of the principal incidents of the Gospel story
was gradually extended to religious legends, thus
giving rise to semi-liturgic mysteries, miracle-plays,
and moralities, and leading to a revival of the
secular drama. The clergy encouraged hilarity
and gaiety, ·because they wished to attract the
vulgar throng, and to keep their hold on the
masses by providing for their amusement. In this
desire originated such festivals as the Feast of
Fools and of Innocents, and the Ass's Feast.

At Rouen at Christmas, twelve of the clergy,
dressed to represent six Jews and six Gentiles,
were placed respectively on the right and the left
of a pyre burning in the centre of the choir. Two
young priests then call upon them to recognize and

revere the mystery of the divine Incarnation. They refuse to do so, and in order to convince them of the truth, the principal personages of the Bible are made to appear : Moses with long beard and horns, the greater and lesser prophets, Balaam on his ass with the messengers of Balak and the angel standing in the way, Shadrach, Meshach, and Abednego in the fiery furnace, apostles, sibyls, and Vergil, who had foretold the advent of Christ, and many other witnesses of the true God. This overwhelming testimony admits of no contradiction, and the stubborn Jews and ignorant Gentiles are converted from the error of their ways. Whether the burning pyre was reserved as an *ultima ratio* in case of final obduracy is not stated, but would seem to be suggested. These spectacles were first given in the nave of the church, but, as the throng increased, they were transferred to the open air, and scaffoldings were erected for the purpose in front of the cathedral.

In 1212, the Council of Paris forbade the nuns to celebrate the Feast of Fools, on account of the excesses and scandals which it occasioned. In 1245, Archbishop Odon found it necessary to suppress the licentious amusements of the nuns in the convents of Rouen, and mentions especially their accustomed dissolute sports ("ludibria consueta"), and their dances either among themselves or with secular priests ("aut inter vos seu cum secularibus choreas ducendo"). These dances, which were performed on the great ecclesiastical feast-days, were accompanied by comical and scurrilous songs and other unseemly exhibitions. The chapter of the cathedral of Senlis issued in 1497 an order permitting the lower clergy to "enjoy their diversions before the principal portal of the church on the eve of the Epiphany, provided they do not sing infamous songs, with ribald and obscene words, or dance in a lewd manner, all of which things," they add, "took place on last Innocents' Day." In an old collection of forty sermons on the destruction of Nineveh (*Sermones quadraginta de destructione Nineva*, Paris, 1525), the author asserts that priests and monks were wont to visit nunneries both by night and by day, and to perform indecent dances with the inmates; "as to the rest," he concludes, "I keep silent, lest perchance I may offend pious ears."

Even within the memory of persons still living, the midnight masses, especially in France, were attended by all sorts of rude horse-play, such as strewing the pavement of the church with "fulminating peas," which exploded when trodden upon, barricading the aisles with chairs or cords, filling the stoups with ink, and embracing young girls in "the dim religious light" of the chapels.

A very queer notion was entertained and inculcated in the middle ages, and seems still to prevail in some less enlightened portions of Christendom, that there is a mysterious and far-reaching analogy between the anatomy of an ass and the architecture of a cathedral. Thus

M. Jérôme Bugeau, in his *Chansons Populaires des Provinces de l'Ouest* (Niort, 1866), gives the following catechism taken down from the lips of children in Angoumois (now in the department of Charente), and evidently forming an important part of their religious instruction—

"*Priest.* What do the two ears of the ass signify?

"*Children.* The two ears of the ass signify the two great patron saints of our city.

"*Priest.* What does the head of the ass signify?

"*Children.* The head of the ass signifies the great bell, and the rein is the clapper of the great bell in the tower of the cathedral dedicated to the patron saints of our city.

"*Priest.* What does the throat of the ass signify?

"*Children.* The throat of the ass signifies the chief portal of the cathedral dedicated to the patron saints of our city.

"*Priest.* What does the body of the ass signify?

"*Children.* The body of the ass signifies the whole structure of the cathedral dedicated to the patron saints of our city."

In this style the catechism goes on, showing the analogies or rather the homologies between the animal and the edifice; the four legs of the ass are the four principal pillars of the building; the heart, liver, kidneys, and other internal organs are the lamps; the paunch is the poor-box, in which the pious put their offerings; the skin is the cope worn by the clergy during divine service; the tail is the aspergill for sprinkling holy water on the people; even the buttocks are not omitted, but stand for "the beautiful stoup, which holds the holy water in the cathedral dedicated to the patron saints of our city."

The Angoumois catechism offers a fair specimen of the weak and vapid pap with which the youthful mind is usually fed in clerical schools, and especially in those conducted by the Jesuits. The late Dr. Döllinger of Munich relates his experience with a student, who had received his preparatory training at such an institute. In answer to the question, "What is that branch of knowledge which we call theology?" the candidate for holy orders replied with the perfunctory promptness of a parrot: "Theology is that branch of knowledge which has St. Catherine for its patroness." "But what is the branch of knowledge of which St. Catherine is the patroness?" asked the doctor, and received the ready response: "St. Catherine is the patroness of theology;" and no ingenuity of interrogation availed to get the young man out of this vicious hagiological circle. It is by the stupefying effects of such teaching that the supreme goal of Jesuitical discipline, namely, the sacrifice of the intellect ("il sacrificio dell' intelletto"), can be most perfectly attained.

It may seem strange that the ass should have been chosen as the homologue of the cathedral; but it must be remembered that in the Orient this animal is noted for its beauty, strength, and intelligence, and that our domestic donkey is the

degenerate scion of a noble stock. There is also
reason to believe that this creature was an object
of peculiar reverence to the early Christians, owing
probably to the fact that Christ made His triumphal
entry into Jerusalem sitting upon an ass, and that
the animal still bears the sign of the cross formed
by a black bar across the shoulders intersecting the
line of the back. Plutarch (*Sympos.*, lib. iv. 5)
and Tacitus (*Hist.*, lib. v.) assert that the ass was
adored by the Jews because it discovered springs
of water in the desert during the exodus, and this
tradition might have easily been accepted by the
Christians as typical of the Saviour, the well-spring
of eternal life. Tertullian says: "There are some
who imagine that our God has the head of an ass,"
and indignantly denies the truth of this statement,
which, nevertheless, seems to have been quite
generally entertained. Indeed, this ardent and
eloquent apologist himself declares that the enemies
of the Gospel exposed publicly a picture representing a person with a book in his hand and
wearing a long robe, but with the ears and legs of
an ass, and under it the inscription : "The Christian
God with the ass's hoof." Again, Cecilius Felix
remarks in the *Dialogue* of Minutius Felix: "I
hear that this basest of creatures is worshipped by
the Christians, though I know not upon what
inane persuasion." In a rude drawing scrawled on
the walls of the barracks or guard-room on the
Palatine, is a man kneeling before a crucifix, on
which is a human being with an ass's head, and a

legend informs us that this person is "Anaxomenos worshipping his God." Epiphanius affirms that the Gnostics believed that the Lord of Sabaoth had an ass's head.[1]

In the church of Saint-Esprit, a suburb of Bayonne, is the wooden effigy of an ass bearing the Virgin and the infant Jesus; the latter is holding a bird in His hand. It was originally in the convent of St. Bernard, built in the thirteenth century and now demolished, and is still known as the ass of St. Bernard. One belonged to each of the cathedrals of Rheims and Paris; there is one in Santa Maria in Organo at Verona, and formerly nearly every church was provided with such an image, of which a good specimen is now preserved in the Germanic Museum at Nuremberg. It was not an object of worship, but was used sometimes instead of the living animal in celebrating the Feast of the Ass, which took place at Christmas in honour of Christ's entry into Jerusalem, and likewise on the fourteenth of January, as a memorial of the flight into Egypt, and was one of the most popular of Church festivals.

There is an old tradition that the ass on which Christ made His entry into Jerusalem left Judea immediately after the Crucifixion, and passing over the sea dry-shod to Rhodes, Cyprus, Malta, Sicily, and Aquileia, finally reached Verona, where it lived to a very old age. After its death its bones were collected and deposited in the belly of the wooden ass of Santa Maria in Organo, which was made as

[1] Cf. *Annales Archéologiques*, xv. p. 383.

a memorial of it and in its exact image. It was
once a popular belief, which may yet linger among
the lower class of Veronese, that all the asses of
that region are scions of this sacred stock ; but their
supposed origin does not appear to insure them
less cruel treatment than low-born donkeys are subjected to in all parts of Italy.

An ass caparisoned with a cope and other sacerdotal apparel, and sometimes ridden by a young
girl with an infant in her arms, was met at the
principal entrance of the church by the canons and
other clergy, and conducted up the nave into the
chancel. The officiating priests held in their hands
urns or pitchers full of wine, and goblets of glass
or pewter. The censer contained, instead of the
usual fragrant gums and spices, fat black-pudding
and sausage, which in burning exhaled anything
but a pleasant perfume. The Introit, the Kyrie, the
Gloria, and the Credo were sung in a harsh braying
tone, after which the following ass's litany in Latin
was chanted, the whole body of the clergy and the
congregation joining vociferously as a chorus in the
refrain, which was French—

> " Orientis partibus
> Adventavit asinus,
> Pulcher et fortissimus,
> Sarcinis aptissimus.
> Hez, sire asne, car chantez
> Belle bouche réchignez
> Vous aurez de foin assez,
> Et de l'avoine à planté.

> " Lentus erat pedibus,
> Nisi foret baculus,

Et cum in clunibus,
Pungeret aculeus.
   Hez, sire asne, etc.

" Ecce magnis auribus,
Subjugalis filius,
Asinus egregius,
Asinorum dominus.
   Hez, sire asne, etc.

" Hic, in collibus Sichem
Enutritus sub Rubem
Transiit per Jordanem,
Saliit in Bethlehem.
   Hez, sire asne, etc.

" Saltu vincit hinnulos,
Dagmas et capreolos,
Super dromedarios
Velox madianeos.
   Hez, sire asne, etc.

" Aurum de Arabia
Thus et myrrham de Saba,
Tulit in ecclesia
Virtus asinaria.
   Hez, sire asne, etc.

" Dum trahit vehicula,
Multa cum sarcinula
Illius mandibula
Dura terit pabula.
   Hez, sire asne, etc.

" Cum aristis hordeum
Comedit et carduum
Triticum a palea
Segregant in area.
   Hez, sire asne, etc.

" Amen dicas, asine,
Jam satur ex gramine,
Amen, amen, itera ;
Aspernare vetera.
   Hez, sire asne, etc."

T

This remarkable hymn may be rendered into English as follows—

> "From the regions of the East
> Came the ass, the worthy beast,
> Strong and fair beyond compare,
> Heavy burdens fit to bear.
>   Huzza, Sir Ass, because you chant,
>   Fair mouth, because you bray,
>   You shall have enough of hay,
>   And also oats to plant.

> " Slow of foot the beast would fare,
> Should the staff you on him spare,
> Or should fail with many a thump
> To goad him on and prod his rump.
>   Huzza, Sir Ass, etc.

> " Lo, with what enormous ears
> This subjugal son appears,
> Most egregious ass, we see
> Lord of asses all in thee.
>   Huzza, Sir Ass, etc.

> "He in Sichem's hills was bred,
> Under Reuben's care was fed,
> Passed through Jordan's sacred stream,
> Skipped about in Bethlehem.
>   Huzza, Sir Ass, etc.

> " Leaping he outruns the hind,
> Hart and he-goat leaves behind,
> Dromedaries doth surpass
> This our swift and sturdy ass.
>   Huzza, Sir Ass, etc.

> " Gold from Araby the blest,
> Frankincense that's much in quest,
> To the church a precious fraught
> Asinary strength hath brought.
>   Huzza, Sir Ass, etc.

> " As he draws along the cart
> Heavy-laden to the mart,
> He his jaws doth ever ply,
> Grinding fodder hard and dry.
> Huzza, Sir Ass, etc.

> " Barley with the awn he eats,
> And himself to thistles treats;
> While on threshing-floors are beat
> From the chaff the grains of wheat.
> Huzza, Sir Ass, etc.

> "Amen thou now mayst bray, O ass,
> Satiate with corn and grass ;
> Amen repeat, amen reply,
> And antiquity defy.
> Huzza, Sir Ass, etc."

Sometimes the refrain was simply " Hez, sire ass, hez "; in fact, the service as well as the song varied slightly in different places, and was modified somewhat by circumstances, but the essential character of the performance remained everywhere the same. The music of this chant, which was of a grave and solemn character, befitting a religious service, has been published by M. Félix Clément in his *Choix des principales Séquences des Moyen Âge tirées des Manuscrits.* With a courage born of enthusiasm, M. Clément had this music of the thirteenth century actually performed at the College Stanislas, April 29, 1847, before a select audience, composed chiefly of musicians of the Opera and Conservatoire of Paris, who are said to have received it with applause.[1]

---

[1] Cf. Didron, *An. Arch.*, vii. *et al.*

Not unfrequently this festival began in the morning, and continued without interruption all night till the evening of the following day. The singing of the anthem, *Conductus ad Poculum* (" Brought to the Cup "), was the signal for the distribution of wine among the choristers, who drank very freely, and often got fuddled. While they were thus refreshing themselves with bottles of wine, the ass was regaled with what the transmogrified Bottom so greatly desired, "a bottle of hay" and a bucket of water. With the intonation of the second anthem, *Conductus ad Ludos* ("Brought to the Sports"), the ass was led into the nave of the church, and danced round by the priests and the people, who imitated its bray. After the dance the ass was reconducted into the chancel and provided with fresh rations of provender. The feast ended with the anthem, *Conductus ad Prandium* (" Brought to the Banquet "), which was sung after vespers on the second day, and was an invitation to the final repast.[1] At the close of the service the priest, instead of uttering the usual formula of dismissal, " Ite, missa est," broke forth into a loud " Hee-haw," which he repeated three times as a parting benediction to the worshippers, and a trinal tribute to the animal which formed the centre of interest and of homage in this strange religious ceremony.

There was also a preparatory meeting or con-

[1] Cf. William Hone, *Ancient Mysteries*, p. 165 ; London, 1823.

vocation held on the eve of the feast, when the
clergy in full canonicals went in procession to
meet the ass at the door of the cathedral, accompanied by two choristers, who chanted the following
invocation—

> " Lux hodie, lux letitiæ me judice tristis
>   Quisquis erit, removendus erit, solemnibus istis,
>   Sicut hodie, procul invidia, procul omnia moesta,
>   Læta volunt, quiscumque celebret asinaria festa."

> " O light to-day, O light of joy, I banish every sorrow ;
>   Wherever found, be it expelled from our solemnities to-
>   morrow.
>   Away with strife and grief and care from every anxious
>   heart,
>   And all be filled with mirth who in the Ass's Feast take
>   part."

The ass was then conducted to a table, usually in
the vestry, at which the dean sat with two pre-
bendaries, who read the order of proceedings as
arranged for the following day, and the names and
offices of the participants. The ass, offering no
objections, was supposed to give silent consent to
the programme, which was accordingly approved.

M. Pierre Louvret, in his *Histoire du Diocèse de
Beauvais*, published in 1635, gives an account of
the manner in which this feast was celebrated in
the cathedral of that city, whose bishops bore the
rank and title of princes, and held the highest place
among the civil and ecclesiastical dignitaries of the
realm. The ass in a cope, sculptured on an archi-
volt in St. Peter's Church in Aulnay, and dating
from the twelfth century, is a survival of the festive

observance just described; indeed, the ass in sacerdotal vestments, painted in fresco, or more frequently carved in relief, may be seen in many sacred edifices.

In an essay entitled *L'Âne au Moyen-Âge*, printed in Didron's *Annales Archéologiques* (vols. vii., xv., and xvi.), M. Félix Clément interprets the ass as a symbol of the Saviour, and thus comments on the first verse of the ass's litany: " It is from the Orient that the light comes to us; the Orient is the cradle of the human race; from the Orient came the wise men, the Magi, with whose gifts the ass was laden; in the Orient appeared the star which guided them to Bethlehem." He also quotes St. Bernard, who calls Jesus Christ *Oriens in vespere. Pulcher* refers to the moral beauty of Christ, *fortissimus* to His strength in overcoming the great adversary, the prince of darkness, and in conquering death and hell, and *sarcinis aptissimus* to His fitness to bear the burden of a sinful world, symbolized by the heavy weight of the Cross. In the fourth verse Sichem is mentioned because it was the ancient capital of Israel and the chief place of worship of the Samaritans, and Bethlehem because Christianity began there. The superiority of the ass to the other animals enumerated in the fifth verse signifies that Christ surpassed in excellence all the Hebrew prophets. The eighth verse indicates the office of Christ as winnower, who with His fan in His hand will purge the floor, gathering the wheat into the garner, but burning the chaff with unquenchable fire. *Aspernare vetera* implies that old things have passed away, and that the Synagogue has been supplanted by the Church. Even the refrain of the hymn, " Hez, sire asne," is interpreted as an abbreviation of " Hatez vos pas, divin Messie," and an earnest injunction to the Lord Jesus to come quickly and complete the work of human redemption. Nevertheless, M. Clément does not seem to have full confidence in the correctness of this explanation, since he afterwards proposes another theory, by which the ass from the East, so full of strength and courage, becomes a type of the Jewish people, the "depositary and transmitter of the belief in the true God."

But whatever symbolism there may have been originally, or is still discernible to the ecclesiological eye in this feast, was soon swallowed up and lost sight of in gross buffoonery, and the religious service degenerated into a sort of Saturnalian amusement, which suited the coarse tastes of the time, and is not to be judged by our modern sense of the sacredness of things, or by the standards of delicate and even fastidious feeling developed by centuries of intellectual culture and inherited refinement. The age of faith, as it is called, was not at all squeamish, and did not suffer itself to be shocked in the slightest degree by grotesque and farcical exhibitions in sacred places. Mediæval monks and ecclesiastics were neither thin-skinned nor dainty-minded, and, like the lower classes of the people, from which the great majority of them

sprung, they indulged in the coarsest jokes, appre-
ciating and enjoying them all the more when they
were at the expense of their cloth. The Church
aimed to take everything under her control, and
to direct the pleasures as well as to dictate the
penances of the masses. The bishops, as Viollet-le-
Duc observes, preferred to throw open their cathedrals to the crowd, and to permit such jollities
within the consecrated walls, rather than to run the
risk of dangerous fermentations of popular ideas
outside. It was especially necessary to maintain
ecclesiastical jurisdiction and supremacy, and not
let men get the fatal notion into their heads that
they could even indulge in merrimakes and pas-
times otherwise than under the auspices of the in-
dulgent Mother Church. Such a presumption and
precedent would have been as perilous to hierarch-
ical authority as it would be prejudicial to medical
prestige to let a man die without the prescription
of a doctor. Whatever concerned the moral or
material interests of the community, whether it
was to rebuke the vicious habits of mendicant
monks and wandering minstrels, or to exterminate
locusts, weevils, and other destructive vermin by
anathematisms, the Church did not deem it alien
to her office or injurious to her sanctity to draw
within her pale, and to make contributory to her
power and glory.

The capitals of the columns on the doorway
leading to the south aisle of St. Sebald's Church in
Nuremberg are adorned with quaint forms of

beasts which are to be interpreted in part as ministering spirits outside of the precincts of the sanctuary, and in part as types of human weakness under temptation, and especially of priestly frailties. Guy de Munois, Abbot of St. Germain d'Auxerre (1285—1309), had for his official seal the figure of a cowled ape with an abbot's staff in its hand, and the legend, "Abbé de singe air main d'os serre." The seal of the Bishop of Pinon in Picardie was an ape in episcopal robes, with crosier and mitre. Ecclesiastical dignitaries, who took delight in satirizing the infirmities of their order and in caricaturing themselves and their sacred office, would not find anything offensive in celebrating the Feast of the Ass, and would not scruple to permit animals in copes and stoles to be carved on the stalls and portals of consecrated edifices, or to be represented in painting and sculpture in the act of burlesquing the holy Mass and the burial service.

Sincere and even ardent Catholics did not hesitate to ridicule many practices which were authorized and encouraged by the see of Rome. Such was the sale of relics, a scandalous abuse sanctioned by the Church, but satirized by John Heywood, a graduate of Oxford and favourite of the bigoted Queen Mary, a zealous papist, whom the accession of Elizabeth in 1558 forced to take refuge on the Continent at Mechlin, where he died towards the close of the sixteenth century. In a play called "The Four P.P., a very merry Enterlude of a Palmer, a Pardoner, a Pothecary, and a Pedler," this sturdy and scholarly Romanist exposes the frauds perpetrated by preaching friars as itinerant vendors of saints' bones. Pardoner exhibits and extols the wonder-working virtues of his wares, and bids his hearers kiss with devotion

> " Of All-Hallows the blessed jaw-bone."

Pothecary, who claims to be an expert in antiquities of this sort, declares that the relic is in bad odour, and enough to turn the strongest stomach—

> " For by All-Hallows, yet methinketh
> That All-Hallows' breath stinketh."

Pardoner replies that Pothecary must have caught a sniff of his own foul breath, and proceeds to cry his merchandise with the impudence and volubility of a mountebank—

> " Nay, sirs, behold, here may ye see
> The great toe of the Trinitie.
> Who to this toe any money vowth,
> And once may role it in his mouth,
> All his life after, I undertake,
> He shall never be vext with toothake."

To this assurance Pothecary retorts sarcastically—

> " I pray you turn that relique about :
> Either the Trinity had the gout,
> Or else, because it is three toes in one,
> God made it as much as three toes alone."

Pardoner, who has a large assortment of "holy particles," and is not to be bluffed by having a seeming blur cast upon any one of them, brings out another specimen and says—

> "Well, let that pass, and look at this.
> Here is a relique that doth not miss
> To help the least as well as the most:
> This is a buttock-bone of Pentecost."

He has also "a slipper of one of the seven sleepers,"
"an eye-tooth of the Great Turk," and

> "a box full of the humblebees
> That stang Eve as she sat on her knees,
> Tasting the fruit to her forbidden."

Again, in *The Pardoner and the Friar* a similar
assortment of relics is exposed for sale : "the great
toe of the Trinity"; "All-Hallows' jaw-bone," an infallible antidote for poisons ; "of Saint Michael eke
the brain-pan," commended as a specific for head-
ache ; the "bongrace of our gracious lady, which
she wore with her French hood when she went out
as a protection gainst sun-burning"; "a holy Jew's
hip-bone," which, if cooked in the pottage, will cure
a man of jealousy, and inspire him with perfect
confidence in the virtue of his wife, even "had she
been taken with friars two or three." As the pardoner is about to show the pope's bull and other
credentials from Rome, the friar begins his sermon,
and the preaching and peddling go on simultan-
eously, until the two competitors for popular favour
fall to blackguarding each other, and finally come
to blows. The village parson, with the help of
"neighbour Prat," who acts as constable, tries to
separate them ; but his reverence is no match for
the burly friar, and soon finds, to use his own expression, that he has more tow on his distaff than he

can spin, while the pardoner, who proves to be as
adroit in pugilism as in pious mendacity, quickly
"punishes" the officious Prat.

The authors of coarse satires like these were not
heretics or infidels, but staunch adherents of the
Romish Church, who were ready to endure exile
or to suffer death for the faith that was in them.[1]
That their descriptions of this traffic are scarcely
exaggerated is proved by the kind and quantity of
relics still preserved and exposed to adoration in
Catholic churches. In the middle ages, when such
articles were in great request, and the bones of
saints, in the jargon of the exchange, were "lively"
and often became "excited," the economical law of
demand and supply, which is as universal and un-
escapable as that of gravitation, worked in a marvellous and quite miraculous way, and produced some
astounding results.

Some years ago a distinguished anatomist, who
visited an old church on the Hradshin in Prague,
observed that a skeleton in one of the shrines had
two right thigh-bones. It was suggested that this
idiosyncrasy might be due to the transforming effect
of canonization, and some devotees were inclined to
regard it as a sign of peculiar sanctity; but only
the most credulous of the faithful accepted this view
as an adequate explanation of the phenomenon.
It was generally admitted that such abnormities

---

[1] Cf. Dodsley's *Old Plays*, 1. 88, 101, etc.; William Hone's
Ancient Mysteries, 87-88 ; Hazlitt's edition of *The Four P.P.*,
with modernized orthography. London, 1874.

of structure were unbecoming in persons whom
the public had been taught to revere as patterns of
piety, and to imitate as models of perfection ; and
although they may have despised the vanities and
seductions of the flesh during their lives, they ought
not to give offence or occasion for scoffing by any
conspicuous irregularity in the arrangement of their
bones after death. Accordingly an inquest was
held ; the worshipful relics were "sat upon" by a
jury of experts, who, as the result of their investigations, recommended a general overhauling and
reparation of the remains of the saints kept in the
churches of the Bohemian capital. The celebrated
anatomist, Professor Joseph Hyrtl, was induced to
undertake the task, which had to be performed with
the greatest secrecy and circumspection, and he
finally succeeded in ridding the enshrined skeletons
of their most obtrusive deviations from the organism
of the natural man, and establishing a certain
degree of harmony between the provinces of sacred
and scientific osteology.

It must not be inferred, however, that the saints
of Prague were exceptional in their variations from
the common sinful human type. The critical
examination of all the treasuries of relics in Christendom would disclose the remains of holy men
and of godly women not a few, who seem to have
had as many arms as Briareus, and as many legs
as a centipede. It is well known that St. Anna
had three arms, only one less than Vishnu ; and
this tribrachial characteristic appears to have been

hereditary in her family, otherwise it would be difficult to account for the fact that one arm of the Virgin Mary is revered in Rome, another in Nuremberg, and a third in Cologne. St. Vitus was unquestionably quadrumanous; one of his hands is in Sienna and another in Bamberg, whilst his entire skeleton, including both hands, is shown in the cathedral at Prague. Perhaps the anthropologist, who has hitherto searched for "the missing link" among chimpanzees, orang-outangs, and other simian tribes, will at last come upon the object of his quest in the voluminous and wondrous annals of hagiology. Some saints were evidently in the habit of shedding their skulls at different periods of their growth, just as stags throw off their antlers and serpents cast their skins. This was the case with St. Peter, whose skull as a child may be seen in one shrine, while his fully-developed cranium as an adult is kept in another. As a matter of convenience for future collectors, and kind consideration for a devout posterity, such forethought is most remarkable, and cannot be too highly praised. When the abbot Marolles of Amiens was shown a head of John the Baptist, he exclaimed : "Glory be to God, that is the sixth head of the Redeemer's forerunner I have had the good fortune to adore ! "

The miraculous power of self-multiplication with which the "particles" of the saints are endowed extends also to their personal effects. There are now in existence about a dozen equally well authenticated originals of the seamless vesture, upon which the Roman soldiers cast lots. The most celebrated specimen of this garment is the " holy coat " in the cathedral of Trier, where it has been repeatedly exhibited as an object of worship and a source of revenue, and even as recently as 1891 attracted crowds of fetichistic pilgrims. Its history, as recorded in a German poem of the twelfth century entitled *Orendel*, surpasses in extravagance the wildest inventions of classical and Oriental mythology. Scores of churches possess pieces of the true cross, which nevertheless may be seen intact in Paris; the same is the case with Aaron's rod, a portion of which is at Bamberg, although the whole is in an excellent state of preservation at Milan.

The superstitious fondness for sacred relics in the middle ages, like the modern enthusiasm for antiques and masterpieces of the Renaissance, incited the dealers in such wares to wholesale perpetrations of fraud. The skeleton of many a malefactor, whose head was deservedly severed from his body by the executioner's axe, is now revered as the remains of a blessed martyr; and countless bones, set with jewels and deposited in costly shrines, were originally taken from the gallows-pit. That the author of *The Four P.P.* gave a true picture of the extent to which this fraudulent traffic was carried on, can be clearly shown, as we have already suggested, by examining the lists of relics in the older Catholic churches.

Thus, for example, in Santa Prassede at Rome, among other queer things of this kind, are a tooth of St. Peter and one of St. Paul, as well as bits of their respective skulls, a scrap of the Virgin's chemise, a bottle of her milk, and a piece of her sepulchre, fragments of the Saviour's girdle and of His swaddling-clout, the pillar at which He was scourged, some of the earth on which He kneeled in prayer before the Passion, the reed and sponge with which He was given vinegar to drink on the cross, parts of His vesture for which the Roman soldiers cast lots, and three thorns from the crown of thorns; near by, in Santa Croce in Gerusalemme, are the superscription which Pilate put on the cross, one of the thirty pieces of silver paid to Judas, and the finger with which the doubting Thomas was told to touch the print of the nails in the hands of the risen Lord; in the cloister of St. Barbara in Coblence is the fore-skin of the infant Jesus, which in the last century is said to have wrought a startling and somewhat unseemly miracle on one of the nuns. Before the Reformation, Schaffhausen was proud of possessing some of the breath of St. Joseph enclosed in one of the gloves of Nicodemus; Halle boasted of having fragments of Noah's ark, and of the chemise worn by the Virgin during her confinement; and the church of Notre-Dame-en-Vaux at Chalons guarded as a rare treasure the navel of Jesus Christ until 1707, when the rationalistic bishop Noailles had it removed. An additional and

exceedingly strong evidence of the extent to which
this utterly absurd "fad" prevailed, and duped
with vile counterfeits even the shrewdest and most
sensible men, is the fact that Duke Frederic III.,
surnamed the Wise, the Elector of Saxony and
the protector of Luther, had a collection of nearly
four thousand relics, among which were such
choice specimens as milk of the Virgin, yarn which
she spun—the yarn we suspect was of the nautical
sort, and spun at a much later period—remains of
the children slain in Bethlehem, straw and hay
from the manger in which Jesus was born, teeth
and hair of Christ, and portions of His raiment.
Boccaccio, in the *Decameron* (Giorn. vi., Nov. 10),
gives some specimens of Fra Cipolla's sacred collection : the jaw-bone of Lazarus, a feather of the
angel Gabriel, the hood of the seraph which appeared to St. Francis, the toe-nail of a cherub,
some vestments of the Holy Catholic Faith, a finger
of the Holy Ghost, a few rays of the star of Bethlehem, and a vial containing tones of the bells of
Solomon's temple. Curiously enough, the scoffing
poet took a religious turn in the fiftieth year of his
age, and became himself a diligent and devout
collector of religious relics.

Coarse caricatures and obscene characterizations
of the Jews are quite common in Christian
churches. Thus on the north-east corner of the
lofty choir near the roof in the parish church at
Wittenberg is a rude high-relief, hewn in stone, of
a sow with a litter of pigs, and among them a lot

U

of Jews, who are assiduously sucking her dugs to the dispossession and great discomfort of her own young. Behind the sow stands a rabbi, who, lifting her right leg with one hand, and holding her by the tail with the other, earnestly endeavours to peer into her insides, as though he saw something there worthy of his closest and keenest scrutiny. According to Luther's interpretation of this remarkable work of art, the Jewish doctor of the law is engaged in searching into the mysteries of the Talmud.[1]

Satire on the Jews.
(*Wittenberg Parish Church.*)

Above this sculpture stood originally a semi-Hebrew inscription in Latin characters : " Rabini Schemhamphoras," which seems to have accidentally disappeared or been purposely removed during the restoration of the church in 1570. Schemhamphoras is the hidden name of God, which, if spoken or written, works magically and is used for con-

---

[1] " Es ist hie zu Wittemberg an vnser Pfarrkirchen eine Saw in Stein gehawen, da ligen junge Ferckel vnnd Jüden vnter, die saugen. Hinder der Saw stehet eyn Rabin, der hebt der Saw das rechte bein empor, und mit seiner lincken hand zeucht er den pirtzel vber sich, bückt vnnd kuckt mit grossem vleis der Saw unter dem pirtzel inn den Thalmud hinein, als wolt er etwas scharffes vnd sonderliches lessen und ersehen."—Dr. Mar. Luther, *Von Schemhamphoras vnnd Geschlecht Christi.* Wittenberg, 1543, 4to.

juration. Also the passage describing the miracle of the pillar of the cloud and the division of the waters (Ex. xiv. 19-21) consists in the original of two hundred and sixteen letters, out of which the cabalists form seventy-two words of three letters each. They pronounce these words as numbers, and understand by them the names of seventy-two angels, which correspond to as many special powers and attributes of God, and are exceedingly potent as charms.[1]

A rhymed chronicle preserved in the city archives of Wittenberg states that the aforesaid relief was intended to deride and vex the Jews, who, by their chafferings and bickerings on Sunday near the sanctuary, disturbed and scandalized all good Christians. After due deliberation, it was resolved to have this work made in order to heap contempt upon the Jews, and to compel them to seek some other place of barter. The ingenious plan, the chronicler informs us, was crowned with complete success, and the Hebrew traffickers felt so insulted that they not only ceased to transact their business in the vicinity of the church, but gradually withdrew wholly from the city.

This explanation is a mere afterthought and pure invention, and is not sustained by any historical records, nor is it at all probable that the Christians of Wittenberg would have been obliged to resort to such indirect means of suppressing

---

[1] Cf. *Zeitschrift für deutsche Kulturgeschichte*, i. 463 *sqq.*

the alleged abuse. In cases of this kind, they
were not wont to deal in innuendoes, but to take
more summary measures. Besides, similar representations exist elsewhere. Thus, on one of the
buttresses on the north side of the church of St.
Nicholas in Zerbst, the former capital of the
principality of Anhalt, is the relief of a sow with
two Jews sucking her teats, while two others are
holding her fast by the head and tail. It was
carved there as a memorial of the banishment of
the Jews from that city, as can be proved by
existing documents ; and the Wittenberg sculpture
had undoubtedly the same origin, and was intended
to satirize Jewish extortion and greed of gain.
It is well known that a pretty general persecution
and banishment of the Jews took place in 1348
and 1349 under divers pretexts; among other
accusations was that of producing pestilence by
poisoning the wells, the pollution of the water caused
by the common filthiness of the inhabitants being
ascribed to the wickedness of one class of the
population.

There is no doubt that the position to which
Christian intolerance condemned the Jews for
many centuries, closing to them all branches of
industry except usury, developed in them a peculiar
talent for finance, together with certain hard and
offensive traits of character naturally growing out
of money brokerage, and finally becoming almost
innate and hereditary. In the middle ages they
were made to serve as sponges to suck up the

people's substance in order that it might be
squeezed out of them at the convenience of the
rulers.   King John II., surnamed the Good, issued
in 1360 a decree permitting the Jews in his realm
to take, as a compensation for loaning money,
"quatre deniers par livre par semaine," equivalent
to ninety per cent. per annum, not from any feeling
of favouritism for the Israelites, but, as he expressly stated, because "the greater the privileges
enjoyed by the Jews in this respect, the better
they will be able to pay the taxes levied on them
by the king."   This "good" monarch was wont to
confiscate periodically a large portion of the pillage
thus obtained, in order to replenish his exhausted
exchequer, and was actually praised by his deluded
subjects for punishing Jewish rapacity.   It was a
crafty system of indirect taxation worthy of modern
tariff legislators.   Also in the early part of the
thirteenth century, Frederic II., the Hohenstaufe,
ordained that the Jews should be permitted to
dwell in Nuremberg and to lend money on interest,
stating that, "inasmuch as this sinful business is
essential to trade and to the commerical prosperity
of the city, it would be a lesser evil to let the Jews
carry it on, than that Christians should imperil the
salvation of their souls by such iniquitous practices,
since the former, owing to their notorious obduracy,
will doubtless persist in their religious perversity
and be damned anyhow."   If the children of Israel
now "take a breed of barren metal," as naturally
as a pointer takes to pointing, or a hound to the

trail of a fox, this tendency is due in part at least
to circumstances which they did not create and
could not control. The chief accusation brought
against the modern representatives of this race by
Anti-Semitic agitators, is that they are unwilling
to follow industrial and especially agricultural
pursuits, in utter forgetfulness of the fact that, until
a comparatively recent date, they were forbidden
by Christian legislation either to engage in mechanical occupations or to own land, a condition of
things still existing in portions of Russia and other
half-civilized countries.

The gross method of outraging the feelings just
described had not even the merit of being original
with those who employed it. The Emperor Hadrian,
after having suppressed the revolt of Bar-Cochba
and recaptured Jerusalem, A.D. 135, caused images
of swine to be sculptured over the gates of the city
as a sign of the exclusion of the Jews, who were
forbidden to dwell within the walls. He then restored it as a Roman city under the name of Ælia
Capitolina, and converted the tabernacle of Jehovah
into a temple dedicated to Jupiter.[1]

On the synagogue in Heidingsfeld is an armorial
shield, on which are emblazoned two swine. It is
the escutcheon of the Prince Bishop of Würzburg,
Adam Friedrich von Seinsheim, who had it placed
there instead of the arms of Heidingsfeld, which
the Jews wished to adorn their sanctuary with, but

---

[1] Cf. Adrichomius, *Descriptio urbis Hierosolymorum.*

were forbidden by the magistracy to use for this
purpose.   The Rabbis were obliged to accept these
heraldic porkers as *gosh* or ceremonially clean in
consecrating the edifice.

A painting formerly on the lower part of the

Satire on the Jews.   (*Tower of Bridge at Frankfort.*)

tower of the bridge across the Main in Frankfort
represented an old Jew with spectacles on his nose
sitting backwards on an enormous sow, and holding
her tail in his right hand.   A young Jew is lying
on his back under the sow and eagerly sucking her

dugs; another old Jew is kneeling on the ground
and receiving the sow's excrement into his mouth,
while Satan with hoofs and horns steals up behind
him and seizes him by the shoulder.   Standing a
little to one side is a Jewess arrayed in fine attire,
holding a goat (the symbol of lechery) by the
horns and looking the devil boldly in the face;
underneath the picture is the following verse :

> " Sauf du die Milch, friss du den Dreck,
> Das ist doch euer bestes Geschleck."

> " Drink the milk and eat the dung,
> That's a dainty for your tongue."

Above is the naked and scarred body of a Christian child, reputed to be the victim of a ritual
murder committed by the Jews in the year 1275.
This is the description of the painting in its original
form.   Other accounts differ somewhat from this
one, probably owing to the disappearance of portions of it in the lapse of time, and to the introduction of slight changes by later renovators.
The Jews of Frankfort offered large sums of money
to have it removed, but in vain; only a finer sense
of propriety, and a higher standard of public decency,
resulting from the progress of civilization, availed
to do away with the scandalous libel.[1]

[1] Engravings of this painting are published in *Der
Antiquarius des Neckar- Main- Lahn- und Moselstroms*,
Frankfurt a. M., 1740, p. 342; and in Scheible's *Schaltjahr*,
iii. p. 212.   The former corresponds to the description just
given; in the latter a tree stands in the place of the
Jewess.   Cf. also Schmidt, *Jüdische Merkwüdigkeiten*, 1741,
ii. 256 *sqq.*

A sow with two Jews as sucklings is carved
on one of the stalls of the choir in Bâle Minster;
and in the cathedral of Magdeburg a chapel
dedicated to the Virgin Mary contains a similar
representation, dating from the fifteenth century.
It is a strange irony of fate that the Jewish race
should be thus held up to derision in a place
especially devoted to the worship of a Jewish
maiden. Among the gargoyles on the collegiate
church (Stiftskirche) of Wimpfen im Thal, a fine
Gothic edifice of the thirteenth century, is the figure
of a Jew sucking a sow and pushing aside a little
pig, which is anxious to have its turn at the
maternal breast. Sculptures of a like character
are found on the city hall (Rathhaus) of Salzburg,
on the chapel of St. Anna in Heiligenstadt on the
Leine, and among the grotesque carvings with
which a monk adorned the high altar and the stalls
of the chancel in the church at Heilbrunn, founded
in 1132, and once famous as a place of pilgrimage.

The Jew suckled by a sow seems to have been
the one great Anti-Semitic joke of the middle ages,
and, judging from its frequent repetition and wide
diffusion, must have been regarded as a wonderfully clever and altogether matchless stroke of
Christian wit and satire. It was chiselled on the
cathedral of Ratisbon, probably at the time of the
expulsion of the Jews from that city in 1519, an
event of sufficient importance to be deemed worthy
of commemoration by an inscription on an apothecary's shop in Kelheim: " Anno Dom. 1519 jar

wurden die juden zu Rengsburg ausgeschafft." It occurs again in the cathedral of Freising on the Isar with the following distich, which takes a rather discouraging view of the missionary work undertaken by the Society for the Propagation of the Gospel among the Jews—

> " So wahr die Maus die Katz nit frisst,
>   Wird der Jud kein wahrer Christ."

> " Sure as the mouse the cat won't chew,
>   No Jew 'll become a Christian true."

The promoters of such proselytism may derive some consolation from the fact that the ambiguity caused by the feminine gender of " Maus " and " Katz," either of which may be the subject or the object of the verb, render it possible for this rather clumsy verse to be so construed as to express the very opposite of the sentiment intended by the rhymster.

Jews formerly complained of being obliged to take an oath standing on a swine's skin, but this method of swearing may have been a survival of the old German custom of solemnly affirming the truth of any statement by the golden-bristled boar, Gullinbursti, sacred to the sun-god Freyr, which the Jews would naturally look upon as a particular grievance and intentional persecution. The Romans sacrificed a swine in forming treaties and making alliances, and the animal was also in this case a symbol of the sun, the great revealer of secrets and detecter of falsehood. In the *Eumenides* of Æschylus, Apollo the purger (Ἀπόλλων καθάρσιος) cleanses Orestes from the stains of matricidal pollution with swine's blood, and Circe purifies the Argonauts, the abettors of the murder of Absyrtus, in the same manner.

It would be foreign to the purpose of the present work to describe the various means devised to throw derision upon the Jews ; only such satirical delineations as are conspicuously connected with ecclesiastical architecture come within its scope.[1] It would be unjust, however, not to mention the heroic spirit of self-sacrifice which such trials tended to develop, and of which the following is a noteworthy instance. During a religious procession in Worms, a report was spread abroad that a crucifix had been mutilated. Of course the Jews, who served as scapegoats for all such offences, were accused of the sacrilege, and a mob of Christian zealots, hastening to the Jews' quarter, demanded with loud cries the surrender of the culprits, and threatened, in case of refusal, to wreak vengeance on the whole Jewish population. A three days' respite was granted in order to discover the persons who had committed the outrage. Towards evening two Hebrew strangers appeared at the closed entrance to the Jewry and

---

[1] The reader who is interested in the general subject is referred to F. L. Bösigk's essay " Ueber die Judenspottbilder des Mittelalters" in *Zeitschrift für deutsche Kulturgeschichte*, i. 463-469; and to Strobel's *Geistliches deutsches Kartenspiel*, published in 1691 at Sulzbach, and containing an account of Schellensau, a game of cards designed to ridicule the Jews.

begged for admittance. They were informed of
the terrible fate impending over the whole Israelitic
community, but insisted in sharing the lot of their
brethren, whatever it might be. At the expiration
of the three days' grace the infuriated and fanatical
rabble assembled again at the gate of the ghetto and
clamoured for the punishment of the sacrilegists.
Then the two stranger guests gave themselves up
as the guilty ones, and were put to death. In the
old synagogue at Worms are two ever-burning
lamps, which, as a Hebrew inscription informs us,
were lighted in memory of two unknown men,
who innocently suffered a cruel death for the sake
of their brethren.

Classical mythology was another source from
which Christian symbolism derived many conceptions and forms subsequently embodied in ecclesiastical architecture. It could hardly be expected
that the first Gentile converts, however sincere in
their profession of the new faith, would be able to
break away entirely from the teachings and traditions of their early life and education. They were
also told that the pagan religions were not merely
old wives' fables, but had a certain heavenly
origin and historical justification as preparatory to
Christianity, which they foreshadowed. The real
significance and *raison d'être* of the deities of
Olympus were to be sought in their prototypical
relation to the expiatory sacrifice on Mount Cal-
vary. Hermes, who was represented in heathen
works of art as the protector of the herds, the

conductor of souls, and the reviver of the dead, would be readily accepted as prefigurative of the Saviour of mankind, and Perseus rescuing Andromeda as signifying Christ redeeming the human soul. On a sarcophagus in the Museo Pio-Clementino at Rome is the relief of a satyr bearing a lamb, and having features strongly resembling those of the traditional good shepherd. There is no doubt, too, that the fear of persecution led the Christians of the first century to make this symbolical use of the old mythology; and it may have been the same dictate of prudence that prevented them from encircling the head of Christ with a nimbus, the earliest example of which, in the catacomb of St. Domitilla, belongs to the beginning of the second century.

Some of the Fathers held the views still entertained by Mr. Gladstone, that all mythologies are corruptions and distortions of a primitive revelation supernaturally communicated to " the chosen people." The applications of this theory are sometimes very odd. Thus it was affirmed that the ass's colt bound to the vine mentioned by the patriarch Jacob in blessing Judah (Gen. xlix. 11) is not only a prefiguration of Christ's entry into Jerusalem, but also the original source of the myths of Bacchus, Bellerophon, and Pegasus. The asininity of many a one who essays to bestride the winged horse of the Muses is lamentably true; but that the fiery steed itself is the foal of Shiloh's ass may be reasonably questioned. Isaiah prophesies

that a virgin shall conceive and bear a son; and
nothing is more common than for Orientals to
speak of the first-born as the child of a virgin; but
the patristic exegetist maintains that this passage,
besides being a prediction of the birth of Christ,
suggested to the Greeks the legend of Danaë, the
mother of Perseus. In like manner the labours
and wanderings of Hercules are based upon the
Psalmist's description of the bridegroom, who
rejoiceth as a strong man to run a race, and whose
going forth is from the end of the heaven. Whim-
seys of this kind have been long since relegated to
the waste-garret of mythological curiosities; but
they are not a whit more extravagant than many
hermeneutical expositions still in vogue.

The magic power ascribed to the music of
Orpheus, which tamed wild beasts and even moved
trees and stones, was applied to the miraculous
power of Christ, who declared, on His entry into
Jerusalem, in reply to the protests of the Pharisees
against the noisy enthusiasm of the people, that, if
the multitude should hold their peace, the stones
would immediately cry out. The descent of the
mythical Greek poet and minstrel into the lower
world, and his success in rescuing his spouse
Eurydice from the dominion of Pluto, rendered the
analogy more complete, and may have given rise
to the legend of Christ's descent into hell for the
purpose of delivering the imprisoned spirits.
Orpheus thus became a prototype of the Saviour,
and as such found a place in the Christian pantheon

at a very early period.   In the centre of the ceiling
of a cubiculum in the catacomb of St. Domitilla near
Rome, we see him seated on a rock and playing on
his lyre, surrounded by beasts and birds, which his
music has attracted to the spot. He figures
frequently on Christian sarcophagi and in the
frescoes of old churches.

The Bacchanal scenes which adorned the temples
of the son of Semele were copied or imitated by
the early Christians in order to illustrate the conception of the Church as a vineyard, which is
expressed in the parables of the householder and
his husbandmen, and of the labourers.   An interesting example of this adaptation is seen in the
mosaics of the fourth century in the cupola of
St. Costanza in Rome, representing the genii of
the vintage.

In the Gothic choir of the minster at Aix-la-
Chapelle is an ambo, dating from the early part of
the eleventh century, with ivory reliefs of a similar
but still more elaborate character : Bacchus with
the symbols of his cult, the vine, the lion, the
panther, and the dog, Pan and the satyrs, the
triumph of Galatea, centaurs, sirens, tritons, nereids,
dolphins, the sea-born Venus, Cupids blowing shells
as trumpets, and the myths of Demeter and Isis
and Horus in their assumed prefigurative relation
to the Virgin Mary.

Scenes from the pagan poets were occasionally
portrayed, as, for example, in the curious sculptures
of the twelfth century on a column in the choir of

the cathedral church of Bâle, giving in four reliefs
the old Babylonian tale of the tragic fate of "a
pair of star-crossed lovers," Pyramus and Thisbe
as related by Ovid in the fourth book of the
Metamorphoses. In the first scene Thisbe has
taken refuge in a tree, at the foot of which a lion
is rending her mantle, while Pyramus approaches
with an uplifted sword to slay the lion, which has
a bit of Thisbe's mantle in its mouth. In the

Pyramus and Thisbe. (*Cathedral of Bâle.*)

second scene Pyramus is smiting the lion. He
then goes in search of Thisbe, but, not finding her,
is convinced that she has been devoured by the
savage beast, and in a fit of despair falls on his
own sword. Thisbe now returns to the place of
rendezvous, and seeing her lover dead throws herself upon his sword. The final relief shows them
both pierced through by the same weapon. This
story of youthful passion thwarted by cruel parents
was exceedingly popular in the middle ages, and

was therefore fitly chosen by Shakespeare to be theatrically caricatured by Nick Bottom the weaver, Peter Quince the carpenter, and other "rude mechanicals," as an episode of *A Midsummer-Night's Dream*, from which it was taken by Andreas Gryphius in his *Absurda Comica oder Herr Peter*

Pyramus and Thisbe. (*Cathedral of Bâle.*)

Squenz. What religious significance the reliefs in Bâle Minster may have it would be difficult to determine. The lion which disturbs the meeting of the lovers, and eventually causes them to commit suicide, probably denotes the snares and terrors of Satan.

After the conversion and accession of Constantine, it was the settled policy of the Christians to erect their churches on the sites of demolished pagan temples, in order that the people might the more readily assemble for the worship of the true God in the places where they had been wont

X

to pay their devotions to idols. Gregory the Great, towards the end of the sixth century, wrote a letter of instructions to the missionaries to the Anglo-Saxons directing them to pursue this plan. Sometimes the ancient edifice was simply transformed and reconsecrated to the new cult, in which case the statues and symbols of the heathen deities remained and received a Christian signification as objects of worship. Thus the Florentine Baptistery superseded a temple dedicated to Mars, and John the Baptist succeeded the Roman god of war as the patron and protector of the city. The statue of Mars, which once adorned the temple, was placed on a tower, but was taken down when Attila sacked the city in 452, and thrown into the Arno, from which it was subsequently recovered and set up on a bridge, where it was still standing in the fourteenth century, as is evident from the references to it by Dante.[1]

In the gallery of the Vatican are two portrait statues of the Greek comic poets, Posidippus and Menander, made of Pentelican marble probably by Kephisodotos, the son of Praxiteles, for the theatre at Athens. After their discovery in Paneperna towards the end of the sixteenth century they were for a long time adored as saints. Under the church of S. Clemente in Rome is a temple dedicated to the worship of Mithras, with the ancient altar still standing. In a village church on the

---

[1] Cf. *Inf.*, xiii. 143-150; *Par.*, xvi. 49, 145.

Danube, not far from Linz, is a statue of Isis made
of black basalt, to which pious Catholics pay their
devotions, regarding it as an image of the Virgin
Mary. A statue of the same goddess was worshipped in the church of St. Germain des Près in
Paris for nearly ten centuries. This church was
originally built by Childebert I. about the middle of
the sixth century on the ruins of a temple of Isis,
whose image was transferred to the new edifice,
where it was an object of adoration till 1514, when
it was destroyed. Three gilded bronze statues of
Alemannic gods were revered in the chapel of St.
Aurelia at Bregenz, until St. Gallus in his prose-
lytic zeal broke them in pieces and threw them
into the lake in order to put an end to this idolatry.
Underneath the church of the Benedictine cloister
of St. Martin near Trier was found, at the time of
its demolition in 1802, an altar with reliefs of
Bellona, Minerva, Mercury, and Hercules. As late
as the sixteenth century a marble statue of
Hercules slaying the Nemean lion stood in the
vestibule of St. Ambrosius in Milan; and in St.
Pietro in Cora the marble altar of a temple of
Hercules served as a font, on the front of which
was carved the head of Apollo encircled with a
halo as a solar deity. Antique sarcophagi and
cinerary urns were often used as Christian fonts
and stoups. This origin accounts for the reliefs
representing the myth of Hippolytus on the font,
or what was formerly the font, in the cathedral of
Girgenti, and for the scenes from the infancy of

Bacchus on a vessel which once served as a
baptismal ewer in the cathedral of Gaeta, but is
now in the Neapolitan Museum.

Cameos and other carved stones representing
mythological personages or narrations were prized
merely as jewels, and set as ornaments in crosiers,
crosses, and the shrines of saints, without regard
to the subjects engraved upon them.   In the so-
called cross of Lothair in the minster of Aix-la-
Chapelle is an amethyst, on which the three Graces
are carved in relief; the story of Leda and the
swan is cut on a canonical seal of the twelfth
century; and an ivory reliquary in the Schloss-
kirche of Quedlinburg is studded with precious
stones, among which is an amethyst wrought into
the head of Bacchus.[1]

The earliest Christian art was purely symbolical,
rudely indicating instead of fully expressing the
idea it was intended to convey.   Thus a simple
cross symbolized the doctrine of the Atonement,
and it was not until a later period that the figure
of Christ was affixed to the cross, which thus
became a crucifix, and gradually acquired an
artistic character.   So, too, the cross-bearing lamb
or Agnus Dei, the Good Shepherd, and similar
emblems, have no claim to be regarded as works of
art, but were nothing more than hieroglyphics or
monograms.   This was due not so much to the
inwardness or spirituality of the new religion

---

[1] Cf. Piper, *Myth. der christl. Kunst*, i. 59-63, for numerous
examples of this kind.

doctrinally, as to its crudeness and incapacity artistically. The best productions of early Christian art are copies or close imitations of contemporary pagan art, such as tutelar genii, victories, Amor and Psyche taken as emblems of the love of God and the human soul, the golden apples guarded by a dragon in the garden of the Hesperides interpreted as a tradition of the tree of knowledge and the subtle serpent in the garden of Eden, Apollo on the chariot of the sun transformed into Elias borne to heaven on a fiery chariot, and Mercury or Hermes with a ram on his shoulder expressive of the Christian conception of the Saviour as the Good Shepherd.

In the eleventh and twelfth centuries this servile imitation is followed by a conscious appropriation and independent elaboration of pagan myths by Christian artists, as the result of a better appreciation of the antique. Sibyls as well as saints and prophets stand in the niches of Giotto's tower, and are sculptured in relief on the bronze doors of Ghiberti in Florence, and on the Casa Santa of Loreto. A mosaic in San Michele at Pavia celebrates the humane and heroic feat of Theseus in slaying the Minotaur; on one side of the entrance to the labyrinth is a dragon, and on the other side a Pegasus; on the left hand, as the biblical counterpart of the classical myth, is David fighting Goliath. It is probably a work of the eleventh century.

Petrarch calls God "living Jove" and "eternal

Jove"; and Dante apostrophizes Christ as "supreme Jove, who for us on earth was crucified "—

"O sommo Giove,
Chi fosti'n terra per noi crocifisso."

Indeed, Jupiter was used as synonymous with Jesus in poetry long before the features of the sovereign of Olympus were borrowed by painters and sculptors to lend dignity and majesty to the portraitures of Christ, especially in His character as stern and avenging Judge on the last day.

Giotto, whose pencil wrought in the spirit of the Divine Comedy, and whose pictures are often mere embodiments and illustrations of Dante's ideas, introduced similar elements of ancient mythology into Christian art by way of allegory. So, too, in the famous frescoes of the triumph of death and the last judgment by Andrea and Bernardo Orcagno in the Campo Santo at Pisa, and in the Strozzi chapel of Santa Maria Novella at Florence, we find Charon the grim ferryman of souls, a triple-necked Pluto as the personification of hell swallowing the damned, Cerberus devouring the envious, the morasses of the Styx, the bull-headed anthropophagous Minotaur, in short the whole scenery of the lower world as conceived by the poets of classical antiquity and seen through mediæval eyes.

The peacock, being sacred to Juno, became a symbol of the apotheosis of Roman empresses, as Jupiter's eagle was of Roman emperors. For this reason these birds were carved on the tombs of the

apotheosized, and on funeral lamps. From pagan
monuments of the dead they passed to Christian
sepulchres, on which they signified the Christian's
conception of apotheosis, the ascension of the
sanctified soul and its union with God. Owing
to the belief that the flesh of the peacock was
incorruptible, this fowl was made an emblem of
the resurrection of the dead, sown in corruption,
but raised in incorruption. On this point Augustine
says (*De Civ. Dei*, xxi. 4): " Quis enim nisi Deus
creator omnium dedit carni pavonis mortui ne
putrescerent ? " " For who except God, the Creator
of all things, endowed the flesh of the dead peacock with the power of never decaying ? " There
is a tradition that the acute and inquisitive suffra-
gan of Hippo experimented with the flesh of
this fowl, and found the popular superstition to
be correct.

The splendour of its plumage made it also an
emblem of the glories
of heaven. In many
mediæval paintings,
for example, in Hans
Memling's picture of
the Last Judgment

Peacocks. (*Psalter of Isabella of France.*)

in the Dorothy Chapel of St. Mary's Church in
Dantzig, the angels have peacocks' feathers in their
wings. The Christian moralist, however, in his condemnation of all sensual beauty as diabolical in its
origin and influence, prefers in general to indicate
and emphasize the imperfections and less attractive

features of the bird, which it endeavours to conceal under its showy qualities. Thus, in Freidank's *Bescheidenheit* (p. 43), the peacock is said to have the slinking gait of a thief, the voice of the devil, and an angel's garb—

> "der phâwe diebes sliche hât,
> tiuvels stimme, und engels wât."

On account of this peculiarity of its walk it is called Petitpas ("Mincing-step") in the *Roman de Renart*. The striking contrast between the ugly feet, the awkward movement, the harsh strident cry of the peacock, and its brilliant hues furnished material for moralization exceedingly welcome to didactic poets and homilists.[1]

The *Physiologus* says that when the peacock wakes suddenly in the night, it cries out as if in distress, because it dreams that it has lost its beauty, thus typifying the soul, which in the night of this sinful world is constantly fearing to lose the good gifts and graces with which God has endowed it. In the bestiaries a man devoid of prudence is likened to a peacock that has lost its tail; because, as the author argues, the tail of the peacock denotes foresight, since the tail being behind is that which is to come; and foresight is the faculty of taking heed to that which is to come. As a burlesque on all reasoning from analogy, nothing could be better than this.

---

[1] Cf. Victor Hehn, *Kulturpflanzen und Hausthiere*, Berlin, 1874, p. 311.

The Christian version of the story of Argus and Io is an excellent example of the naïve manner in which classical myths were diverted from their natural course into the channel of moral and religious instruction. " There was once a lady who had a very beautiful cow. In order that it might not be stolen, she hired a herdsman named Argus, who had a hundred eyes, but slept with only two at a time, and kept watch with all the others. Nevertheless her precaution was of no avail, and she lost her cow. For a certain man, who coveted the animal, had a son called Mercurius, who was very skilful in playing on a long, hollow reed. This clever young man took occasion to visit Argus, and began to talk about one thing and another and to play on his pipe ; and as he went on talking and playing, Argus fell asleep at first with two eyes, then with four, and so on until finally the hundred eyes were all closed in slumber. Thereupon Mercurius cut off the head of the herdsman, and drove away the cow to his father. This incident is an admonition and a warning for us. We are Argus, and the cow is our precious soul, which we are set to keep with vigilance, and the hundred eyes are the good deeds and pious services by which the safety of the soul is secured. The man who wished to steal the cow is the devil ; and his son and emissary lulls us to sleep by luxury, pride, vicious habits, and worldly pleasures, and at last carries away the soul captive, and delivers it to his father, the author of all evil.'

A miniature of this scene from the Arsenal manuscript has been published by
Cahier (*Mél. d'Arch.*, II. xx.
AB), and it is easy to conceive how by such a process
of transformation all the
fables of pagan mythology
might serve as apt illustrations of Christian teachings,

Myth of Argus. (*Bestiary.*)

and appropriate decorations of Christian architecture.

In the Septuagint the word σειρῆνες occurs
frequently where owls and ostriches are spoken of
in the English version. Thus the prophet Isaiah
(xiii. 21-22) is made to declare that "sirens and
satyrs shall dance in Babylon, and onocentaurs
and demons shall dwell in their habitations." The
sirens are said to be of three kinds: half woman

Sirens. (*Psalter of Isabella of France.*)

and half fish, half woman and half bird, and half
woman and half ass. Some play on flutes, others
on harps, and others sing, attracting men by the
sweetness of their music, lulling them to sleep and
rending them in pieces. They symbolize the power
of female blandishment, and the allurements of the

flesh, and are often portrayed in missals and on different parts of ecclesiastical edifices. The ship of Ulysses sailing by the island of the sirens, himself bound to the mast, and the ears of the mariners stopped with wax, was a favourite subject with ancient artists, who delineated the scene on gems, mosaics, urns, and vases. In Christian art the ship of the wandering king of Ithaca was transformed into the ship of the Church, which bears those who entrust themselves to its care and keeping safely through the temptations of the world. Thus in the crypt of Santa Lucia, in the catacombs of Callistus, is a representation of Ulysses and the sirens, which St. Maximus of Turin interprets as a Christian allegory. " This ship," he says, "is the Church, and the mast symbolizes the cross of Christ, to which the faithful must cling in order to escape the seductions of the senses. As our Lord Jesus Christ was nailed to the cross, and remained sinless among temptations, so let us navigate the perilous sea of life as if our ears were stopped."

As servants and messengers of Proserpina the sirens, like the Scandinavian Valkyrias, carried the souls of the departed to Hades, and were therefore often sculptured on tombs and cinerary urns, usually playing musical instruments. On the sepulchres of illustrious orators like Isocrates or eminent poets like Sophocles, the sirens personified the magic power and irresistible persuasiveness of eloquence and the charms of poetry, which captivate the souls of men. Patristic theologians and exegetists confounded sirens and mermaids, and believed them to be real creatures expressly intended to serve as deterrent types of carnal appetites and sensual enticements. In mediæval poetry the siren symbolizes the delusive fascinations of this world, which Konrad von Würzburg by a bold metaphor calls "die syrene trügesam" ("the deceitful siren"), from whose allurements the holy Virgin rescues us on the voyage of life, and brings us safely to the haven of eternal rest.

The siren is often represented in sacred art with a fish in her hand, signifying the soul held in the grip of libidinous passion, as for example on the capitals of some of the columns in St. Germain des Près, the oldest of the Parisian churches; in the arcades of the cloister of St. Aubin, where the siren has a fish in one hand and a knife in the

Siren presenting a Fish to a man.
(*Church at Cunault-sur-Loire.*)

other; on capitals in the churches at Civaux, where the siren is handing the fish to a man in a boat, while another is plunging from the opposite side

of the boat into the sea, as though he feared the
seductress even when bringing gifts, and risked his
life to save his soul; and at Cunault-sur-Loire,
where a similar scene is represented, the man in
the boat receiving the fish with an affrighted mien,
and his companion standing in a deprecating
attitude on the shore. This sculpture dates from
the twelfth century. Sirens are carved on the
stalls of the chancel in the cathedral of Poitiers
and in Notre Dame of Rouen, in the church of
St. Nicholas at Anclam, and on the portal of the
Schottenkirche in Ratisbon; also winged virgins
with birds' legs and tails adorn the four corner
pillars which support the candelabra wrought in
bronze by Peter Vischer.

In classical mythology centaurs were associated
with sirens in Bacchanal processions and orgies,
because they both embodied and symbolized over-
ruling animal impulses and passions. They dis-
charged similar functions as agents of the gods of
the lower world, and for this reason were sculptured
on pagan sarcophagi and other funeral monuments,
from which they were borrowed by Christians, who
conceived of them as demons armed with bows and
arrows, and going about annoying believers and
assailing them with what Paul calls "the fiery darts
of the wicked."

St. Jerome records that when St. Anthony, in the
ninetieth year of his age, went to visit Paul the
Hermit in the desert, he met a creature half man
and half horse. The saint made the sign of the

cross, as a protection against diabolical influences, and then inquired the way to Paul's hermitage. Thereupon the strange hybrid uttered some harsh semi-articulate whinnying sounds, and, pointing with his right hand in the proper direction, galloped off. Jerome maintains that this apparition was an emissary of Satan sent to frighten St. Anthony, and to deter him from his purpose; but if this theory be correct, the willingness with which the devil's agent acted as a guide-post and helped the holy man on his way is rather remarkable.   The monks were wont to people the desert, and other lonely places in which they dwelt, with monstrous shapes or entrancing visions, like those which so sorely tempted St. Anthony, products of their own suppressed but ineradicable passions, and abortions of an imagination morbidly excited by asceticism and solitude.

The centaur figures very frequently in architecture from the tenth to the sixteenth century, especially on the doors of churches. Thus, in the reliefs on the bronze doors of Augsburg Cathedral one centaur is shooting at a man and another at a lion; on a frieze in the church at Brenz are reliefs of centaurs shooting arrows, and the same subject is on the bronze doors of St. Sophia in Novgorod; on the west side of St. John's, in Gmünd, is a centaur with a knife; on the portal of St. Gilles are two centaurs, one shooting at a stag and another pursuing a lion; on the portal of St. Trophine at Arles we find seven reliefs of centaurs shooting at

lions, and of men fighting with divers wild beasts,
illustrating the conflict of fierce passions, or men
contending against their own lower natures, and
trying to subdue them. In the cloister of Zurich
Minster are two female centaurs, one shooting
an arrow at a dragon, and the other thrusting
a spear down its throat; in the former cloister-
church at Ibbenstadt in Wetterau, on the base of
a pillar surmounted by a cross, is a centaur dis-
charging an arrow into the extended jaws of a
dragon; in the Liebfrauenkirche (Church of our
dear Lady) at Halberstadt are reliefs on the frieze
of the stone enclosure of the chancel, representing
female centaurs nursing their young, and male
centaurs tearing each other's hair; and in Freiburg
Minster a man fighting a winged centaur with
sword and shield, and a couple of female centaurs
contending with similar weapons. It is not easy
in every case to determine the precise spiritual
significance of such scenes, and in some instances
they are doubtless purely decorative, although a
lingering tradition of the original symbolism of the
centaur underlies them all, and accounts for the
introduction of these fabulous monsters even as
merely ornamental forms.

Dante (*Inf.*, xii.) condemns those who have
been guilty of deeds of violence against life and
property, Alexander, Attila, and other great con-
querors and ravagers of the earth, to suffer for
their crimes in a turbulent stream of boiling blood,
guarded by centaurs armed with darts, and running

along the shore; and Vergil (*Æn.*, vi. 286) is met
by them as he is about to enter the lower world,
where they seem to have acted as warders of the
gate to the nether regions.   In Bernardo Orcagna's
famous fresco of the Last Judgment in the Strozzi
Chapel of Santa Maria Novella, in Florence, which
is essentially a pictorial illustration of Dante's description of Inferno, the damned are pursued by
centaurs.   In the church of the Franciscan cloister
at Assisi, on the groined arch over the grave of
St. Francis, is a centaur painted by Giotto as a
symbol of self-will, together with other frescoes by
the same master, representing allegorical figures of
poverty, chastity, obedience, prudence, humility, and
kindred virtues with which the saint was supposed
to have been pre-eminently endowed.   In a painting
by Andrea Mantegna in the gallery of the Louvre
the vices are delineated as satyrs and centaurs;
and on a stoup by Jacopo della Quercia in the
cathedral of Sienna are reliefs of David rending the
jaws of a lion and Hercules slaying a centaur,
forming a part of a series of sculptures giving the
history of creation from the birth of light to the
expulsion of Adam and Eve from the garden of
Eden.   In older works of Christian art, which have
for their subject the fall of man, centaurs often
appear as personifications of criminal impulses
rashly and recklessly obeyed.   At a later period,
like other real or fabulous creatures, they gradually
lost their symbolical meaning, and were used for
satirical purposes in accordance with the general

law of degeneracy that governs this hieroglyphic mode of expression. Thus, on some of the seats of the stalls in the choir of Bâle Minster, belonging to the end of the fifteenth century, are carvings of centaurs with the heads of bishops and of merry-making monks and nuns, and other caricatures of the clergy.

In the crypt of the cathedral at Freising, near Munich in Bavaria, is a column adorned on all sides with sculptures of the eleventh century, representing the chief incidents of the old German myth of Sigurd (Siegfried). In the first group two persons—one in armour, and wearing spurs (Sigurd), and the other in a kirtle (Regino)—are slaying the dragon. Next we see a naked man letting himself down into the jaws of the dead dragon; it is Sigurd bathing himself in the dragon's blood, which would render him invulnerable. A branch of leaves hanging down covers a part of his shoulder, and indicates the fatal spot which remained unwashed by the monster's blood, and therefore capable of being wounded. Two birds are perched on the capital of the column. An animal, probably an ichneumon (also a legendary killer of monsters in the form of crocodiles), is rushing into the jaws of another dragon resembling an alligator. On the fourth side is a woman with long hair, a valkyrie, or perhaps Brunhild. The legend of Sigurd symbolized the vernal freshness and vigour of the sun slaying the demon of winter, and freeing earth's treasures from its icy grasp, and was therefore easily

Y

turned into the channel of
Christian ethics and theology,
and made to signify the redeeming power of the Sun
of Righteousness. For this
reason scenes from it are frequently found depicted on
monuments of Christian art.
In Norway the Sigurd Saga
seems to have been a favourite
theme of Christian architects,
and the adventures of this old
Scandinavian ideal of heroic
valour and strength were frequently carved on the door-
posts and stalls of sacred edifices, especially in the southern
provinces. The most com-
plete of these delineations
are the curious wood-carvings
from the portal of the church
at Hyllestad, in Saetersdal,
now in the University collection of Northern Antiquities
at Christiania, and dating
probably from the thirteenth
century. The scenes represented are as follows: 1. The
smith, Regino, forges the
sword "Nothung," while Sigurd blows the bellows.

Siegfried Saga. (*Freising.*)

Siegfried Saga. (*Freising.*)

2. Sigurd tests the sword by smiting the anvil in twain. 3. Sigurd slays Fafnir the dragon. 4. Sigurd cuts Fafnir's heart in three pieces and roasts them on a spit; while Regino is asleep Sigurd touches one of the pieces with his finger to see if it is done; as the juice of the roast is hot he licks his finger, and thus gets a taste of it, and is able to understand the language of the birds which are singing in the branches above his head. The steed Grane is also visible, laden with the Andvaregold, known as the Rhinegold or Nibelungen Hort (treasure). 5. Sigurd kills Regino, whose meditated treachery has been revealed to him by the birds. 6. Gunnar is lying in a pit of serpents with his hands bound, and playing a harp with his feet in order to charm the venomous reptiles and render them innoxious; one of them, however, is of the kind mentioned by the Psalmist, "which will not hearken to the voice of

charmers, charming never so wisely," and has bitten him. This last legend is more fully rendered on two carved planks from the portal of the church at Austad (Saetersdal), where we find two scenes from the Gjukungasaga: Hogne's heart is cut out of his breast by Atle and shown to the brother of the slain, Gunnar, who is exposed to serpents, and plays the harp with his feet. The portal of the church at Vegusdal, also in Saetersdal, is adorned with delineations of Sigurd's exploits similar in character, but less fully represented. Indeed, as we have already stated, more or less fragmentary episodes of old Norse Saga-cycles are found in a great number of churches, as, for example, at Nesland in Thalemarken, at Hemsedal in Hallingdal, at Lardal in Jarlsberg, at Opdal in Numedal, and elsewhere. A carving at Lardal represents the ex-

Siegfried Saga. (*Freising.*)

Siegfried Saga. (*Freising.*)

piation made for the death of the otter by heaping up gold sufficient to cover its skin; round its neck is the fatal Andvare ring. In the church of Hitterdal, a remarkably interesting specimen of the Norwegian "stavekirker" of the twelfth century, are decorative carvings of Sigurd and Gunnar riding up the mountain towards the spot where Brynhildr (Brunhild) is asleep, encircled with a barrier of fire, and, as they return, Sigurd holds the ring of Andvare in his hand. Doubtless many monuments of this kind, formerly existing in Scandinavia and in other northern countries, have perished. Fragments of sculptures treating the Sigurd Saga in the manner already described may be seen still, although in a very mutilated condition, on a cross-shaft at Kirk Andreas, in the Isle of Man.[1]

[1] Cf. Dr. L. Dietrichson and H.

Christianity, it must be remembered, was forced upon the Norwegians by sovereigns who, like King Olaf Tryggvason, had been converted in foreign lands, and endeavoured to introduce the new religion in a summary manner by royal decree. There was no change, however, in the religious beliefs of the masses of the people, who continued to worship the ancestral gods and to revere the mythical and semi-mythical heroes whose deeds, as celebrated in ancient songs and sagas, were anything but illustrations of Christian virtues. Chief of these popular demi-gods was Sigurd, the most perfect embodiment of the Norseman's conception of manly force and fearlessness. Even Christian priests themselves were not wholly free from this feeling, and

Munthe, *Die Holzbaukunst Norwegens in Vergangenheit und Gegenwart*, Berlin, 1893, pp. 25-27; *Journal of the British Archæological Association*, vol. xliii., p. 260.

Sigurd Saga. (*Hyllestad.*)

Sigurd Saga.   (*Hyllestad.*)

cherished a lingering fondness for the outworn creeds and discarded superstitions of their fathers. Partly as an expression of this sentiment, and partly as a matter of policy, Sigurd, the slayer of Fafnir, was made to symbolize Christ, the subduer of Satan, or was regarded as the pagan prototype of the Christian dragon-killers, St. George and St. Michael, and placed at the portal of the church as its protector. By the same process of adaptation and assimilation Gunnar in the serpents' pit came to typify man in the bondage of sin, trying to comfort himself and to calm his conscience by resorting to worldly pleasures, but doomed to spiritual death.

Another favourite theme of mediæval art was the weighing of souls, which plays such a prominent and decisive part in the eschatology of the ancient Egyptians, on whose sepulchral monuments the Supreme Judge is seen determining the worth of souls by weight, and condemning each to be reimbodied in the animal form to which the habits of life cultivated in a previous existence rendered it best suited. Thus a glutton is scourged with rods by cynocephali, who are re-conducting his spirit to the earth, where it is doomed to pass its next period of incarnation as a hog. Most probably, however, the mediæval artist knew nothing of the Egyptian method of procedure in determining the destiny of souls, but simply intended to illustrate the words of Daniel to King Belshazzar: "Thou art weighed in the balances, and art found wanting;" although this metaphorical phrase is evidently based upon the Oriental conception of the method by which retributive justice is meted out in accordance with the theory of metempsychosis.

In a bas-relief on a church at Velay an angel is engaged in weighing souls; the devil in the shape of a pig is carrying off a woman, whose virtues have been found of too light a quality, and keeping one eye on the scales to see that the angel does not cheat him out of the rest of the ponderable wares. It is a competition in which neither will bate the other even one poor scruple. In a sculpture of the thirteenth century on the portal of the church at Louques, in the province of Aveyron, the devil is slyly touching the beam with his finger in order to make it incline in his favour; and in a stained window of the cathedral of Bourges we see the

arch-fiend putting his foot on the scale and pressing
the lever with his hand, while one of his imps is
pulling at it from be-
low so as to make the
side of virtue kick the
beam. Here the good
and evil qualities are
incarnate as heads.
A relief on the pedi-
ment over a doorway
of the cathedral of
Autun represents a
crowd of naked and

Weighing Souls.   (*Bourges Cathedral.*)

clawfooted devils eagerly watching a balance, in one
scale of which are the vices of the soul incorporate
in a hideously-deformed creature, and in the other
scale its virtues personified by a young child under
the protection of a lean and lank angel in exceedingly stiff and angular drapery.   Here, too, the devil
in charge tries to push the doubtful beam, but is
caught in the act and thwarted by the vigilant
angel.   Behind the devil stands a long procession
of trembling souls, and in the background a fiery
furnace, into which a serpent-headed imp as stoker
is vigorously thrusting those who have been found
deficient in saving qualities.   In Egyptian eschatology the office of weighing souls was performed
by Osiris and Typhon ; in Christian art the function
of balancing good and evil deeds and thus determining the future destiny of men is commonly
assigned to the archangel Michael and Satan.

Sometimes the scales are held by the hand of God reaching out of the clouds, as, for example, on the arch of the principal doorway of the cathedral of Autun, and on a capital in the church of Saint-Croix in Saint-Lô; usually, however, it is St. Michael who superintends this weighty business, and prevents any cheating on the part of the great deceiver. There is a vivid representation of this scene on the portal of St. Trophine in Arles-sur-Rhone (eleventh century), where the good souls under the care of the tutelar archangel mount upwards and join the assembly of the elect in heaven, while the bad ones are seized by a gigantic demon, who already has two in his clutch, holding them with their heads downward. Essentially similar scenes are sculptured on the portals of the cathedral St. Nicholas at Fribourg in Switzerland, the metropolitan church Notre-Dame-de-Paris, the old cathedral church of Bazas in Gironde, and in many other ecclesiastical edifices.

On the portal of the minster at Bonn are sculptured an angel and a devil, each diligently writing in a scroll held on the knee; and cowering between the ribs of the arch of the famous pulpit in Bâle Minster (hewn in 1486 in the form of a Gothic chalice out of a single stone) is a devil busily engaged in taking notes, not probably of the sermon, but of the conduct of the congregation; underneath is the inscription *Prope est dies Domini* ("the day of the Lord is near"). In a fresco painting of the thirteenth century in the cathedral of Freising

depicting the Last Judgment the archangel Michael
and Satan are each presenting their books to
Christ; this picture might serve as an illustration
to the fine Latin hymn also of the thirteenth
century, and ascribed to the Franciscan monk
Thomas of Celano—

> "Liber scriptus proferetur,
> In quo totum continetur,
> Ex quo mundus judicetur.
>
> Judex ergo cum sedebit,
> Quidquid latet apparebit,
> Nil inultum remanebit."

In Indian mythology of the Post-Vedic period
it is Yama who fixes the fate of the soul after
hearing the report of his secretary Chitragupta,
who keeps a strict record of human actions in a
book called Agrasandhâni. Sometimes, however,
in works of art this clerk is represented as weighing
a person with a steelyard in the presence of the
Judge of the Dead.

Characteristically enough, the procession waiting
for judgment in Christian delineations of the scene
consists almost entirely of women. The notion
that woman is, in an emphatic and peculiar sense,
the ally and satellite of Satan originated in the
legend of the fall of man, and was strengthened by
the institution of sacerdotal celibacy. By yielding
to the suggestions of the devil she brought ruin
upon the human race, and is still the most efficient
agent of the evil one in disturbing the meditations
of pious men. From her first appearance on the

stage of history her seductive influence has been the cause of all the social, political, and domestic intrigues that have disturbed the peace and happiness of the world. "*Cherchez la femme*" is always a pertinent mandate in the presence of any such calamity. This prejudice was firmly rooted in the mediæval mind, and finds drastic expression in the painting and sculpture as well as in the poetry and theology of that period. A troubadour of the thirteenth century, in a poem entitled *Les Blasme des Fames*, compares woman to various animals, each of which is distinguished for some undesirable quality : she stings like a serpent, is fiery like a horse, double-natured like a dragon, deceitful like a fox, greedy like a bear, and loves darkness like a bat; she is not even admitted to have that "excellent thing in woman," a "voice ever soft, gentle, and low," but hoots and screeches like an owl—

"Fame est huans, fame est fressaie."

A picture in Notre Dame de Recouvrance in Brest portrays the devil noting down the idle words of two women, who are gossiping during mass. This subject is often treated in sculpture in the miniatures of manuscript missals and in the designs of tapestries, and is thus referred to in a poem written by Pierre de Grosnet in 1553—

"Notez en l'ecclise de Dieu,
Femmes ensemble caquetoyent.
Le diable y estoit en ung lieu
Escripvant ce qu'elles disoyent.

Son rollet plain de poinct en poinct,
Tyre aux deus pour le faire croistre :
Sa prinse eschappe et ne tient poinct,
Au pillier s'en cobby la teste."

On a gable-window of the Château de Villeneuve in Auvergne, dating from the sixteenth century, is a painting of three frightful devils forging the head of a woman, and three angels moulding the head of a man—the female head, being of diabolical workmanship, is full of diabolical propensities. The artists who conceived and executed such things, it must be remembered, were in the service of a Mariolatrous and yet misogynistic religion. In a carving in the church of Saint-Spire, in Corbeil, a woman has got the better of the devil, and is sawing off his infernal majesty's right ear.

The devil is by no means a prominent figure in the oldest monuments of Christian art, and it is difficult to determine with precision when he began to claim the attention of painters and sculptors. The general panic produced by the belief that the end of the world was at hand, and that Christ would come to judge the quick and the dead in the year 1000, caused the thoughts of men to turn more and more anxiously to the person of his satanic majesty, who was expected to play a prominent and fatal part in that final scene. In consequence of this state of fearful anticipation, we find the devil and his acolytes making their appearance in the latter half of the tenth and the beginning of the eleventh century on the capitals

and friezes, the doorways and pediments of
churches, frequently as human monsters with jagged
wings and forked tail, or that hideous abortion of
an affrighted imagination, the dragon.   The object
of such creations was to exert a religious influence
by inspiring terror.   But after the period so pain-
fully looked forward to had passed, and the day of
vengeance seemed to be indefinitely postponed, a
reaction of feeling set in, and men began to treat
the devil as a bugaboo to be ridiculed rather than
to be dreaded.   The imps which are sculptured in
bas-relief on the churches of the fifteenth century
are far more comical than terrible forms.   They
are devils who are fallen into dotage and visible
decay, and with whom the artist can take all sorts
of liberties, turning them into clowns and buffoons
for the amusement of the populace.

This tendency was intensified by the scepticism
which attended the Renaissance movement and led
to the Reformation, and was naturally and inevitably
fostered by the success of these intellectual and
ecclesiastical revolts.   Luther's devil was a poor
discrowned potentate, whom it was perfectly safe
to deride and vilify.   No hurling of inkstands
would have sufficed to discomfit the devils of the
tenth and eleventh centuries, nor would any good
Christian of that day have ventured to address
them in such offensive terms as Luther employs
in his *Table Talk*, lest they should take him at his
word and effect an anal possession of his person
that would defy the most vigorous crepitus as a

means of expulsion. Luther's attitude towards the prince of darkness, however bold and reckless it may seem, was in reality nothing but the cheapest and coarsest sort of swagger. The great devil in the pediment over the portal of the cathedral of Autun, belonging to the twelfth century, would have "grinned horribly a ghastly smile" at the scurrile scoffings and obscene jocularities in which the Wittenberg Reformer was so fond of indulging at the expense of the arch-fiend.

As Maupertuis was passing through a cemetery, a friend, pointing to a heap of skulls, said, "What are they grinning at?" "At us who are living," was the reply. This is the moral of the Dance of Death. A Tyrolese priest, preaching to a congregation of peasants, naïvely remarked, "All men must die, even I myself." The grim skeleton is no respecter of persons, so far as riches and rank are concerned; the crown, the mitre, the tiara, the surplice, and the stole do not avail to ward off the inevitable fate. Death's touch paralyzes the strongest arm, and his scythe strikes through the heaviest helmet and pierces the network of the most impenetrable coat of mail. The artists who delineated such scenes enforced in the most emphatic manner the doctrine of human equality so impressively taught by Hamlet in his churchyard soliloquy: "Now get you to my lady's chamber, and tell her, let her paint an inch thick, to this favour must she come." The lawyer with "his quiddits, his quillets, his cases, his tenures, and his tricks," the jester with his gibes, his gambols, his songs, his "flashes of merriment, that were wont to set the table on a roar," pope, emperor, courtier, beggar, miser, spendthrift, knight, peasant, soldier, judge, and criminal—all join in the measured movement directed by the untiring and unrelenting corypheus.

The oldest Dance of Death of which we have any knowledge dates from 1312, and was a fresco-painting in the cloister of Klingenthal at Little Bâle, consisting of forty representations of the manner in which death arrests the activity and cuts short the career of all classes and conditions of men, and accompanied with explanatory verses. More than a hundred years later the churchyard of the Minorite cloister of the Innocents at Paris was adorned with similar scenes, "begun," as a contemporary record states, "in the month of August, 1424, and finished in the following Lent." It was called La Dance Macabre, and woodcuts of it were published in a volume printed at Paris in 1485, and bearing the title: *Chorea ab eximio Macabro versibus alemanicis edita*, etc., from which it appears that the word Macabre was then supposed to be derived from a distinguished German poet, Macabrus, who composed the rhymes. Unfortunately for this theory, no poet of this name ever existed in Germany, although he may have owed his origin to a confusion with Marcabrus, a Provençal poet of the fourteenth century, who, however, sang wholly different themes. Nearly a dozen

more or less ingenious interpretations have been
given of this phrase, which is probably a translation and corruption of the mediæval Latin *Chorea
Machabæorum*, so called because the seven Mac-
cabean brothers with their mother were originally
the principal characters in it, or because it was first
celebrated in their honour on the day (August 1)
devoted by the Church to their memory as martyrs;
for the Dance of Death was represented dramati-
cally as well as pictorially, and was doubtless
acted in cloisters and in public places long before
it became the subject of artistic delineation. The
verses explanatory of the oldest paintings are
always in the form of a dialogue between the in-
exorable destroyer and his victims, and may be
regarded as fragments of the original play.

In England, France, Germany, and Switzerland
some fifty cities are mentioned as having had
paintings of the Dance of Death, the most famous
of which was that on the outer wall of the churchyard of the Dominican cloister in Great Bâle, made
in free imitation of the Klingenthal fresco about
the middle of the fifteenth century, renovated by
Hans Hugo Klauber in 1568, and ruthlessly destroyed by order of an over-zealous iconoclastic
municipal council on account of its being "a terror
to children and a bugaboo to the people"—"ein
Kinderschreck und eine Leutescheuche."

The libraries of Heidelberg, Munich, and Paris
contain quite a number of manuscripts with miniatures of the Dance of Death, some of which are

Z

really superb in execution, while others are crude
in form, but not without a certain vigour of movement and vividness of expression. By far the
finest delineation of this subject is Hans Holbein's
Imago Mortis, the original drawings of which, now
in St. Petersburg, are artistically as superior to all
former productions of the kind as Goethe's *Faust*
is to the folk-books and puppet-plays that describe
the uncanny career of the mediæval master of the
black art. Holbein's drawings were engraved on
wood by Hans Lützelburger. These cuts, the
proof-impressions of which, published at Lyons
and Bâle, resemble the best work of the artist's
pencil, and to which several posthumous sheets
were added in the early part of the present century, have passed through more than a hundred
editions, to say nothing of copies on copper and
lithographic reproductions.

In the *Book of Hours* of Geoffroy Tory are
miniatures of a like character : the grim skeleton
is mounted on a black horse, with a scythe on his
shoulder, a folded letter in his hand, a raven, the
ominous bird of Odin, flying over his head, and his
pathway strewn with corpses. In a copper-plate
by the Nuremberger Hans Sebastian Beham, dated
1541, and bearing the inscription, *Omnem in homine
venvstatem Mors abolet* (" Death does away with
all beauty in man "), Death in the guise of a
court-fool surprises a richly-dressed maiden of patri-
cian birth, while gathering a bouquet of flowers.
Beham was a genial artist, but a lewd fellow. In

the Berlin Museum is an engraving of Death looking with lustful emotions on a lascivious pair, on
the margin of which are written these words:
"propter quam picturam ex civitate ejectus est."
His fellow-burghers were so outraged by this superfluity of obsceneness that they compelled him to
quit the city. After his exile he went rapidly from
bad to worse, kept a brothel in Frankfort, and, in
1550, was drowned in the Main. Well-preserved
representations of Death's triumphs, painted by
Meglinger in the sixteenth century, may still be
seen in the pediments under the roof of the long
wooden bridge (Spreuer Brücke) over the Reuss at
Lucerne.

The spirit of the Dance of Death is thoroughly
democratic, and inculcates the doctrine of human
equality in the most emphatic and impressive
manner. The great leveller shows no consideration for rank or dignity; the lowest is not beneath,
nor the highest above his notice; neither emperor
nor pope can escape his dominion or refuse to obey
his behest. He clutches the rich and powerful with
a rude hand, gently lulls the infant to sleep, and
closes the weary eyes of the poor and oppressed
with a touch of tenderness and compassion. He
delights to turn the tables on his victims, to make
a mockery of human faculty and function, and

> "to have the engineer
> Hoist with his own petard."

Thus he presents the monarch a fatal potion in a
goblet set with jewels, capers with the king's jester

towards an open grave, breaks the judge's staff of
office over his head, strikes down the miser with
his heavy bag of hoarded wealth, pierces the cook
through with a spit, combats the cavalier on horseback, tilts with a lance against the knight in the
lists, plays the gallant with coquettes, catches the
fowler in a snare, points to the doctor's pills and
tinctures and bids him heal himself, seizes the
apothecary in the midst of his drugs, snatches the
priest from the altar as he is praying souls out of
purgatory, gives the astronomer a skull in the form
of a globe, and says to the astrologer, who casts
the horoscope of others, but is ignorant of his own
fate—

> " Tu dis par amphibologie
> Ce qu'aux aultres doibt advenir ;
> Dys-moy donc par astrologie
> Quand du debvras a moy venir."

> " You tell by amphibology
> What unto others is to be ;
> Now tell me by astrology
> When are *you* to come to me."

Honoré de Sainte Marie, a popular and sensational preacher of the latter half of the seventeenth
century, was wont to take skulls into the pulpit
and address them in the sarcastic moralizing style
of Hamlet. To the skull of a judge he would say :
" Speak now, hast thou not sold justice for gold,
and refused to listen to the pleadings of the poor ? "
The skull of a flirt he would apostrophize in the
following strain : "Art thou not the head of one
of those fair dames whose chief occupation was to

lay snares for human hearts, and to catch them
with honeyed words as birds are taken with lime?
Well then, empty and musty sconce, where are
those fine eyes, with their fond and furtive glances?
Where are those beautiful teeth, which bit so many
hearts, and made them more easily devoured by the
devil? Where those delicate ears, into which fops
have so lovingly whispered, seeking through these
avenues easy access to the heart? What has
become of those lilies and roses, which thou didst
suffer to be plucked by unchaste kisses?" It
would be interesting to know whether the idea of
delivering such discourses was original with the
French divine, or borrowed from Hamlet's meditations in the churchyard. The most probable
supposition is that these sermons were suggested
by the Dance of Death, inasmuch as the Shake-
sperian dramas were little read and indeed hardly
known in France at that time, and it was not until
a much later period that they began to be generally
appreciated even in England.

It would be wholly foreign to the scope of the
present work to consider at length the different
forms in which death has been represented in art.
To the poetic imagination and fine æsthetic sense
of the Greeks the genius of death was not a grim
monster, but a graceful youth leaning on an inverted
torch, the twin brother of sleep, as Homer calls him,
and it was not till the twelfth century of the Christian era that he began to be personified and portrayed as a mummy or a skeleton. The Dance of

Death doubtless originated in the Dance of the Dead (Todtentanz, Danse des Morts), which according to popular superstition took place in church-yards at the ghostly hour of midnight. The remarkable fascination of the theme is evident from the frequency with which it has been por-trayed by modern artists, as, for example, by Alfred Rethel in six admirable xylographs of Death on the barricades and in revolutionary and reactionary contests suggested by the political events of 1848, in the woodcuts of Ille, Pocci, and Barth, the ex-cellent series of India-ink drawings by Otto Seitz, and the more recent and uncommonly clever sketches by Lührig. In these and similar works Death figures as a working-man in a blouse preach-ing insurrection, as the "walking delegate" of a labour union organizing a general strike, as a Jesuit urging a monarch to resist by force of arms the will of the people, as a diplomatist seated at a table and kindling war by a single stroke of his pen, as a Swiss guide leading a company of tourists through a mist over a precipice, as a careless switchman plunging an express train into an abyss, and finally in the newest and most destructive rôle of an anarchist and dynamiter.

BIBLIOGRAPHY

ADELINE, JULES: Les Sculptures Grotesques et Symboliques (Rouen et environs). Rouen, 1879.

AHRENS, KARL : Zur Geschichte des sogenannten Physiologus, Programm des Gymnasiums zu Ploen, 1885, No. 251.

ALLEN, J. ROMILLY: Christian Symbolism in Great Britain and Ireland before the Thirteenth Century. London, 1887.

—— On the Norman Doorway at Alne in Yorkshire. Art. in The Journal of the British Archæological Association. Vol. xlii., pp. 143-158.

AUBER, L'ABBÉ CHARLES AUGUSTE : Histoire et Théorie du Symbolisme religieux avant et depuis le Christianisme. 4 vols. Poitiers, 1872.

AUDSLEY, WM., Manual of Christian Symbolism. London, 1865.

BERGER DE XIVREY: Traditions Tératologiques. Paris, 1836.

BOYLESVE, MARIN DE: Les Animaux et leurs Applications Symboliques à l'Ordre Spirituel. Paris, 1881.

BREYSIG, J. A.: Wörterbuch der Bildersprache oder Angaben symbolischer und allegorischer Bilder. Leipzig, 1830.

Bulletin Monumental. Vols. xi.—xxix. Caen, 1846—1854.

CAHIER, CHARLES: Mélanges d'Archéologie. 4 vols. Paris, 1847—1856.

CAHIER, CHARLES: Nouveaux Mélanges d'Archéologie.
4 vols. Paris, 1874—1877.

—— Monographie de la Cathédral de Bourges, ou
Vitraux de Bourges. Paris, 1841—1844.

—— Caractéristiques des Saints dans l'Art Populaire.
Paris, 1844.

CARUS, J. VICTOR: Geschichte der Zoologie. Vol. xii.
of Geschichte der Wissenschaften. Munich, 1872.

CHAMPFLEURY (pseudonym of JULES FLEURY): Histoire
de la Caricature moderne. Paris, 1865.

—— Histoire de la Caricature au Moyen Âge et sous
la Renaissance. 2nd ed. Paris, 1875.

—— Les Sculptures Grotesques et Symboliques.
Rouen, 1879.

—— Histoire de la Caricature sous la Réforme et la
Ligue. Paris, 1880.

CLEMENT, FELIX: L'Âne au Moyen Âge (Annales
Archéologiques, vols. xv., xvi.).

CROSNIER, L'ABBÉ: Iconografie Chrétienne. Caen, 1848.

DAHLERUP, VERNER: Bibliography of the Physiologus in
Aarboger for Nordisk Oldkyndighed og Historie ud-
given af Det kongelige Nordiske Oldskrift-Selskab.
1889.

Denkwürdiger und Nützlicher Antiquarius des Neckar-
Mayn- Lahn- und Moselstroms. Frankfurt am Mayn,
1740.

DIDRON, A. N.: Histoire de Dieu, Iconographie des
Personnes Divines. Paris, 1843.

—— Manuel d'Iconographie Chrétienne. Paris, 1845.

—— Annales Archéologiques. Paris, 1844—1872.

DIETRICHSON, L.: De Norske Stavkirker; studier over
deres system, aprindelse og historiske Udvikling.
Kristiania og Kjobenhavn, 1892.

DIETRICHSON, DR. L. und MUNTHE H.: Die Holzbaukunst Norwegens in Vergangenheit und Gegenwart.
Berlin, 1893, pp. 25-27.

DOUCE, F.: Dissertation on the Dance of Death.
London, 1833.

DU CANGE (CHARLES DUFRESNE): Glossarium. Festum,
1678.

DUMONTIER, G.: Les Symboles, les Emblemes et les
Accessoires du Culte. Paris, 1891.

DURSCH, G. M.: Der Symbolische Charakter der
Christlichen Religion und Kunst. Schaffhausen,
1860.

DU TILLOT: Mémoires pour servir à la Fête des Fous.
1741.

EBERS, GEORG: Sinnbildliches, Die Koptische Kunst,
ein neues Gebiet der Altchristlichen Sculptur und ihre
Symbole. Mit 14 Zinkotypien. Leipzig, 1892.

FIORILLO, J. D.: Kleinere Schriften artistischen Inhalts.
2 vols. Göttingen, 1803—1806.

GARRUCCI, RAFFAELE: Storia della Arte Cristiana. 4
vols. Prato, 1879.

GUERARD, F.: Recherches sur la Fête des Fous.
Amiens, 1861.

GUILLAUME, CLERC DE NORMANDIE: Le Bestiaire Divin.
Best edition by Reinsch. Leipzig, 1890.

HEIDER, GUSTAV: Über Thiersymbolik und das Symbol
des Löwen in der Christlichen Kunst. Wien, 1849.

—— Die Romanische Kirche zu Schöngrabern in
Nieder-Oesterreich. Ein Beitrag zur Christlichen
Kunst-Archäologie. Wien, 1855.

KNIGHT, GALLY: Ueber die Entwickelung der Archi-
tectur vom x. bis xiv. Jahrhundert unter den Nor-
manen. Leipzig, 1841.

KOLOFF, EDUARD: Die sagenhafte und symbolische Thiergeschichte des Mittelalters. Raumer's Hist. Taschenbuch, 1867, pp. 179-269.

KRAUS, FRANZ XAVER: Kunst und Alterthum im Unter-Elsass. Strasburg, 1876.

KREUSER, JOH.: Der christliche Kirchenbau, seine Geschichte, Symbolik, Bildnerei nebst Andeutungen für Neubauten. 2 vols. Bonn, 1851 ; revised ed., Regensburg, 1860.

KUGLER, FRANZ: Kleine Schriften und Studien. Vol. i. Stuttgart, 1853.

LANGE, KONRAD: Der Papstesel. Ein Beitrag zur Kultur- und Kunstgeschichte der Reformation. Göttingen, 1891.

LANGLOIS, E. H.: Les Stalles de la Cathédral de Rouen. Rouen, 1838.

LAUCHERT, FRIEDRICH: Geschichte des Physiologus. Strasburg, 1889.

   (This exhaustive work contains a very full account of editions and translations.)

L'ÉSPRIT: Histoire des Chiffres et des 13 Premiers Nombres. Paris, 1893.

LUTHER, MARTIN: Abbildung des Bapstum. Wittenberg, 1545.

—— und MELANCHTHON: Deutung der czwo grewlichen Figuren Bapstesels czu Rom und Munchkalbs zu Freyberg. Wittenberg, 1523.

LYCOSTHENES: Prodigiorum ac Ostentorum Chronicon. Basil, 1557.

Maxima Bibliotheca Veterum Patrum. 27 vols. Leyden, 1677.

MEISSNER: Articles in Herrig's Archiv für das Studium der neueren Sprachen und Literatur. Vols. lvi.—lviii.

MENZEL, WOLFGANG: Christliche Symbolik. 2 vols.
Regensburg, 1854.

MÜLLER, SOPHUS: Die Thierornamentik im Norden.
Aus dem Dänischen von J. Mestorf. Hamburg,
1881.

NAPIER, ARTHUR S.: History of the Holy Rood-Tree,
a Twelfth-Century Version of the Cross-Legend. With
notes by the editor, Professor Arthur S. Napier.
London, 1894.

NEALE, J. M., and WEBB, BENJ.: Du Symbolisme dans
les Églises du Moyen Âge. Avec une Introduction,
des Additions et des Notes par M. L'Abbé J. J.
Bourassé. Tours, 1847.

(The second part (pp. 255-402) is an extended
summary of William Durand's Rationale Divinorum
Officiorum, which was printed at Mayence in 1459.)

NORDSTERN (pseudonym of NOSTITZ und JÄNCKENDORF),
GOTTL. ADOLF ERNST: Sinnbilder der Christen.
Leipzig, 1818.

PAULUS, EDUARD: Kunst- und Alterthums-Denkmale im
Königreich Württemberg. Stuttgart, 1889-93. Text,
with numerous illustrations and large plates.

PEIGNOT, E. G.: Recherches sur les Danses des Morts
et sur l'Origine des Cartes à jouer. Paris, 1826.

PHILIPPE DE THAUN: Le Livre des Créatures. Vide
Wright's Popular Treatises on Science during the
Middle Ages, pp. 74-131.

[PINDER ULRICH]: Der beschlossen gart des rosen-
krants Marie. 2 vols. Nürnberg, 1505.

(According to the colophon this work was Gedrükt
vn volendet zu Nürmberk durch doctor Vlrichen
Pinter / an tag Dyonisiy / Nach Cristi vnsers lieben
herren geburt M. fünff hundert vnd fünff jar.)

PIPER, FERDINAND: Mythologie und Symbolik der christlichen Kunst von den ältesten Zeiten bis in das 16 Jahrhundert. 2 vols. Weimar, 1847—1851.

PITON, FRÉDÉRIC: La Cathédral de Strasbourg. Strasbourg, 1861.

PITRA, J. B. : Spicilegium Solesmense complectens Sanctorum Patrum scriptorumque Ecclesiasticorum anecdota hactenus opera selecta e græcis orientali-busque et latinis codicibus. Tom. i.—iv. Paris, 1851—1858.

Publications of Early English Text Society. Vols. xlvi.—xlviii. London, 1865-66.

Revue Archéologique. Paris, 1844—1892.

Revue de l'Art Chrétien. Especially vols. vi.—xx. Paris, 1845—1877.

RICHTER, CHRISTIAN : Über die fabelhaften Thiere. Gotha, 1797.

RUDOLPHI, FRIEDRICH : Gotha Diplomatica oder Aus-führliche Historische Beschreibung des Fürstenthums Sachsen-Gotha. Vol. ii., p. 310. Frankfurt am Main und Leipzig, 1717.

SCHADOW, J. G. : Wittenberg's Denkmäler der Bild-nerei, Baukunst und Malerei, mit historischen und artistischen Erläuterungen. Wittenberg, 1825.

SCHEIBLE, J. : Das Kloster, weltlich und geistlich, meist aus den ältesten deutschen Volks-Wundercuriositäten und komischen Literatur. A curious compilation in 13 vols. Stuttgart, 1845—1849. Vide especially vols. vii., ix., and xii.

SCHNAASE, KARL : Geschichte der bildenden Künste im Mittelalter. Especially vol. iv. Düsseldorf, 1843—1864.

SEPET, MARIUS : Le Drame Chrétien au Moyen Âge. Paris, 1878.

VILLETTE, CLAUDE : Raisons de l'Office. Paris, 1601.

VIOLLET-LE-DUC: Dictionnaire Raisonné de l'Architecture Française du 11me au 16me Siècle. Paris, 1853.

VOLLMÖLLER, CARL : Romanische Forschungen, Erlangen, 1890. Bd. v. pp. 1-12, 13-36, 392-418.
    1. Zum Physiologus von Fried. Lauchert. (An account of Cecco d'Ascoli's " Acerba.")
    2. Der äthiopische Physiologus von Fritz Hommel. (A revised German translation.)
    3. Der waldensische Physiologus von Alfons Mayer. (The first publication of the original text.)

[VULPIUS, AUG.]: Curiositäten der physisch- literarisch-artistisch- historischen Vor- und Mitwelt zur angenehmen Unterhaltung für gebildete Leser. 10 Bände. Weimar, 1811—1823. Especially vol. vi., pp. 133-142.

WEERTH, ERNST AUS'M: Kunstdenkmäler des christlichen Mittelalters in den Rheinlanden. 5 Bände Text und Tafeln. Leipzig, 1857—1868.

WESSELY, J. E.: Die Gestalten des Todes und des Teufels in der darstellenden Kunst. Leipzig, 1876.

WRIGHT, THOMAS: Popular Treatises on Science during the Middle Ages. London, 1841.

—— History of Caricature and the Grotesque. London, 1875.

—— and HALLIWELL : Reliquæ Antiquæ. London, 1841—1843.

ZEDDEL, F. C.: Beiträge zur biblischen Zoologie. Quedlinburg, 1836.

Zeitschrift für deutsche Kulturgeschichte. Vol. i., pp. 463-69 ; 708 sq.

ZOCKLER, O.: Geschichte der Beziehungen zwischen Theologie und Naturwissenschaft. 2 vols. Gütersloh, 1887—1889.

INDEX

Richard Clay & Sons, Limited, London & Bungay.